SECOND EDITION
Challenger

Teacher's Manual

ADULT READING SERIES

FOR STUDENT BOOKS 5-8

New Readers Press

Challenger Teacher's Manual 5–8, 2nd Edition
ISBN 978-1-56420-577-3

Copyright © 2010, 1988 New Readers Press
New Readers Press
ProLiteracy's Publishing Division
104 Marcellus Street, Syracuse, New York 13204
www.newreaderspress.com

Printed in the United States of America
9 8 7

Proceeds from the sale of New Readers Press materials support professional development, training, and technical assistance programs of ProLiteracy that benefit local literacy programs in the U.S. and around the globe.

Developmental Editor: Terrie Lipke
Contributing Editor: Terry Ledyard
Contributing Writer: Practical Strategies, Inc.
Creative Director: Andrea Woodbury
Production Specialist: Maryellen Casey
Cover Design: Carolyn Wallace

CONTENTS

CONTENTS

Book 6

INTRODUCTION

LESSON NOTES

Book 7

INTRODUCTION

LESSON NOTES

CONTENTS

Book 8

INTRODUCTION

LESSON NOTES

Answer Key for Writing Books

INTRODUCTION TO THE *CHALLENGER SERIES*

The *Challenger Adult Reading Series* is a program designed to develop reading, writing, and reasoning skills in adult and adolescent students. The first four books in the *Challenger* series emphasize *learning to read*, developing basic decoding, vocabulary, comprehension, and writing skills. Beginning with Book 5, the emphasis shifts to *reading to learn*, developing higher-level comprehension and reasoning skills while expanding the student's knowledge base.

Components of the Series

The *Challenger* series contains:

- 8 student books
- 2 teacher's manuals
- 8 writing workbooks
- online *Challenger Placement Tool*
- online puzzles correlated to the student book lessons

The Student Books

Each book in this controlled vocabulary series contains 20 lessons, plus reviews. Each lesson includes:

- word study
- a reading selection
- a wide variety of exercises and activities

In Books 1, 3, 5, and 7, each lesson begins with a word chart that introduces new words according to specific phonics principles. In all books, new words that appear in the lesson are listed before each reading selection.

The reading selections in the odd-numbered books are mostly fiction. Books 1 and 3 contain original stories about a group of adults in a variety of situations. Most reading selections in Books 5 and 7 are minimally adapted well-known works of fiction. The even-numbered books contain engaging informational readings. The selections in Books 2 and 4 are on topics similar to those in magazines and encyclopedias. Most selections in Books 6 and 8 are adapted from highly respected works of nonfiction that enable students to broaden the scope of their knowledge.

The varied exercises and activities help students to develop their reading, writing, speaking, and listening skills and to increase their basic knowledge. Comprehension exercises based on the reading selections focus on the development of literal, inferential, and applied comprehension skills. In addition, comprehension exercises in Books 5 through 8 develop literary understanding, interpretation, and critical reading skills.

Other exercises are designed to increase vocabulary and develop reading and reasoning skills. They include vocabulary reviews; word associations; classifying, sequencing, and categorizing exercises; using context clues; forming analogies; using dictionaries and reference materials; and several types of puzzles.

There are reviews after every four or five lessons, except in Books 1 and 3. Each book has a final review. Also included in Books 1 through 5 are indexes of the words introduced so far in that book. The word indexes for Books 6 through 8 are available online. These word indexes can be used in developing reinforcement activities and vocabulary reviews.

The Teacher's Manuals

There is a single *Teacher's Manual for Books 1–4* and a single *Teacher's Manual for Books 5–8*. These comprehensive manuals explain the concepts underlying the *Challenger* series and offer practical suggestions about procedures and techniques for working with students. Separate chapters deal with preparing to teach, teaching the lessons, writing, doing reinforcement activities, and using the lesson notes. These chapters should be read before you begin to use this program. Individual lesson notes contain suggestions for pre-reading, post-reading, and writing activities. Comments on specific exercises should be read before teaching the lessons. In the teacher's manuals, there are also introductions to each book, scope and sequence charts, and answer keys for each book. Finally, the *Teacher's Manual for Books 1–4* contains a chart of the common phonics principles and elements in English words.

Student Writing

Students are encouraged to write from the very first lesson. Early in the series, exercises focus on writing at the sentence level and are designed to simultaneously improve spelling, sentence structure, and students' skill in expressing themselves clearly. Most lessons in Books 5 through 8 have exercises that require students to write brief paragraphs. Suggestions for providing additional writing activities are given in the individual lesson notes.

Significant Educational Features

FLEXIBILITY AND ADAPTABILITY

The *Challenger* series has been used successfully with students in many different types of instructional settings:

- adult volunteer literacy programs
- ABE, pre-GED, and GED programs
- secondary remedial reading programs
- secondary special education programs
- community college reading programs
- educational programs in correctional institutions
- workforce tutorial programs for employees

Challenger can be used in one-to-one tutoring situations, as well as in a variety of group settings. The lessons can be adapted to fit a variety of formats, allowing you to introduce additional activities and topics related to individual student interests and needs.

An Integrated Approach

Challenger integrates reading, writing, speaking, and listening skills. Reading comprehension is developed through oral discussion of inferential- and applied-level questions. These discussions help students to develop speaking and listening skills. Students build writing skills through follow-up writing activities. Critical thinking and reasoning skills are developed as students discuss the readings, the exercises, and their writing activities.

Sequenced Skill Building

Each lesson builds on the skills developed and the content introduced in previous lessons. Students are continually challenged as the lessons increase in length and difficulty. As reading selections become longer, the content, vocabulary, and sentence structure become more sophisticated and demanding. The exercises and writing activities build on and expand students' knowledge and abilities. Students experience a sense of progress as they learn to apply their skills to new situations.

Highly Motivating Material

Students who have used the *Challenger* series have commented that this reading program has many characteristics that help to hold their interest and maintain their motivation. The characteristics they most frequently cite include:

- exceptionally motivating reading selections
- mature and diverse material
- information that increases background knowledge
- emphasis on using reasoning powers
- challenge of increasingly difficult materials
- feelings of success and confidence generated by the program

Placement

The *Challenger Placement Tool,* used in conjunction with information you have about a student's background knowledge, speaking and writing abilities, and motivation, can help you to decide where to place the student in the *Challenger* series. Scores on standardized reading inventories can also be used. For Books 5–8, scores in the following reading level ranges are appropriate:

Book 5:	5.0–6.5
Book 6:	6.0–7.5
Book 7:	7.0–8.5
Book 8:	8.0–9.5

Keep in mind that numerical reading levels by themselves are not adequate descriptors of adult reading abilities. For students already using the series, scoring 85 percent or better on the final review in each book indicates that they are ready to go on to the next book.

SCOPE AND SEQUENCE: Student Book 5

Phonics

Lesson	1	2	3	4	R	5	6	7	8	R	9	10	11	12	R	13	14	15	16	R	17	18	19	20	R
1. Use phonic skills to decode unknown words	●	●	●	●	●	●	●	●	●	●	●	●	●	●	●	●	●	●	●	●	●	●	●	●	●
2. Recognize long and short vowel sounds	■	▲	▲	▲	▲	▲	▲	▲	▲	▲	▲	▲	▲	▲	▲	▲	▲	▲	▲	▲	▲	▲	▲	▲	▲
3. Recognize sounds for consonant blends	▲	■	■	■	▲	■	■	■	▲	▲	▲	▲	▲	▲	▲	▲	▲	▲	▲	▲	▲	▲	▲	▲	▲
4. Recognize sounds for digraphs	▲	■	▲	■	▲	■	▲	▲	■	▲	■	▲	▲	▲	▲	▲	▲	▲	▲	▲	▲	▲	▲	▲	▲
5. Recognize sounds for vowel combinations	▲	▲	▲	▲	▲	▲	▲	▲	■	▲	■	■	▲	▲	▲	▲	▲	▲	▲	▲	▲	▲	▲	▲	▲
6. Recognize sounds for *r*-controlled vowels	▲	▲	▲	▲	▲	▲	▲	▲	▲	▲	▲	▲	■	▲	▲	▲	▲	▲	▲	▲	▲	▲	▲	▲	▲
7. Recognize sounds for *c*	▲	▲	▲	▲	▲	▲	▲	▲	▲	▲	▲	▲	▲	▲	▲	▲	▲	▲	▲	▲	▲	▲	▲	▲	▲
8. Identify sounds for *c*													■												
9. Recognize sounds for *g*	▲	▲	▲	▲	▲	▲	▲	▲	▲	▲	▲	▲	▲	▲	▲	▲	▲	▲	▲	▲	▲	▲	▲	▲	▲
10. Identify sounds for *g*														■											
11. Recognize sounds for *y*	▲	▲	▲	▲	▲	▲	▲	▲	▲	▲	▲	▲	▲	▲	▲	▲	▲	▲	▲	▲	▲	▲	▲	▲	▲
12. Recognize the sound for *ph*																							●		
13. Contrast sounds									■						■						■				■

Word Analysis

Lesson	1	2	3	4	R	5	6	7	8	R	9	10	11	12	R	13	14	15	16	R	17	18	19	20	R
1. Use syllabication to decode words	●	●	●	●	●	●	●	●	●	●	●	●	●	●	●	●	●	●	●	●	●	●	●	●	●
2. Divide words into syllables	■			■	■	■						■													
3. Form compound words							■	■	■		■			■		■									
4. Recognize common word beginnings: *re–*											▲														
pre–, per–														■											
dis–													■												
5. Recognize common word endings: *–er*																			■						
–y																	■								
–ment																		■							
–ness																■									
–ful, –less																					■				
el, ture, ale																						■			
le, al, et, tion, sion, ish																						■			
et, age, ice, ive																								■	

Vocabulary

Lesson	1	2	3	4	R	5	6	7	8	R	9	10	11	12	R	13	14	15	16	R	17	18	19	20	R
1. Learn unfamiliar vocabulary	●	●	●	●	●	●	●	●	●	●	●	●	●	●	●	●	●	●	●	●	●	●	●	●	●
2. Infer word meanings from context clues	●	●	●	●	●	●	●	●	●	●	●	●	●	●	●	●	●	●	●	●	●	●	●	●	●
3. Identify definitions/descriptions of terms	●	●	●	●	●	●	●	●	●	●	●	●	●	●	●	●	●	●	●	●	●	●	●	●	●
4. Complete word associations	■					■									■										
5. Identify synonyms		■	■	■	■					■					■	■		■	■	■		■			■
6. Identify antonyms			■	■	■			■		■					■			■	■	■		■		■	■

KEY: ● = Primary emphasis   ■ = Secondary emphasis   ▲ = Integrated with other skills

Vocabulary, cont.

Lesson	1	2	3	4	R	5	6	7	8	R	9	10	11	12	R	13	14	15	16	R	17	18	19	20	R
7. Identify multiple meanings of words			▲																				■		
8. Complete analogies			■										■			■							■		
9. Learn/review idiomatic expressions/common sayings				■				▲														■			
10. Complete puzzles (double crostics and cryptograms)																			■						

Comprehension

Lesson	1	2	3	4	R	5	6	7	8	R	9	10	11	12	R	13	14	15	16	R	17	18	19	20	R
1. Identify words using context clues	●	●	●	●		●	●	●	●	●	●	●	●	●		●	●	●	●		●	●	●	●	
2. Read stories independently	●	●	●	●		●	●	●	●	●	●	●	●	●	●	●	●	●	●	●	●	●	●	●	●
3. Complete exercises independently	●	●	●	●	■	●	●	●	●	●	●	●	●	●		●	●	●	●		●	●	●	●	
4. Improve listening comprehension	■	■	■	■	■	■	■	■	■	■	■	■	■	■	■	■	■	■	■		■	■	■	■	
5. Group words appropriately when reading orally	■	■	■	■		■	■	■	■	●	■	●	■	■		■	■	■	■		■				
6. Interpret punctuation correctly when reading orally	■	■	■				■			■		■	■			■					■				
7. Develop literal comprehension skills:																									
– Recall details	●	●	●	●		●	●	●	●		●	●	●	●		●	●	●	●		●	●	●	●	●
– Locate specific information	●	●	●	●		●	●	●	●		●	●	●	●		●	●	●	●		●	●	●	●	●
– Identify cause-and-effect relationships	●	●						●					●						●			●			
– Recall sequence of events								●					●									●			
8. Develop inferential comprehension skills:																									
– Infer word meanings from context clues	●	●	●	●		●	●	●	●	●	●	●	●	●		●	●	●			●	●	●	●	●
– Infer information from the story	●	●	●	●		●	●	●	●	●	●	●	●	●		●	●	●			●	●	●	●	●
– Use context clues to predict correct responses	●	●	●	●	●	●	●	●	●		●		●	●		●	●	●			●		●	●	●
– Draw conclusions based on story	●		·					●													●	●			
– Infer cause-and-effect relationships		●																							
– Classify words under topic headings													■			■									
9. Develop applied comprehension skills:																									
– Relate reading to personal experience		●	●	●			●	■		●	●	●		●		●	●	●				●		●	
– Draw conclusions based on personal experience																			●			●			●
10. Learn/review basic factual information					●						●	●													
11. Locate/infer information from a circle graph			●								●														

Literary Understanding

Lesson	1	2	3	4	R	5	6	7	8	R	9	10	11	12	R	13	14	15	16	R	17	18	19	20	R
1. Identify/interpret characters' actions, motivations, feelings, and qualities	●	●	●	●		●	●	●	●	●	●	●		●		●	●	●	●		●	●	●	●	
2. Identify/interpret plot	●	●	●	●		●	●	●	●	●	●	●		●		●	●	●	●		●	●	●	●	
3. Identify/interpret setting (time and/or place)	●	●	●	●							●	●													
4. Identify/infer narrator	●																								
5. Relate characters' names to qualities			●																						
6. Create ending for story											●														

KEY: ● = Primary emphasis   ■ = Secondary emphasis   ▲ = Integrated with other skills

Scope and Sequence: Level 5   TEACHER'S MANUAL   **9**

Literary Understanding, cont.

Lesson	1	2	3	4	R	5	6	7	8	R	9	10	11	12	R	13	14	15	16	R	17	18	19	20	R
7. Relate to characters' motivations and feelings							●	●	●		●		●	●		●					●				
8. Identify theme								●								●	●	●			●				
9. Predict outcome of story								●	●			●						●						●	
10. Recognize personification											●												●	●	
11. Identify surprise ending											●														
12. Recognize fables																●									
13. Infer moral of fable																●									
14. Contrast stories																									
15. Recognize autobiography																		●	●						
16. Infer narrator's attitude toward character																			●		●				
17. Identify tone																						●			

Writing

Lesson	1	2	3	4	R	5	6	7	8	R	9	10	11	12	R	13	14	15	16	R	17	18	19	20	R
1. Copy words accurately	●	●	●	●	●	●	●	●	●	●	●	●	●	●	●	●	●	●	●	●	●	●	●	●	●
2. Capitalize words appropriately	●	●	●	●	●	●	●	●	●	●	●	●	●	●	●	●	●	●	●	●	●	●	●	●	●
3. Spell words with greater accuracy	●	●	●	●	●	●	●	●	●	●	●	●	●	●	●	●	●	●	●	●	●	●	●	●	●
4. Form new words by adding the ending -y																									
5. Change the y to i before adding -ness																■		■							
6. Change dialect to standard English																			■						
7. Use homonyms correctly																			■						■
8. Write sentence or paragraph answers to questions	●	●	●	●		●	●	●	●		●	●	●			●	●	●			●		●	●	

Note: Specific suggestions for additional writing assignments appear in the individual lesson notes of this manual.

Study Skills

Lesson	1	2	3	4	R	5	6	7	8	R	9	10	11	12	R	13	14	15	16	R	17	18	19	20	R
1. Increase concentration	●	●	●	●	●	●	●	●	●	●	●	●	●	●	●	●	●	●	●	●	●	●	●	●	●
2. Skim story to locate information	●	●	●	●	●	●	●	●	●	●	●	●	●	●	●	●	●	●	●	●	●	●	●	●	●
3. Use a dictionary to look up word meanings	●	●	●	●	●	●	●	●	●	●	●	●	●	●	●	●	●	●	●	●	●	●	●	●	●
4. Apply reasoning skills to exercises: context clues	●	●	●	●	●	●	●	●	●	●	●	●	●	●	●	●	●	●	●	●	●	●	●	●	
process of elimination	●	●	●	●	●	●	●																		
"intelligent guessing"	●		●			●																			

KEY: ● = Primary emphasis   ■ = Secondary emphasis   ▲ = Integrated with other skills

SCOPE AND SEQUENCE: Challenger Writing 5

The following scope and sequence chart indicates the introduction and major practice for writing skills. It also shows the introduction of grammar and mechanics rules that are most helpful to emerging writers. Reinforcement and practice of these rules are spread throughout the various exercises.

Lesson	STRAND 4 — Unscramble the Sentences (transitions that add information)	STRAND 5 — Put These Sentences in Order (transitions that show time order)	STRAND 6 — What Do You Think? (questions w/o starters)	STRAND 6 — What Would You Like to Know? (writing questions)	STRAND 10 — Write Paragraphs (3 guided: different topics, transitions)	STRAND 10 — Write a Paragraph (introduction, body, conclusion)	STRAND 10 — Write a 3-paragraph essay	STRAND 10 — Write a 3-par essay (topic sentence, transitions that add information)	STRAND 10 — Write a descriptive paragraph	STRAND 10 — Write a 1-par summary paragraph	STRAND 10 — Write a 3-par summary (topic sentence that shows time order)
1			X		X						
2			X		X						
3			X		X						
4			X		X						
5			X		X						
6			X			X					
7			X			X					
8			X			X					
9		X	X			X					
10		X		X			X				
11	X			X			X				
12	X						X				
13									X		
14									X		
15									X		
16										X	
17											X
18											X
19								X			
20								X			
R		X					X		X		X

Lesson	Use These Words in Sentences	Use These Words and Phrases in Sentences	List Words and Phrases to Use in Sentences	Add Details (vivid words, specific nouns, action verbs)	Try Your Hand at Using Details	Choose the Best Descriptive Words and Phrases	Combine Sentences (comma fault)	Combine Sentences (subordinating conjunction, comma)	Combine Sentences (run-on)	Combine Sentences (sentence fragments)	Combine Sentences (subject-verb agreement)
1	X						X				
2	X							X			
3	X							X			
4		X									
5		X							X	X	
6		X								X	
7		X					X	X	X	X	
8		X					X	X	X	X	
9			X								
10			X								
11			X								
12		X		X							
13			X	X							
14					X	X					
15					X	X					
16		X	X				X	X	X	X	
17						X					X
18						X					
19						X					
20											
R	X		X								

Lesson	STRAND 13		STRAND 14			STRAND 15	STRAND 16		
	Punctuation (end marks)	Punctuation (capitals)	What Will You Write About? (brainstorming)	What Will You Write About? (5 W's and H)	What Will You Write About? (T-chart)	Is It One or More Than One? (subject-verb agreement)	Use Pronouns in Sentences (personal)	Use Pronouns in Sentences (relative)	Use Pronouns in Sentences (interrogative, question marks)
1									
2									
3									
4									
5									
6									
7									
8									
9									
10	X	X							
11									
12									
13									
14			X						
15			X						
16				X		X			
17				X					
18				X			X		
19					X			X	
20					X				X
R			X						

SCOPE AND SEQUENCE: Student Book 6

Word Analysis

Lesson	1	2	3	4	5	R	6	7	8	9	10	R	11	12	13	14	15	R	16	17	18	19	20	R
1. Use syllabication to decode words	■	■	■	■	■	■	■	■	■	■	■	■	■	■	■	■	■	■	■	■	■	■	■	■
2. Recognize word families		■			■	■		■								■						■		
3. Form compound words					■	■		■								■						■		
4. Recognize/form abbreviations								■		■		■						■						
5. Recognize/form contractions		■											■					■						■
6. Form/use words with common suffixes:																								
–ment	■				■						■													
–ness						■					■													
–or				■		■					■													
–ly						■				■		■												
–ence/–ance						■			■		■													
–tion						■				■								■						
–ful							■				■								■					
–less						■	■				■													
–sion																■								
–ize														■									■	
7. Recognize/use common prefixes:																								
un–												▲			■									
il–														■	■									
im–															■									
in–															■									
ir–													■		■									
non–																■								
re–																							■	
pre–																								

Vocabulary

Lesson	1	2	3	4	5	R	6	7	8	9	10	R	11	12	13	14	15	R	16	17	18	19	20	R
1. Learn unfamiliar vocabulary	●	●	●	●	●	●	●	●	●	●	●	●	●	●	●	●	●	●	●	●	●	●	●	●
2. Infer word meanings from context clues	●	■	●	●	●	●	■	●	■	■	●	■	●	●	●	●	●	●	●	●	■	●	●	■
3. Identify definitions/descriptions of terms			■		■		●		■		■				■	■	●	●	●	●	■	■		●
4. Identify synonyms			●	●		●	●		■	■			●			●	●				●		●	
5. Identify antonyms			●	●		●	●		■				●											
6. Form/use compound words									■			●												■
7. Identify symbols								●		■				■		●	■			■				■
8. Complete analogies					■						●			●										
9. Complete word associations							■																	●
10. Complete word puzzles							■			■		■					■				■	■	■	
11. Learn/review sayings and idiomatic expressions										▲		▲					●	▲			●		▲	▲

KEY: ● = Primary emphasis   ■ = Secondary emphasis   ▲ = Integrated with other skills

Comprehension

Lesson	1	2	3	4	5	R	6	7	8	9	10	R	11	12	13	14	15	R	16	17	18	19	20	R
1. Read selections independently	●	●	●	●	●	●	●	●	●	●	●	●	●	●	●	●	●	●	●	●	●	●	●	●
2. Complete exercises independently	●	●	●	●	●	●	●	●	●	●	●	●	●	●	●	●	●	●	●	●	●	●	●	●
3. Identify words using context clues	●	●	●	●	●	●	●	●	●	●	●	●	●	●	●	●	●	●	●	●	●	●	●	●
4. Improve listening comprehension	▲	▲	▲	▲	▲	▲	▲	▲	▲	▲	▲	▲	▲	▲	▲	▲	▲	▲	▲	▲	▲	▲	▲	▲
5. Improve oral reading	▲	▲	▲	▲	▲	▲	▲	▲	▲	▲	▲	▲	▲	▲	▲	▲	▲	▲	▲	▲	▲	▲	▲	▲
6. Develop literal comprehension skills:																								
– Recall details	●	●	●	●	●	●	●	●	●	●	●	●	●	●	●	●	●	●	●	●	●	●	●	●
– Locate specific information	●	●	●	●	●	●	●	●	●	●	●	●	●	●	●	●	●	●	●	●	●	●	●	●
7. Develop inferential comprehension skills:																								
– Support statements with appropriate details	●	●			●					●	●	●			●	●	●		●	●		●	●	
– Infer word meanings from context clues	■	■	●		●		■	■	■	■	■	■	■				■	■	■	■	■	■	■	■
– Use context clues to fill in missing words	●	■	●		●	■	■	■	■	■	■	■	■			■			■	■	■	■	■	■
– Infer information from reading	■										■	■	●		■				■	■	■	■	■	
– Draw conclusions based on reading		●			●								●										●	
– Identify/infer cause-and-effect relationships		■		■	■		▲	■		■	▲							■			▲			
– Distinguish between positive and negative statements																		■						
– Classify words under topic headings										●						●	●	●						●
– Distinguish between fact and opinion									■	●					●									
– Translate Middle English																			■					
8. Develop applied comprehension skills:																								
– Draw conclusions based on personal experience	●	●							●	●		●		●			●		●	●	▲	●	■	
– Relate reading to personal experience	■	■			■	■	▲	●	●	●	●	■	■		■	■	■	▲	■	●	■	▲	●	■
9. Locate/review basic factual information									■		●	●							■					
10. Locate/infer information from:																								
– classified or online ads																			■					
– diagram or label		■																						
– travel brochure				●																				
– driver's test			■													■								
– editorial cartoon				●												●					●			
– chart or table	■																					●		
– time line											●													

Literary Understanding

Lesson	1	2	3	4	5	R	6	7	8	9	10	R	11	12	13	14	15	R	16	17	18	19	20	R
1. Distinguish between fiction and nonfiction	■	▲			▲		▲			▲			▲				▲		▲	▲		▲	▲	
2. Identify/interpret characters' actions, motivations, feelings, and qualities				●			■	■					■		●	■				●	●			
3. Identify/interpret plot/setting											●				■									

KEY: ● = Primary emphasis   ■ = Secondary emphasis   ▲ = Integrated with other skills

Literary Understanding, cont.

Lesson	1	2	3	4	5	R	6	7	8	9	10	R	11	12	13	14	15	R	16	17	18	19	20	R
4. Predict outcome																								
5. Interpret poetry															●						●		●	
6. Interpret drama																					●			
7. Recognize autobiography													◄											
8. Recognize biography								◄					◄											
9. Relate to characters' motivations and feelings				■				■			■		■		■	■					■		■	■
10. Infer author's attitude toward material	◄	◄	◄	◄	◄	◄	◄	■	■	■	■	◄	◄	◄	■	■	◄	◄	◄	◄	◄	◄	◄	◄

Writing

Lesson	1	2	3	4	5	R	6	7	8	9	10	R	11	12	13	14	15	R	16	17	18	19	20	R
1. Write sentence or paragraph answers to questions	●	●	◄	●	●	●	●	●	●	●	●	●	●	●	●	●	●	●	●	●	●	●	●	
2. Form a reasoned opinion	●	●	■	●	●	●	●	●	●	●	◄	●	●	●	●	●	●	●	●	●	●	●	●	
3. Copy words accurately	◄	◄	◄	◄	◄	◄	◄	◄	◄	◄	◄	◄	◄	◄	◄	◄	◄	◄	◄	◄	◄	◄	◄	◄
4. Fill out a job application										●														
5. Spelling:																								
– Form the plural of words ending in *f* or *fe*	■								■															
– Change *y* to *i* before adding suffix			■	■							◄													
– Use an apostrophe to show ownership									■		■										■			
– Spell words with greater accuracy	◄	◄	◄	◄	◄	◄	◄	◄	◄	◄	◄	◄	◄	◄	◄	◄	◄	◄	◄	◄	◄	◄	◄	◄
6. Learn capitalization rules	■	■	■	■							●						■							
7. Capitalize words appropriately	◄	◄	◄	◄	◄	◄	◄	◄	◄	◄	◄	◄	◄	◄	◄	◄	◄	◄	◄	◄	◄	◄	◄	◄

Note: Specific suggestions for additional writing assignments appear in the individual lesson notes of this manual.

Study Skills

Lesson	1	2	3	4	5	R	6	7	8	9	10	R	11	12	13	14	15	R	16	17	18	19	20	R
1. Increase concentration	■	■	■	■	■	■	■	■	■	■	■	■	■	■	■	■	■	■	■	■	■	■	■	■
2. Skim selection to locate information	■	■			■		■	■	■	■		■	■	■				■	■		■		■	■
3. Apply reasoning skills to exercises:																								
– context clues	●	●	●	●	●	●	■	■	■	■	■	■	■	●	■	■	●	■	●	■	●	●	●	●
– process of elimination	■	■	■	■	■	■	■	■	■	■	■	■	■	■	■	■	■	■	■	■	■	■	■	■
– "intelligent guessing"	■	■		■	■		■	■	■	■	■	■	■				■	■		■		■		■
4. Use a dictionary:																								
– to look up word meanings	◄	◄	◄	◄	◄	◄	◄	◄	◄	◄	◄	◄	◄	◄	◄	◄	◄	◄	◄	◄	◄	◄	◄	◄
– to form compound words						■						◄				■								
– to identify bodies of water					◄																			
5. Use reference materials:																								
– to identify bodies of water																	●							
– to identify state capitals	■																						■	

KEY: ● = Primary emphasis   ■ = Secondary emphasis   ◄ = Integrated with other skills

SCOPE AND SEQUENCE: Challenger Writing 6

The following scope and sequence chart indicates the introduction and major practice for writing skills. It also shows the introduction of grammar and mechanics rules that are most helpful to emerging writers. Reinforcement and practice of these rules are spread throughout the various exercises.

Lesson	STRAND 10							STRAND 11			
	Write a 1-paragraph summary	Write a 3-paragraph summary (topic sentences, intro, body, conclusion)	Write a descriptive paragraph	Write a 3-paragraph expository essay (topic sentences, intro, body, conclusion)	Write an expository paragraph	Write a 4-paragraph expository essay	Write a persuasive paragraph	Use These Words and Phrases in Sentences	Add Details (vivid words, specific nouns, action verbs)	Try Your Hand at Using Details	Choose the Best Descriptive Words and Phrases
1	X							X	X		
2	X							X	X		
3	X							X	X		
4	X							X			
5		X						X			
6			X								X
7			X								X
8		X									X
9				X						X	
10				X							X
11					X					X	
12						X					
13				X						X	X
14				X							
15							X				X
16							X			X	X
17							X				
18				X						X	
19				X						X	X
20				X						X	
R		X	X	X			X	X			X

Lesson	STRAND 12 Combine Sentences (coordinating, subordinating conjunction; comma fault)	Combine Sentences (run-on)	Combine Sentences (sentence fragments)	STRAND 14 What Will You Write About? (listing)	What Will You Write About? (brainstorming)	What Will You Write About? (5 W's and H)	What Will You Write About? (T-chart)	STRAND 15 Is It One or More Than One? (subject-verb agreement)	STRAND 16 Use Pronouns in Sentences (personal)	Use Pronouns in Sentences (relative)	Use Pronouns in Sentences (interrogative, question marks)
1				X							
2				X							
3				X							
4	X					X					
5	X			X							
6		X			X						
7		X			X						
8			X	X							
9			X	X							
10	X	X	X			X					
11					X						
12				X							
13							X				
14							X				
15				X	X						
16					X			X			
17				X				X	X		
18							X			X	
19				X					X	X	X
20				X							X
R					X						

| Lesson | STRAND 17 | | |
	Add Transitions (time order)	Add Transitions (cause, effect)	Add Transitions (compare, contrast)
1			
2			
3			
4			
5			
6			
7			
8			
9			
10			
11	X		
12		X	
13	X	X	
14			X
15			X
16			
17			
18			
19			
20			
R	X		

SCOPE AND SEQUENCE: Student Book 7

Lesson	1	2	3	4	R	5	6	7	8	R	9	10	11	12	R	13	14	15	16	R	17	18	19	20	R
Word Analysis																									
1. Use phonics and syllabication skills to decode words	■	■	■	■	■			■	■	■	■	■	■	■	■	■	■	■	■	■	■	■	■	■	■
2. Review basic phonics sounds/patterns	■	■	■	■	■	■	■	■	■	■	■	■	■	■	■	■	■	■	■	■	■	■	■	■	
3. Recognize/use word families					●				●					■						●		■			
4. Use homonyms correctly	■																							●	
Vocabulary																									
1. Learn unfamiliar vocabulary	●	●	●	●	●	●	●	●	●	●	●	●	●	●	●	●	●	●	●	●	●	●	●	●	●
2. Infer word meanings from context clues	●	●	●	●	●	●	●	●	●	●	●	●	●	●	●	●	●	●	●	●	●	●	●	●	●
3. Identify definitions/descriptions of terms	●	●	●	●	●	●	●	●	●	●	●	●	●		●	●	●	●	●	●	●	●	●	●	●
4. Learn/use rules pertaining to standard English usage	■	●	●		●	●																			
5. Complete word associations			●	●	●		●									●								●	
6. Identify synonyms		●					●									●							●		
7. Identify antonyms				●	●		●																●		
8. Learn common affixes and roots:																									
−al																									
−ly				■																					
−ness																									
−ist									■																
uni−														■											
bi−																	■								
tri−											■														
cred																									
9. Complete analogies	▲	■				●				■	■							■						●	●
10. Learn/review idioms, sayings, and proverbs	▲			▲	▲										▲	▲		▲	▲					▲	
11. Complete word puzzles			■						■		■						■				■				●
Comprehension																									
1. Identify words using context clues	●	●	●	●	●	●	●	●	●	●	●	●	●	●	●	●	●	●	●	●	●	●	●	●	●
2. Read selections independently	●	●	●	●	●	●	●	●	●	●	●	●	●	●	●	●	●	●	●	●	●	●	●	●	●
3. Complete exercises independently	●	●	●	●	●	●	●	●	●	●	●	●	●	●	●	●	●	●	●	●	●	●	●	●	●
4. Improve listening comprehension	▲	▲	▲	▲	▲	▲	▲	▲	▲	▲	▲	▲	▲	▲	▲	▲	▲	▲	▲	▲	▲	▲	▲	▲	▲
5. Improve oral reading	▲	▲	▲	▲	▲	▲	▲	▲	▲	▲	▲	▲	▲	▲	▲	▲	▲	▲	▲	▲	▲	▲	▲	▲	▲
6. Develop literal comprehension skills:																									
− Recall details	●	●	●	●	●	●	●	●	●	●	●	●	●	●	●	●	●	●	●	●	●	●	●	●	●
− Locate specific information	●	●	●	●	●	●	●	●	●	●	●	●	●	●	●	●	●	●	●	●	●	●	●	●	●
− Recall or establish sequence of events				■																					

KEY: ● = Primary emphasis ■ = Secondary emphasis ▲ = Integrated with other skills

Comprehension, cont.

Lesson	1	2	3	4	R	5	6	7	8	R	9	10	11	12	R	13	14	15	16	R	17	18	19	20	R
7. Develop inferential comprehension skills:																									
– Support statements with appropriate details	●	●	●	●	●	●	●	●	●	●	●	●	●	●	●	●	●	●	●	●	●	●	●	●	
– Infer word meanings from context clues	●	●	●	●	●	●	●	●	●	●	●	●	●	●	●	●	●	●	●	●	●	●	●	●	●
– Infer information from the reading or exercises	●	●	●	●	●	●	●	●	●	●	●	●	●	●	●	●	●	●	●	●	●	●	●	●	●
– Use context clues to fill in missing words	●	●	●	●	●	●	●	●	●	●	●	●	●	●	●	●	●	●	●	●	●	●	●	●	●
– Draw conclusions based on reading	●	▲	▲	●	●	●	▲	●	●	●	▲	▲	▲	●	●	●	▲	▲	▲	▲	▲	▲	●	▲	
– Identify/infer cause-and-effect relationships	▲	▲	▲	●	▲	▲	●	■	●	●	▲	▲	●	●	●	●	●	●	▲	●	●	▲	▲	●	
– Classify words under topic headings	■				■	■		■										■			■				
– Identify tone of voice														●											
8. Develop applied comprehension skills:																									
– Relate reading to personal experience	■	▲	▲	●	●	■	■	▲				▲	▲	▲		▲					●	●		▲	
– Draw conclusions based on personal experience	■	▲	▲	▲	▲	■	■	▲					▲	▲	▲	▲					●				
9. Learn/review basic factual information	■	■	▲	■	■	■	■	■	■	■	■	■	■	■	■	■	■	■	■	■	■	■	■	■	■

Literary Understanding

Lesson	1	2	3	4	R	5	6	7	8	R	9	10	11	12	R	13	14	15	16	R	17	18	19	20	R
1. Identify/interpret characters' actions, motivations, feelings, and qualities	●	●	●	●	●	●	●	●	●	●	●	●	●	●	●	●	●	●	●	●	●	●	●	●	
2. Identify/interpret plot	●	●	▲	●	●	●	●	●	●	●	●	●	●	●	●	●	●	●	●	●	●	●	●	●	
3. Infer attitudes/qualities of characters	▲	●	▲	●	●	●	▲	●	●	●	●	▲	▲	▲	●	●	▲	●	●	●	▲	▲	▲	▲	
4. Relate to characters' motivations and feelings	●	▲	▲	●	■	▲	▲	●	●	▲	●	▲	▲	▲	▲	●	▲	▲	▲	●	▲	▲	▲	▲	
5. Distinguish between fiction and nonfiction	▲	▲	▲	▲	●	▲	▲	●	▲	▲	▲	▲	▲	●	▲	▲	▲	▲	▲	●	●	●		▲	
6. Relate sayings/concepts to reading	●			●			●		●				●	●										●	
7. Infer/interpret author's purpose/attitude		▲				●		▲		▲					■	●					●				
8. Interpret poetry					●					●				●	●	●				●					
9. Infer attitude of speaker in a poem					●							●		●	●	●									
10. Interpret figurative language	▲	▲			●	●				●									●	■	●	●			
11. Predict outcome/aftermath of selection	■										■														
12. Identify theme of selection		▲			■	▲	■	●		▲				●	▲	●					■				
13. Compare and contrast characters							▲		●	●					●			●	●	●					
14. Identify/interpret setting		▲	▲					▲				▲	▲	▲		▲		▲	▲					▲	
15. Describe personal reaction to reading										▲		▲		▲		▲	●		●						
16. Recognize symbols																	●							▲	
17. Interpret drama																							●	●	
18. Recognize biography																	▲		▲					▲	

KEY: ● = Primary emphasis ■ = Secondary emphasis ▲ = Integrated with other skills

Scope and Sequence: Level 7 TEACHER'S MANUAL **21**

Writing

Lesson	1	2	3	4	R	5	6	7	8	R	9	10	11	12	R	13	14	15	16	R	17	18	19	20	R
1. Write sentence or paragraph answers to questions	●	●	●	●	●	●	●	●	●	●	■	■	●	●	●	●	●	●	●	●	●	●	●	●	
2. Form a reasoned opinion	●	●	●	●	●	●	●	●	●	●	●	●	●	●	●	●	●	●	●	●	●	●	●	●	
3. Copy words accurately	▲	▲	▲	▲	▲	▲	▲	▲	▲	▲	▲	▲	▲	▲	▲	▲	▲	▲	▲	▲	▲	▲	▲	▲	▲
4. Spelling:																									
– Spell words with greater accuracy	▲		▲	▲	▲	▲	▲	▲	▲	▲	▲	▲	▲	▲	▲	▲	▲	▲	▲	▲	▲	▲	▲	▲	▲
– Identify misspelled words					●		■																		
– Change *y* to *i* before adding suffix									■																
– Recognize hyphenated words																			■						

Note: Specific suggestions for additional writing assignments appear in the individual lesson notes of this manual.

Study Skills

Lesson	1	2	3	4	R	5	6	7	8	R	9	10	11	12	R	13	14	15	16	R	17	18	19	20	R
1. Increase concentration	■	■	■	■	■	■	■	■	■	■	■	■	■	■	■	■	■	■	■	■	■	■	■	■	■
2. Skim selection to locate information	■	■	■	■	■	■	■	■	■	■	■	■	■	■	■	■	■	■	■	■	■	■	■	■	■
3. Apply reasoning skills to exercises:																									
– context clues	●	●	●	●	■	■	■	■	●	■	●	●	●	●	●	●	●	●	●	■	●	●	●	■	■
– process of elimination	■	■	■	●	■	■	■	■	■	■	■	■	■	■	■	■	■	■	■	■	■	■	■	■	■
– "intelligent guessing"	■	■	■	■	■	■	■	■	■	■	■	■	■	■	■	■	■	■	■	■	■	■	■	■	■
4. Use a dictionary or the Internet:																									
– to look up word meanings	■				■			■	■	■	■	■	■	■	■	■		■	■	■	■	■	■	■	■
– to learn word origins																									
5. Use reference materials:																									
– to find factual/geographical information		■		■		■	■	■		■	■	▲				■		■					▲		
– to establish chronological order								■																	

KEY: ● = Primary emphasis   ■ = Secondary emphasis   ▲ = Integrated with other skills

SCOPE AND SEQUENCE: Challenger Writing 7

The following scope and sequence chart indicates the introduction and major practice for writing skills. It also shows the introduction of grammar and mechanics rules are most helpful to emerging writers. Reinforcement and practice of these rules are spread throughout the various exercises.

Lesson	STRAND 10				STRAND 11			STRAND 12		
	Write a 3-paragraph summary	Write a 3- to 4-paragraph expository essay	Write a 3-paragraph persuasive essay or letter	Write a 5-paragraph expository essay	Add Details (vivid words, specific nouns, action verbs)	Try Your Hand at Using Details	Choose the Best Descriptive Words and Phrases	Combine Sentences (coordinating, subordinating conjunction; comma fault)	Combine Sentences (run-on)	Combine Sentences (sentence fragments)
1	X				X		X			
2		X			X		X			
3	X	X				X	X			
4		X					X			
5	X	X					X			
6							X			
7		X				X				
8		X				X				
9			X			X			X	
10		X				X				
11		X				X			X	X
12		X				X			X	X
13			X			X		X		
14		X				X		X		
15	X					X		X	X	X
16		X				X				
17		X				X				
18		X				X				
19				X		X				
20				X		X				
R	X		X				X			

Lesson	STRAND 14 — What Will You Write About? (listing)	(brainstorming)	(5 W's and H)	(T-chart)	(mapping)	(cause-and-effect chain)	(chart)	STRAND 16 — Use Pronouns in Sentences (personal, relative, interrogative)
1			X					
2					X			
3			X					
4	X							
5			X					
6		X						
7		X						
8				X				
9				X				
10			X					
11				X				
12	X							
13		X						
14		X						
15			X					
16						X		X
17	X							X
18		X						
19		X			X			
20	X						X	
R	X	X	X	X	X	X	X	

Lesson	STRAND 17				STRAND 18		
	Add Transitions (time order)	Add Transitions (cause, effect)	Add Transitions (compare, contrast)	Add Transitions (add info)	Untangle the Confusion (misplaced modifiers)	Untangle the Confusion (missing words)	Untangle the Confusion (antecedents)
1							
2							
3							
4	X						
5	X						
6				X			
7		X					
8			X				
9				X			
10	X			X			
11				X			
12		X		X			
13				X			
14		X	X	X			
15	X						
16		X					
17				X			
18		X		X	X		
19				X		X	
20				X			X
R							

SCOPE AND SEQUENCE: Student Book 8

Vocabulary	Lesson	1	2	3	4	5	R	6	7	8	9	10	R	11	12	13	14	15	R	16	17	18	19	20	R
1.	Learn unfamiliar vocabulary	●	●	●	●	●	●	●	●	●	●	●	●	●	●	●	●	●	●	●	●	●	●	●	●
2.	Infer word meanings from context clues	■	■	■	●	■	●	●	●	■	■	■	●	●	■	■	●	●	●	●	■	●	■	■	■
3.	Identify definitions/descriptions of terms	●	●	●	●	●	●	●	▲	●		●	●	●			■	●	●	●	●	●	●	●	●
4.	Identify synonyms	●		●		▲	●		●			●	●		●						●				
5.	Identify antonyms		■	●			●				■		●	●								■		■	●
6.	Complete word associations		●	●	●		●	●		●	●						●	■			●				●
7.	Complete analogies				●						●					●	●								
8.	Increase understanding of prefixes and suffixes		■	■		■		■			■	■	●							■					
9.	Review homonyms																	●							
10.	Learn etymological origins	■			▲									■								■			
11.	Complete word puzzles							■							■			■							
12.	Use word families correctly														■	■					■				
13.	Form/use compound words																■								
14.	Learn/review idioms, sayings, and proverbs	▲			▲			▲					▲						▲	▲					

Literary Understanding	Lesson	1	2	3	4	5	R	6	7	8	9	10	R	11	12	13	14	15	R	16	17	18	19	20	R
1.	Identify/interpret characters' actions, motivations, feelings, and qualities	●	●			●	●	●	●	▲					●			●			●			●	●
2.	Infer/interpret author's purpose/attitude	●						●	●										▲		●	●		●	
3.	Predict/describe future/alternative events	●				●				▲	●	▲		▲			▲	●	●		●				
4.	Interpret poetry						●				●								●			●		●	
5.	Compare/contrast points of view						●			▲	▲	●	●	●			▲	▲	▲		●		●	●	
6.	Interpret figurative language						●			▲	●				●		▲	●	●		●		●		●
7.	Relate to characters' motivations and feelings	▲				●				●	●	●	●				●	●			●				
8.	Identify setting																▲					●			
9.	Interpret drama	▲										▲					▲				▲				
10.	Identify literary genres	▲				▲	▲	▲		▲	▲	▲	▲	▲			▲	▲	▲		▲		▲		▲

KEY: ● = Primary emphasis   ■ = Secondary emphasis   ▲ = Integrated with other skills

Comprehension	Lesson	1	2	3	4	5	R	6	7	8	9	10	R	11	12	13	14	15	R	16	17	18	19	20	R
1.	Read selections independently	●	●	●	●	●	●	●	●	●	●	●	●	●	●	●	●	●	●	●	●	●	●	●	
2.	Complete exercises independently	●	●	●	●	●	●	●	●	●	●	●	●	●	●	●	●	●	●	●	●	●	●	●	●
3.	Identify words using context clues	●	●	●	●	●	●	●	●	●	●	●	●	●	●	●	●	●	●	●	●	●	●	●	●
4.	Improve listening comprehension	▲	▲	▲	▲	▲	▲	▲	▲	▲	▲	▲	▲	▲	▲	▲	▲	▲	▲	▲	▲	▲	▲	▲	▲
5.	Improve oral reading skills	▲	▲	▲	▲	▲	▲	▲	▲	▲	▲	▲	▲	▲	▲	▲	▲	▲	▲	▲	▲	▲	▲	▲	▲
6.	Develop literal comprehension skills:																								
	– Recall details	■	■	■		■		■	■	■	■			■	■	■	■	■		■	■	■	■	■	■
	– Locate specific information	■	■	■		■		■		■	■	■		■	■	■	■	■		■	■	■	■	■	
	– Establish sequence of events	●										■							●						
7.	Develop inferential comprehension skills:																								
	– Support statements with appropriate details	●	●	●	●	●	●	●	●	●	●	●		●	●	●	●	●	●	●	●	●	●	●	●
	– Infer word meanings from context clues	●	●	●	●	●	●	●	●	●	●	●		●	●	●	●	●	●	●	●	●	●	●	●
	– Infer information from the reading or exercises	●	●	●	●	●	●	●	●	●	●	●		●	●	●	●	●	●	●	●	●	●	●	
	– Draw conclusions based on reading	●	●					▲				▲			▲	▲						●		●	
	– Compare/contrast points of view		●	●			▲	▲	▲	●	●				▲										
	– Relate examples to ideas						▲					▲		■	▲		▲	▲			▲		●	▲	
	– Use context clues to fill in missing words	■				■						■	■			●			●		●		■		
	– Identify/interpret humor					▲	▲		▲	▲		▲			●		▲	▲	▲		▲	●			
	– Identify/infer cause-and-effect relationships													●						●				▲	
	– Organize information in outline form											●	●												
	– Classify words under topic headings			■																					
	– Distinguish between fact and opinion	●							●		●												●		●
8.	Develop applied comprehension skills:																								
	– Draw conclusions based on personal experience	●	●	●	●	●		●		●	●	●		●	●	●	●	●	●	●	●	●	●	●	
	– Relate reading to personal experience	●	●	●	●	▲	▲		▲	▲	●	●		●								●			
	– Design a bar graph											●													
	– Draw a diagram or time line							●																	
9.	Learn/review basic factual information	■				■		■		■			■	●		●		■	●	■		■	■	■	■
10.	Locate/infer information from:																								
	– maps		●																						
	– editorial cartoons			●											●										
	– charts and graphs													●											●
	– diagrams and time lines											■	■												

KEY: ● = Primary emphasis   ■ = Secondary emphasis   ▲ = Integrated with other skills

Writing

Lesson	1	2	3	4	5	R	6	7	8	9	10	R	11	12	13	14	15	R	16	17	18	19	20	R
1. Write sentence or paragraph answers to questions	●	●	●	●	●	●	●	●	●	●	●	●	●	●	●	●	●	●	●	●	●	●	●	●
2. Form a reasoned opinion	●	●	●	●	●	●	●	●	●	●	●	●	●	●	●	●	●	●	●	●	●	●	●	●
3. Support statements with details	●	●	●	●	●	●	●	●	●	●	●	●	●	●	●	●	●	●	●	●	●	●	●	●
4. Copy words accurately	▲	▲	▲	▲	▲	▲	▲	▲	▲	▲	▲	▲	▲	▲	▲	▲	▲	▲	▲	▲	▲	▲	▲	▲
5. Spelling:																								
– Spell words with greater accuracy	▲	▲	▲	▲	▲	▲	▲	▲	▲	▲	▲	▲	▲	▲	▲	▲	▲	▲	▲	▲	▲	▲	▲	▲
– Spell homonyms correctly		▲															●						▲	▲
– Identify misspelled words				■																			■	
6. Write contrasting statements		●						■													●			
7. Write dialogue		▲		▲																▲				
8. Write about an illustration								■	■															
9. Write a biography																						●		

Note: Specific suggestions for additional writing assignments appear in the individual lesson notes of this manual.

Study Skills

Lesson	1	2	3	4	5	R	6	7	8	9	10	R	11	12	13	14	15	R	16	17	18	19	20	R
1. Increase concentration	■	■	■	■	■	■	■	■	■	■	■	■	■	■	■	■	■	■	■	■	■	■	■	■
2. Skim selection to locate information	■	■	▲	■	■	■	■	■	■	■	■	■	■	■	■	■	■	■	■	■	■	■	■	
3. Apply reasoning skills to exercises:																								
– context clues	■	■	■	■	■	■	●	●	■	■	■	■	■	■	■	■	■	●	■	■	■	■	■	■
– process of elimination	■	■	■	■	■	■	■	■	■	■	■	■	■	■	■	■	■	■	■	■	■	■	■	■
– "intelligent guessing"	■	■	■	■	■	■	■	■	■	■	■	■	■	■	■	■	■	■	■	■	■	■	■	■
4. Use a dictionary or the Internet:																								
– to look up word meanings		■	▲		▲	▲	▲	▲	■	▲	■	■	■	■	■	■	▲	■	■	▲	▲	■	■	
– to learn word origins	■												■											
– to learn plural forms of words																■								
– to form compound words								■																
5. Use reference materials to find factual/ geographical information	■				●	▲	▲							■			■		■			■	■	▲

SCOPE AND SEQUENCE: Challenger Writing 8

The following scope and sequence chart indicates the introduction and major practice for writing skills. It also shows the introduction of grammar and mechanics rules that are most helpful to emerging writers. Reinforcement and practice of these rules are spread throughout the various exercises.

Lesson	STRAND 10 Write a 5-paragraph summary	Write a 5-paragraph expository essay	Write a 3-paragraph summary	Write a 4-paragraph expository essay	Write a 5-paragraph persuasive essay	STRAND 11 Add Details (vivid words, specific nouns, action verbs)	Try Your Hand at Using Details	Choose the Best Descriptive Words and Phrases	STRAND 12 What Do you Mean? (run-on sentences)	What Do You Mean? (sentence fragments)	What Do You Mean? (comma faults)
1	X										
2		X									
3		X									
4		X									
5		X	X								
6		X				X					
7		X									
8				X							
9		X									
10		X			X	X					
11	X	X			X	X					
12		X							X		
13		X								X	
14		X									X
15		X							X	X	X
16		X							X	X	X
17		X							X	X	X
18		X					X				
19		X					X	X			
20		X									
R		X									

Scope and Sequence: Level 8 TEACHER'S MANUAL **29**

Lesson	STRAND 14 — What Will You Write About? (listing)	What Will You Write About? (brainstorming)	What Will You Write About? (5 W's and H)	What Will You Write About? (T-chart)	What Will You Write About? (mapping)	What Will You Write About? (chart)	What Will You Write About? (Venn diagram)	STRAND 15 — Is It One or More Than One? (subject-verb agreement)
1					X			
2						X		
3		X				X		X
4		X				X		X
5			X					
6		X				X		
7	X					X		
8							X	
9	X					X		
10	X	X				X		
11	X					X		
12								
13				X		X		
14		X				X		
15		X				X		
16	X	X				X		
17				X		X		
18				X		X		
19						X	X	
20	X	X				X		
R								

Lesson	STRAND 17				STRAND 18			STRAND 19		
	Add Transitions (time order)	Add Transitions (cause, effect)	Add Transitions (compare, contrast)	Add Transitions (add info)	Untangle the Confusion (misplaced modifiers)	Untangle the Confusion (missing words)	Untangle the Confusion (antecedents)	How Will You Organize Your Summary? (chronological order)	How Will You Organize Your Essay? (order of importance)	How Will You Organize Your Essay? (block arrangement)
1						X	X	X		
2					X				X	
3									X	
4									X	
5	X							X		
6									X	
7				X					X	
8			X							X
9		X							X	
10									X	
11									X	
12									X	
13									X	
14								X		
15								X	X	
16									X	
17									X	
18										
19									X	
20										
R										

Chapter 1 Preparing to Teach

The following suggestions are based on the author's experiences and those of other teachers who have used these books. You may find that your own situation renders some of these suggestions either impractical or impossible to implement in your classroom. It is hoped, however, that most of these suggestions can be modified to meet your particular needs.

How Often to Use *Challenger*

In general, it is recommended that teachers use *Challenger* with students two or three times a week for at least 45 minutes per session. If you meet five times a week with pre-GED students who are eager to pass the tests and have time outside the classroom to complete homework assignments, you may want to use *Challenger* every day.

If you meet five times a week with an adult or adolescent reading class that does not have a specific task such as GED preparation to motivate them, the recommended schedule is to focus on the lessons three times a week and devote the other two class sessions to activities that reinforce or enrich material presented in the lessons. Suggestions about these reinforcement activities appear in Chapter 4.

It is important that students recognize the need to work with *Challenger* regularly. This is often an issue for students in volunteer programs or institutions in which class attendance is not mandatory. Whatever the situation, if a student chooses to attend class on a highly infrequent basis, tell him politely but frankly that there is little point in his attending at all because he's not giving himself a chance to make any significant progress.

If only one class meeting a week is possible, try to schedule this class for 90 minutes to two hours. Also, have the students complete two lessons and, if appropriate, a writing activity for homework. When the students look at you as if you are crazy, show them that by completing a few components of the lessons each day, they will not only be able to do the work but also reinforce what they are learning. Sports and music are helpful analogies because most students know that both require daily practice.

The Lesson Format

After the first class, which of course involves no homework review, the procedure for each lesson is basically the same. The overview below gives you an idea of what happens during each class. More detailed procedures for this work appear in later chapters of this manual.

1. **Writing assignment.** If students have been given a writing assignment, begin the class by letting them share their work in pairs or small groups. Chapter 3 gives details on writing assignments.

2. **Homework review.** Discuss the reading selection to make sure students have understood it and to give them a chance to react to the reading. Then go over the comprehension questions and the other exercises, and have students make any necessary corrections.

3. **Reinforcement activity.** If no writing assignment was given and if time permits, have the students do one or more reinforcement activities. See Chapter 4 for suggestions about reinforcement activities.

4. **Homework preview.** Go over the Words for Study listed at the beginning of the lesson. Introduce the reading selection, and call attention to any special features that may be new or confusing. Have students quickly preview the individual exercises for anything they don't understand.

Following this general procedure on a fairly consistent basis helps students because they tend to feel more relaxed and work better when they have a sense of routine. Modifications in the procedure should be made only when they will enhance students' reading development.

Just as you encourage students to see homework assignments as daily workouts, encourage them to see class time as a daily workout, also. These lessons should not be seen as achievement tests but rather as opportunities to move students smoothly toward their reading goals. Students do not have to demonstrate mastery of the material in one lesson in order to go on to the next lesson. Mastery will come with consistent practice.

It is crucial for teachers to think in terms of improvement rather than mastery because students using these books often want to add a fourth component to the lesson format—rationalizing and/or lamenting their mistakes. This uses up valuable classroom time and, if allowed a foothold, will result in students giving up and dropping out. Students must learn to perceive their mistakes as a natural and helpful part of the learning process. They can learn this only by your gentle but firm reminder that consistent practice is the key to mastery.

Remember that both adult and adolescent reading students tend to be overly sensitive to mistakes in their work. In most cases, they firmly believe that if they hadn't made so many mistakes in the first place, they wouldn't have to be working in these books. For example, a woman in her mid-twenties who decided to quit class explained her reason this way: "My teacher told me that it was all right to make mistakes, but every time I had one in my work, she would kind of close her eyes and shake her head like I should have learned all this in the fourth grade." Teachers must think and act in terms of improvement rather than mastery and regard mistakes as natural and helpful.

Do not expect to know at the outset how much time to allot to each segment of the lesson. Understanding exactly how to pace the lessons takes time. By paying attention to students' responses and rate of accuracy, you will gradually learn how to schedule the lessons so that students improve their reading and writing skills in a relaxed but efficient manner.

Preparing the Lessons

In preparing the lessons, develop the habit of following this procedure:

1. Familiarize yourself with the lesson students are to work on that day.
2. Review the appropriate lesson notes in this manual for suggestions to help you teach the lesson. Go over the appropriate answers in the Answer Key in the student book as well.
3. Review any notes you took after the preceding class in which you jotted down vocabulary words or writing difficulties that students need to review. Teacher note-taking is discussed in Chapter 5 of this manual.
4. Decide on any reinforcement activities you may want to use, and complete any preparation needed. Suggestions for reinforcement activities are given in Chapter 4.
5. Skim the lesson to be assigned for homework and the appropriate lesson notes so you can introduce the reading selection and answer any questions students may have about the exercises.

Last and most important, you need to prepare yourself mentally and emotionally for the class. If possible, take several minutes before the students' arrival to unwind from the previous activities of the day. As a general rule, how well the lesson goes is determined by how relaxed and focused you are on the work. As the teacher, your main function is to serve as a smooth "bridge" between the student and the lesson material. Your own patience and concentration will determine how helpful this bridge is.

The Teacher-Student Relationship

Making sure that you are relaxed for the lesson also contributes to the development of a good working relationship with your students. Adolescent or adult reading students rely heavily on your support and encouragement.

It is helpful to remember that most of us, as we grow older, learn to fake or avoid situations in which we feel inadequate. We prefer habits and routines that are familiar and give us some sense of security. Adolescent or adult reading students have entered into a situation in which they cannot avoid the material (unless they give up) or fake their way through it. They are to be admired for having put themselves in this situation. Unless they are extremely motivated or thick-skinned, they must feel a sense of support from you or they will eventually drop out, because exposing their lack of knowledge just gets too painful after a while.

In addition, completing the lessons in these books *is* hard work. No matter how much progress is being made, virtually all students experience a sense of frustration at one time or another. Your encouragement will help them to get through these gloomy periods when they are ready to throw in the towel.

Suggestions for a Good Working Rapport

The following are suggestions to help you consider how best to develop a good working relationship with your students.

- Strive for naturalness in your voice and mannerisms. Some teachers unconsciously treat reading students as if they were mental invalids or victims of a ruthless society. A condescending or pitying approach does not help students become better readers.
- Greet the students pleasantly, and spend a few minutes in casual conversation before you actually begin work. As a rule, do not allow this conversation to exceed five minutes. Students will take their cue from you. If you encourage conversing rather than working, they will be more than willing to oblige.
- Participate fully in this pre-lesson conversation, and listen attentively to the students' remarks. Often you can later refer to these remarks when you are helping students to understand a vocabulary word or a point in the reading selection. Not only do they appreciate the fact that you actually were listening to them, but also they begin to make connections with the material they are studying.
- Use a phrase such as "Shall we get started?" to indicate that it is time to begin the lesson. A consistent use of such transitional statements helps the students feel more comfortable with both you and the class routine.
- If possible, work at an uncluttered table rather than at desks. Try to have straight-backed, cushioned chairs since physical comfort makes developing a good relationship easier.
- Be sure to use positive reinforcement during the lesson. Remind students of the progress they are making. When a student is particularly discouraged, do this in a concrete way. For example, show him how many pages

of work he has completed, or have him look at his composition book to see all the writing he has done.

- Develop the habit of wishing students a good day or a good evening as they leave the class. This is especially important if both you and the students have had a rough session. The students, particularly adolescents, need to know that you don't carry personal grudges.

GENERAL SUPPLIES

For each class, students need to bring their *Challenger* books, their writing notebooks, and pens or pencils. The use of a writing notebook—a slim loose-leaf binder with wide-lined paper—is discussed in Chapter 3.

You need your own copy of *Challenger*, any notes and reinforcement activities pertaining to the lesson, a few sheets of blank paper for notes, and a pen, A pen is recommended because students can spot your marginal notes and corrections more easily. Avoid red ink as it may be associated with bad memories by some students.

Have a dictionary and, if possible, access to the Internet. Keep a map or an atlas within easy reach. The dictionary is a valuable resource because it provides additional information about many of the words, people, and events mentioned in the reading selections and exercises. Be prepared to teach students how to use these resources. Do not assume that students working at a Book 5 or above reading level are familiar with them.

A map or atlas is helpful because it can make the facts presented in the lessons more meaningful to students. Access to the Internet is also very valuable. For example, in Lesson 10, Exercise 6 of Book 6, students are introduced to the Jew's harp. Although they are given a description of the item, this presents a good opportunity for students to research the item online to see what it looks and sounds like.

Encourage students to research additional information as often as their interest, abilities, and time permit, and give them all the assistance you can when they need help. These mini-research experiences help students feel more competent when searching for information.

A Summary of *Dos*

1. Do try to schedule as many sessions each week as possible.
2. Do develop a consistent lesson format.
3. Do take time to decide the pace that works best for your students.
4. Do prepare for each class.
5. Do take a few moments to relax before each class.
6. Do develop a good working relationship with your students because it is essential to their reading progress.
7. Do make sure that the environment in which you teach is as conducive to good learning as possible.

Chapter 2 Teaching the Lessons

In this chapter, suggestions are given for teaching the main components of each lesson. These components include word study, the reading selection, the exercises, correcting the homework, and the homework preview.

Word Study

The *Challenger* series places a great deal of emphasis on learning and/or reviewing word meanings since a major obstacle to reading development is a poor vocabulary. It has been estimated that only about 2,000 words account for 99 percent of everything we say. To be a proficient reader, however, one must be familiar with far more than 2,000 words. Thus, except for the reading comprehension exercises, most of the other exercises focus on vocabulary development.

WORD CHARTS AND DEFINITIONS

As mentioned previously, the word charts in student books 5 and 7 contain new words that are organized around common phonics principles. Most of these principles have been introduced in earlier books and are now simply being reviewed. How much emphasis you give to the phonics principles depends on the needs of your students. Some students enjoy reading the chart words aloud, while others prefer to start each class with the definitions exercise. Words from the chart are repeated frequently in exercises, so it is not essential that students read the chart words aloud. For those who do, however, emphasize pronunciation only. Meanings are stressed in the definitions exercise and in many other exercises.

WORDS FOR STUDY

Keep in mind that the *Challenger* series is a controlled vocabulary series. When students wish to know how the words listed in the Words for Study at the beginning of each lesson have been selected, inform them that these words are appearing for the first time in the series. Most of the other words in each lesson have appeared earlier in the series.

Some students not only find the concept of a controlled vocabulary interesting but interpret this concept in interesting ways. For example, one student who was experiencing difficulty with a synonym exercise in Book 7 remarked: "Well, you can't expect me to know words that were studied in Book 6!"

Behind this statement is a conviction shared by many reading students that once you've studied a word, you should never have to study it again. Unfortunately, this is not true. Words are learned through repetition, practice, and using the dictionary. Do not assume that your students

know this. Simply remind them, when appropriate, that a good reading vocabulary is necessary for good reading and that they will encounter a word in various types of exercises so that they can truly master its meaning.

The best way to encourage your students as they complete the many vocabulary development exercises is to demonstrate an interest in language yourself. This does not mean that you have to use a lot of fancy words when talking to your students. What it does mean is that you do not approach vocabulary study as if it were something merely to be endured.

SUGGESTIONS FOR ENRICHING WORD STUDY

Here are a few suggestions for making vocabulary study more interesting for students:

1. Have students pronounce the Words for Study in the next lesson during the homework preview. Most words will not give them any trouble. By pronouncing the unfamiliar ones, students will gain confidence in their ability to learn the words, and confidence often leads to interest.

2. Encourage students to develop the habit of paying attention to word endings. Words listed in the Words for Study appear in the same form in which they appear in the reading. For example, notice that in Lesson 1, *following* is listed. Emphasis on accurate pronunciations of endings will help students with both their reading and writing.

3. When time permits, spend a few minutes in casual conversation about some of the words. Using the Words for Study in Lesson 2 of Book 5 as an example, you may wish to talk about the different ways the word *grant* can be used, or have students identify the root in *reaction*, or help them to trace the origin of *synonym* in a good dictionary. Occasional discussion of words helps students to see them as more than just a string of letters.

4. Take time during discussions of the readings to highlight vocabulary and/or language features. In Lesson 6, Exercise 3 of Book 8, students use context to figure out the meaning of words.

5. Finally, strive to speak with expression. You needn't be a Broadway star, but a little ham goes a long way.

Reading Selections

The amount of time you allot to oral reading and discussion of the reading selections ultimately depends on both the needs of your students and how much class time you have with them.

PRE-READING AND POST-READING ACTIVITIES

There are many types of pre-reading and post-reading activities to aid students in developing strategies for increasing their literal, interpretive, and critical comprehension skills.

Pre-reading activities should accomplish one or more of the following objectives:

1. to stimulate students' interest by drawing on prior experience and understanding of the subject.
2. to provide essential background information.
3. to give students a purpose for reading.

You can link the subject of the reading to students' own experiences by asking "Have you ever done/been/thought/felt...?" questions. Some of the readings are better understood if the historical setting is first discussed or described. It is also helpful to set a task for students as they read. For example, for the story in Lesson 1 of Book 5, you might say, "As you read, think about what kind of person Grandpa was."

Read the first few paragraphs of each reading selection aloud to the students. Have them follow along in the book as you read. Then ask one or two questions to make sure students have understood what you read. By reading aloud, you can create interest in the reading and give students a feel for the author's style and tone. At the same time, you are modeling good reading for your students.

After students have finished reading the selection for homework, have a general discussion to refresh their memories and to make sure they have understood the reading. Then discuss their responses to any pre-reading task you set for them. Also discuss their responses to the comprehension exercises.

You should make a list of pre- and post-reading questions and/or activities for each reading selection based on your students' backgrounds, capabilities, and needs. The individual lesson notes give some suggestions.

Encourage students to talk about how they feel about the readings. Remember that literature evokes emotional as well as intellectual responses and is meant to be enjoyable.

ORAL READING

Having students read aloud at least part of the reading selection periodically gives you an opportunity to note their strengths and weaknesses and also to help them develop good oral reading habits. Some students are under the impression that good oral reading means that one reads as fast as one can. Remind these students that in oral reading one must always be conscious of the needs of the listeners.

DISCUSSING THE READING

To create an atmosphere in which the reading selections and student thoughts about them can be discussed with a sense of harmony and unity, consider these suggestions.

1. Plan questions that you want to ask in class. Be prepared, however, to put your planned questions aside when a spontaneous question arises in class.
2. Make sure students understand the basic ground rule of all good discussions: one person speaks at a time.
3. Encourage participation, but don't force it. Likewise, discourage students from monopolizing the discussion.
4. Keep the discussion focused.
5. Avoid asking "yes" and "no" questions. Discussions, like travel, should be broadening. "Yes" and "no" questions shut off discussion by being answerable in a single word. They also imply that the student should have reached a conclusion before the discussion has even started.
6. If students seem confused by your questions, rephrase them rather than repeating them word for word. This practice is not only courteous, but it also reminds students that there is usually more than one way to phrase an idea.

These suggestions represent the easier part of moderating a discussion. The harder part is staying out of the way. Your task as the moderator is to get students to react to each other's opinions and comments, not to dominate the discussion yourself.

It is essential to view discussions in the same way that you view the students' other work—in terms of improvement, or growth, instead of mastery. It takes time to develop a good discussion group in which participants can learn to really listen to each other and gain confidence to express themselves as genuinely as possible. Do not expect it to be otherwise.

Through these discussions, students begin to sense a relationship between the lesson material and their own lives. The relationships they have with you and the other students can become more relaxed and real. This, in turn, means that everyone learns better and faster.

The Exercises

In the exercises, students develop their reasoning abilities because they are required to think and infer, to use context clues, to practice the process of elimination, and to apply what they already know to new situations.

Three points that you should emphasize to students are accuracy, legibility, and completeness. They are to spell their responses correctly and legibly, and they are not to leave any item blank. Tell them to answer all questions to the best of their ability. Not only does learning thrive on corrected mistakes, but also much is to be said for the art of intelligent guessing.

Remind students to check over their homework after they have finished all the exercises to make sure they have answered all questions completely and accurately.

Allow enough time at the end of the class period for previewing the exercises that are to be completed for homework. It is important that students understand exactly what is expected of them, so don't rush this segment of the lesson.

You should spend a few minutes during the first class meeting with your students to review the importance of homework. Remember, some of your students haven't been in a school situation for quite a while, and they may need to be reminded of the importance of completing the assignments as well as they can.

Sometimes students try to complete the homework right after a full day's (or full night's) work, or just before going to bed, or while trying to fulfill other responsibilities. Suggest that they schedule definite 30-minute study times in quiet surroundings when they are not exhausted.

Make sure to present your ideas on how to develop better study habits in the form of suggestions. You are not stating policy; you are simply encouraging students to think about how they can better achieve their reading goals within the circumstances of their lives.

CORRECTING THE HOMEWORK

Be sure you allow enough time to go over the homework with the students. You will probably need to observe your students and try out a few different schedules before you hit on the pace that works best for them. But once you establish the appropriate pace, consistency promotes good concentration and effective learning.

Of all the lesson segments—the words for study, the reading selection, and the exercises—the exercises should be covered most thoroughly. All the homework should be corrected. Remember that many patterns are being established. If students develop the habit of doing something incorrectly, they will have a hard time unlearning the procedure. Be sure to explain this to the students. Eventually, they adapt to this procedure because they see that the more they correct in the early stages, the less they have to correct later.

Too often, going over the homework can be nothing more than a dry, mechanical routine in which students simply read their answers. Not only does this deprive them of practice with the words and concepts they've been studying, but also it is unfair. Consciously or unconsciously, the students' efforts are being slighted if the homework critique is being done in a dreary "what's-the-answer-to-number-2?" style.

Take your time and enjoy this part of the lesson. If opportunities arise for brief tangents in which items are related to life experiences or other bits of information, take advantage of them.

Above all, don't forget to express your appreciation for students' efforts. Your supportive remarks should be brief and spoken in a natural voice. Excessive praise is ultimately as counterproductive as no praise at all. Words of encouragement should stress the notion of progress because students are progressing as they complete each lesson.

THE HOMEWORK PREVIEW

During the homework preview, the students note what to do in the next lesson, which they are to complete for homework. Begin by going over the words listed in the Words for Study. Then introduce the reading selection to give students an idea of what they will be reading about. It may be necessary to help students get into the habit of noting the title of the reading selection. They should understand that the title gives them a general idea of what the selection is about and helps to focus their attention. Also, tell students to look at any illustrations that accompany a reading. Explain that illustrations may offer clues to what a reading is about.

Remind students to refer to the reading selection when they cannot recall an answer to a comprehension question. In many instances, they may need to make intelligent guesses based on information that is implied rather than stated directly.

At this point in their reading development, all students are able to skim through the exercises and ask questions about words and/or directions with no assistance from you. The individual lesson notes indicate those instances in which you may want to emphasize certain words or directions.

A Summary of *Dos*

1. Do take time when necessary to explain to students how vocabulary study, the reading selections, and exercises contribute to their reading development.
2. Do make vocabulary study as interesting as possible.
3. Do plan pre-reading and post-reading activities to develop students' literal, interpretive, and critical comprehension skills.
4. Do encourage students to have an attitude of growth rather than fixed opinions in their discussions.
5. Do remind students, when necessary, of the significant role that homework plays in reading development.
6. Do emphasize the need for thoroughness, correct spelling, and accuracy in completing each exercise.
7. Do strive for completeness and enthusiasm in the homework reviews.
8. Do support the students' progress by taking the time to point out growth they have demonstrated in their work.
9. Do allow enough time at the end of each lesson to go over the Words for Study, introduce the next reading selection, and preview the homework exercises.

Chapter 3 Writing

The Challenger *series emphasizes helping students to develop their reading skills. Opportunities for sustained writing in the student books are necessarily limited. This chapter gives suggestions for integrating more writing practice into the lessons on a regular basis. You may also include the correlated* Challenger Writing *student workbooks as part of your* Challenger *curriculum. More information on the writing workbooks is given on pages 39–40 of this teacher's guide.*

Why Writing Is Included

The teacher can assume that a student who has completed some of the books that precede Book 5 can write complete sentences and coherent paragraphs. These students will not be surprised at the exercises that involve writing in the later *Challenger* books.

Students who are new to this series may wonder why writing activities have been included in a reading series. When this is the case, take time to point out the following:

• Writing is part of literacy. To be literate, a person must be able to write as well as read.

• Writing helps students to formulate and express their thoughts more precisely. This type of thinking helps them to complete the other exercises more rapidly.

• The writing that students do in these lessons will help them with other types of writing they may want to do, such as letters, reports, and short paragraphs on job applications or resumés.

• Only through actually writing can students see that they are able to write.

Opportunities for Writing

In the student books, primary emphasis is placed on content rather than on the mechanics of writing. The reading comprehension questions require students to draw conclusions from inferences, to cite reasons to support their opinions, to give explanations for their answers, and to cite examples and details to support their responses. There are also opportunities for imaginative writing, such as predicting the endings to stories.

The individual lesson notes include many suggestions for writing assignments, which can supplement the lessons as reinforcement activities. As stated in the introduction to each level, it is recommended that weekly writing assignments be given. However, the decision on how often to give writing assignments as homework should depend on the teacher's assessment of the students' time, personal needs, and capabilities. The key word is flexibility.

How to Handle Writing Assignments

When students have been given a writing assignment, have them share their work at the beginning of the next class session. Working in pairs or small groups, students can read their assignments aloud to one another and react to each other's writing on the basis of content and organization. Students can then exchange papers and act as editors or proofreaders, checking for mechanical problems such as missing words, spelling, capitalization, and punctuation. Give students the opportunity to revise their assignments before collecting them at the following class session.

When responding to these writing assignments, try to make positive comments as well as noting areas for improvement. Your reactions should be based more on the content, style, and organization of the writing than on the mechanical aspects.

It is recommended that students keep all writing assignments in a slim loose-leaf binder with wide-lined notebook paper. Composition books enable both the students and the teacher to quickly review student progress. Have them date their work. As the weeks and months progress, most students enjoy looking back now and then at all the writing they have done and how much they have accomplished.

Like reading and vocabulary work, writing must be seen in terms of improvement rather than mastery. Most students read far better than they write. It is not uncommon for a student working in Book 6, for example, to write at a Book 4 level: very simple sentences, few modifiers, and underdeveloped thoughts. The most common reason for this is lack of practice. The writing workbooks can help students practice good writing habits. Allow students to develop from their own starting points, making them aware of their strengths as well as helping them to work on their weaknesses. And don't forget to be patient.

Here are a few suggestions to consider in helping students with their writing:

• As often as possible, have students read their written responses or compositions aloud. Students usually enjoy doing this, and it gives them a chance to hear whether or not their writing makes sense. Insist on honest but courteously presented reactions from the other students.

- Occasionally, allot some class time to studying how the professional writers write. Use a reading selection from *Challenger* or an interesting magazine article. Help students analyze the piece of writing on the basis of content organization and style. Make sure students understand that the writing they are analyzing is more than a second, third, or fourth draft. Few students recognize the contribution editing makes in the writing process, and understanding this makes them feel less discouraged about their writing difficulties.
- With their permission, use writing from previous or present students as models to explain a particularly difficult writing assignment. Seeing the work of their peers often helps students realize that the teacher is not asking them to do the impossible.
- With their permission, compile a worksheet using sentences from student work that illustrate common mistakes. For example, a worksheet comprised of student-created run-on sentences is an excellent reinforcement activity. Students can work together in class to correct the errors and better understand how to avoid this particular writing problem.
- Provide the opportunity for students to publicly display their final drafts so other students can read them.

Dealing with Typical Writing Problems

RUN-ON SENTENCES

This situation demands consummate tact on your part because, invariably, the student thinks she has written a terrific sentence and is dismayed to learn that she has to divide it into three or four shorter sentences. Help her to see that by using commas and periods wherever necessary, she helps readers to follow her thoughts more easily. To illustrate how punctuation helps the reader, have her read the sentence aloud, telling her to pause only at commas and to take a breath only at a period. If you prefer, you can demonstrate by reading her sentence to her. When she recognizes the value of punctuation marks, have her revise the run-on sentence as necessary. Be sure to commend her for her effort in helping to make her writing easier for readers to comprehend.

OMITTED WORDS

When reading their sentences aloud, students are often surprised to see that they have omitted words. Remind them that many writers have this problem because the mind can think faster than the hand can write. Suggest that after they have written something, they should read it to themselves, pointing to each word as they encounter it. This strategy will help them learn to monitor their own writing.

CONFUSING SENTENCES

When a student writes a sentence that is confusing, tell him you don't understand what he's trying to express, and ask him to explain what he meant. Once you understand his intent, start a more coherent version of his sentence, and have him finish it. After the student has read the revision, ask him if it matches what he meant. If not, work on the sentence until the revision accurately expresses the student's original idea.

PROBLEMS WITH CONTENT AND ORGANIZATION

Students often have difficulty finding enough to say in their writing assignments and organizing their thoughts in a logical or interesting manner. Suggest that they begin by making notes of everything they can think of pertaining to the topic. The next step is to select from their notes the specific points and details that they want to include in their compositions. Then they should organize those points and details in the order in which they want to include them. They should do all of this *before* writing the first draft. After the first draft is written, they should read it to see if they want to add anything more or to rearrange any of the points.

A Summary of *Dos* and *Don'ts*

1. Do tailor writing assignments to meet the students' needs and capabilities.
2. Do make sure that students understand the purpose and value of writing practice.
3. Do have students keep an orderly composition book for all their writing.
4. Do make sure that written work is evaluated, and when appropriate, have students write at least a second draft.
5. Do provide opportunities for students to share their writing with each other.
6. Don't expect the students' writing levels to be as high as their reading levels.
7. Don't allow writing assignments to become more important than the lessons and other necessary reinforcement activities.

Correlated Writing Workbooks

The eight *Challenger Writing* workbooks have been developed to provide additional writing practice for students at each level of the *Challenger* reading series. Each of the eight writing books contains two pages of exercises for each lesson in the corresponding *Challenger* student book. Comprehension of the reading selections is aided by doing exercises in the writing books. Students are asked to write about personal opinions and experiences related to the readings. Thus, reading comprehension and vocabulary building are reinforced while writing and thinking skills are being developed.

Challenger Writing is designed to systematically develop the skills necessary for writing sentences, paragraphs, and more. Writing skills are developed sequentially throughout the eight writing books, as exercise formats become familiar while increasing in difficulty and sophistication.

Related strands of exercises also become more difficult as the series levels progress. These strands include:
- Filling in missing words
- Putting sentences in order
- Completing sentences and paragraphs
- Writing guided and open-ended paragraphs

As well as helping to develop writing skills, the exercises in the correlated *Challenger* writing books also develop and reinforce critical thinking skills. Questions about time order help develop sequencing skills. Exercises that ask for a reason why an incident in a story may have happened reinforce the concept of cause and effect. Learners develop basic skills in logic and reasoning as they write coherent sentences and responses to questions.

And because *Challenger* is a controlled-vocabulary reading series, the vocabulary in the student writing books is also controlled. Words used at each level of the writing books are those that have been introduced in the corresponding level of student book.

The lesson notes for Books 5–8 include notes about writing activities that are in the correlated writing books.

Chapter 4 Reinforcement Activities

As the term suggests, these activities are designed to reinforce the students' understanding and retention of the lesson material. All students and most teachers occasionally need a break in the routine. Reinforcement activities may throw your schedule off a bit, but it's worth it. Just make sure that you leave enough time at the end of the class period to preview the homework.

Choosing Activities

At this point in students' development, two types of activities are particularly helpful:

- activities that reinforce vocabulary skills.
- occasional, short exercises that focus on mechanical or usage errors most of your students repeatedly make in their compositions.

The types of activities you use and the frequency with which you use them depend on the needs of your students and how often you have an opportunity to meet with them. The suggestions in this section are based on activities that students have found both helpful and enjoyable. This list is by no means complete. Take some time to develop your own "bag of tricks." Through talking with other teachers, skimming puzzle magazines, and using your own imagination, you will soon have reinforcement activities for a variety of skills. Students, too, often recall helpful activities from their earlier schooling. In fact, some of the suggestions that follow come from students.

Word and Information Games

Students working at this level often enjoy games that are modeled after television shows such as *Jeopardy*. These activities take some time to prepare, but they are an excellent way to reinforce vocabulary and information presented in the lessons. Certainly you can prepare the questions, but having the students do it gives them an excellent opportunity to review the material.

Students can create their own *Jeopardy* games by preparing sets of questions based on the reading selections. They can also create sets of vocabulary questions. For example, all the answers in a category might begin with the prefix *pre-* or the letter *s*. Other appropriate categories include State Capitals, Bodies of Water, U.S. Presidents, Roman Gods and Goddesses, Famous Inventors, Abbreviations, and so on.

Other game show formats can also be used. For example, students enjoy playing their own version of *Wheel of Fortune*. They also enjoy their version of *College Bowl* in which two teams compete against each other. In this game, the teacher can prepare the questions and act as the moderator.

PUZZLES

Many puzzles and other activities can be found in puzzle magazines sold in most drugstores and supermarkets. You can create your own puzzles using these formats and vocabulary from past and current word indexes. The word list for Book 5 is at the back of the Book 5 student book. The word indexes for Books 6, 7, and 8 can be found online. You can also go online to access software available for creating crossword puzzles using vocabulary words.

SPELLING BEES OR DRILLS

This activity is most helpful when a specific principle is emphasized, for example, selecting words that all contain a specific suffix or consonant blend, or that belong to the same word family. Again, the word indexes at the back of this manual can be helpful in developing these activities. Drills should be spontaneous, brief—ten words is usually sufficient—and informally presented. In other words, they should not resemble a quiz in which students demonstrate mastery. Rather, they are an opportunity to help students to better understand certain language principles that are giving them difficulty.

Worksheets

One type of worksheet can focus on some principle that is giving students trouble, such as recognizing analogies, using context clues, or making inferences. A popular type of worksheet for context clue or vocabulary reinforcement is to collect sentences from a newspaper or magazine in which troublesome words you have been working with appear. Set them up in a fill-in-the-blank format for the students to complete as a group. As one student once remarked, "You mean people actually do use these words?" You might also tell students to be on the lookout for these words and have them bring to class examples that they find in their own reading.

Another type of worksheet can give students practice with some aspect of writing, such as capitalization or punctuation. For example, many students neglect to use commas after introductory clauses. You might prepare ten sentences that begin with introductory clauses and have the students insert commas appropriately. Students find this type of introduction to grammar both tolerable and beneficial because it helps them to recall a rule they need for their own writing.

Enrichment Projects

Students can spend some time in the library or searching online to find additional information about people or topics presented in the lessons and informally report their findings to the class. These reports can be given during the time set aside for reinforcement activities.

Any additional information that you can present also heightens the students' interest in the material. For example, for Lesson 2 of Student Book 5, you might have copies of easy-to-read collections of myths available so that students can read other myths related to Bacchus or to some of the other gods. You might bring to class photos of statues of the gods or of some of the many paintings that depict the ancient myths. Students could collect references to the gods that they find in newspapers and magazines. The individual lesson notes contain some suggestions for enrichment ideas.

Activities Based on Student Needs

Occasionally students may have specific personal needs, such as filling out an application form or creating a resumé, that can be fit comfortably into the lesson format as reinforcement activities if they tell you about them far enough in advance. However, reinforcement activities are to reinforce, not replace, the lessons. If students are spending most of their valuable class time hearing additional information about the reading selections or getting your assistance with personal needs, they may learn some interesting facts or get forms filled out, but they are not progressing in their reading development.

If you suspect that students are using reinforcement activities to avoid working on the lessons, you probably need to help them clarify their learning goals. Gently but firmly remind them that, in the long run, their reading and writing will progress more rapidly if they concentrate more on the lesson work and recognize that the primary reason for reinforcement activities is to do just that—reinforce.

A Note to the Teacher

Because it takes time to prepare many of these reinforcement activities, be sure to file them away for use with future students.

Also, do not pressure yourself to come up with something new every time you plan a reinforcement activity. It takes a few years to develop a solid file of activities.

A Summary of *Dos* and *Don'ts*

1. Do make sure the scheduled lesson time is not sacrificed for reinforcement activities.

2. Do involve the students in planning and creating reinforcement activities whenever possible.

3. Do plan and implement activities that address both the students' learning needs and their personal needs.

4. Do remember to save materials you develop for future use.

5. Don't foster a "here's-some-more-hard-work" attitude toward reinforcement activities. The students have just finished discussing a reading selection, reviewing their homework, and learning new material. If the reinforcement activities are to benefit them, they need a little more informality from you for this segment of the lesson.

6. Don't foster a "this-is-just-for-fun" attitude either. Some students might not find the activities enjoyable, and you want students who do find them enjoyable to recognize that pleasure and learning can go hand in hand.

Chapter 5 Using the Lesson Notes

Because you are already familiar with the principles and procedures that pertain to the lessons in general from reading the previous chapters in this manual, you have the necessary foundation for sound instructional practices. The lesson notes address some specific points for the individual lessons. As part of class preparation, you should review the notes for the lesson assigned for homework. You should also read the notes for the lesson that you will be previewing to decide on how best to introduce the reading and to note any suggestions and reminders that might be helpful to the students when they are doing their homework.

Keep in mind that the lesson notes are only suggestions based on the experience of other reading teachers. If you try one of the suggestions a few times and find it doesn't work, disregard it.

Items of Primary and Secondary Emphasis

In most cases, the items listed under the "Primary emphasis" heading deal with comprehension of literature and vocabulary development. Using context clues and using the dictionary receive primary emphasis, also. The first time a particular task is introduced as an exercise, it also is listed under "Primary emphasis."

Items listed under "Secondary emphasis" receive less emphasis in the lesson. Many are skills that have been introduced previously and are now being reinforced.

The Reading Selection

The lesson notes contain suggestions for introducing the reading selections and for discussing them. The reading segment of the lesson demands more flexibility on the teacher's part than any other. Students vary greatly in ability and motivation. Remember that the key to helping students make the greatest gains in the least amount of time is observation. Carefully monitoring your students' progress will help you to develop sound procedures for improving reading and comprehension skills.

Developing Your Own Notes

Develop the habit of keeping your own notes. Take time at the end of each class session to write down any remarks or reminders about particular difficulties students may have had with the lesson. Also make note of specific words or skills for which you may want to develop reinforcement activities.

Be sure to also keep notes on any procedures and techniques that seem to work well. Often you will hit upon an excellent way to present a certain skill or concept. Take some time to jot down your idea, especially if you know that you won't have the opportunity to use it again until a much later time. So much patience and concentration are called for in teaching reading that it's easy to forget those great ideas.

Book 5 Introduction

The format of Book 5 corresponds to the one used in earlier odd-numbered books in the *Challenger* series. Each lesson begins with a word chart that introduces words into this controlled-vocabulary series according to specific phonics principles. The sound for *ph,* introduced in Lesson 19, is the only phonics principle that students are studying for the first time in this series.

Definitions of difficult words from the word chart appear in a matching exercise that immediately follows each word chart. All students should own or have access to a dictionary in order to complete these exercises. Dictionary work is more heavily emphasized in Book 5 than in earlier books in this series.

The reading selections in Book 5 are adaptations of well-known and well-written literary pieces. With a few exceptions, all the adaptations are from short stories. You should point out to students that they are reading quality literature. Experience indicates that students' self-esteem and motivation are bolstered when they realize that they are studying widely-acclaimed authors.

The exercises and reviews in Book 5 help the students to develop further their comprehension skills and recall and reasoning abilities. Literary understanding is emphasized in the reading comprehension exercises. In addition, the concepts *synonym, antonym,* and *homonym* are introduced in Book 5.

A review appears after every four lessons. These reviews provide students with additional opportunities to review words and concepts. They also help students to develop the habit of referring to previous lessons for the correct answers to some of the questions. At the end of the reviews are word indexes containing the words introduced so far in Book 5. These indexes can be used when developing reinforcement activities such as spelling and vocabulary reviews.

Book 5 is the appropriate starting point for students who score in the 5.0–6.5 range on standardized reading achievement tests. The final review in Book 4 can also be used as a placement tool. An accuracy rate of 85 percent or better for this review indicates that students are ready for Book 5.

Students who start this series in Book 5 may need extensive oral reading practice because many students who begin work at this level are careless decoders. Their homework often reflects carelessness also. By calling students' attention to oral reading errors and conducting homework critiques, you can correct this pattern. All students who use this book should be given as many opportunities for oral reading practice as time permits. This practice helps to develop confidence, enjoyment, and interest in reading.

Book 5 builds upon procedures and practices emphasized in the earlier books in this series. Thus, you may find it worthwhile to look through the lesson notes for some of these books.

Scheduling Considerations

Book 5 works well in a classroom setting. The most progress is achieved when students work with *Challenger* a minimum of 45 minutes two or three times a week. Students can work independently, in a group, or with partners. When working with other students, they receive the support and stimulation from one another that make learning more enjoyable. Also, the more advanced students can assume much of the responsibility for giving explanations and leading reinforcement activities, which in turn reinforces their own reading skills. Experience indicates that less advanced students usually benefit from peer instruction provided that you are available to supply any necessary clarifications.

The Lesson Components

Later chapters of this manual outline the principles and procedures that form the foundation of this reading series. The major components of the lessons in Book 5 are briefly described below.

WORD CHART

Like the earlier odd-numbered books in this series, Book 5 uses common phonics principles to organize the introduction of new words. Words presented in this manner help students to understand better the many patterns that exist in the English language. This awareness, in turn, contributes to students' reading development. How much emphasis you place on the phonics principles reviewed in these word charts depends on the pronunciation and spelling needs of your students.

WORD MEANINGS

A matching exercise directly follows each word chart. Words in this exercise are taken from the word chart. Students are encouraged to use a dictionary for unfamiliar words. For this exercise, 100 percent accuracy is desired.

WORDS FOR STUDY

This section, which precedes the reading selection in each lesson, lists words in the lesson that appear for the first time in this series. As was the case in the earlier books, these words appear in the same order and form in which they initially appear in the lesson. This gives students additional practice in pronouncing word endings accurately.

STORY

Most of the reading selections in Book 5 are short story adaptations. It is important for students to understand the differences between fiction and nonfiction. These terms should be introduced or reviewed. Familiarize students with the main elements in short fiction: character, setting, plot, and theme.

In addition to the adaptations of short stories, other types of literature presented are myth (Lesson 2), fables (Lesson 13), and autobiography (Lessons 15 and 16).

Introduce the reading selections with appropriate pre-reading activities, and try to link the readings with your students' prior knowledge and experiences whenever possible. It is also a good idea to give students a purpose for reading by setting a specific task for them to keep in mind as they are reading. The individual lesson notes contain some suggestions for pre-reading activities.

With the exception of the first lesson, students should read the selections as homework. Read the first few paragraphs of each selection aloud in class to acquaint students with the author's style and the tone of the selection. Follow this by asking one or two questions about what you read to be sure students understood it.

Have a brief general discussion of each reading selection after students have read it to give them a chance to react to it before discussing their responses to the comprehension questions.

ABOUT THE STORY

The comprehension questions in Book 5 are designed to move students beyond the level of literal comprehension and to help them develop inferential and critical comprehension skills. Most of the lessons contain questions on all three of these levels.

The comprehension exercises call for a variety of different responses: multiple choice, fill in the blank, and complete sentences. This variety gives students practice with formats that appear on both job-placement tests and the GED Test—tests that many students using this book may well encounter.

Other Exercises

A wide variety of exercises has been included to help students improve recall, increase vocabulary, and develop reasoning abilities. As often as seems appropriate, draw students' attention to the fact that reasoning is an essential part of reading. Help them develop such strategies as using the process of elimination, making intelligent guesses, using the dictionary, and referring to previous lessons when completing these exercises.

A score of 80 percent or higher should be considered satisfactory on these exercises. If students consistently score below this figure, take some time to help them pinpoint the problem. Often they are trying to complete the exercises too rapidly.

Because students are encouraged to learn from their mistakes, they should not be penalized for making them. If you work in a school that gives report cards, it is strongly recommended that evaluations be based on corrected work and overall progress rather than on students' initial efforts. In no way does this practice encourage typical reading students to be careless in completing their homework. Rather, they usually become more interested in reading than in report cards, they are more relaxed and patient with themselves in completing assignments, and they develop a more realistic definition of academic progress.

Reinforcement Activities

Suggestions and procedures for reinforcement activities for those words and concepts that give students difficulty are discussed in Chapter 4.

Writing Assignments

Student writing is discussed in Chapter 3. It is recommended that students working in Book 5 complete weekly writing assignments of 100–125 words in addition to the writing that is required to complete the exercises in the individual lessons. Paragraphs or brief essays about discussion topics that interest students and personal and/or business letters are also appropriate writing assignments. Suggestions for writing assignments are also given in the individual lesson notes.

The Lesson Format

The procedure for each lesson should be as consistent as possible.

1. Students go over the writing assignment if one was given and review the work in the previous lesson first. This includes discussing the reading selection and correcting the exercises.

2. If time permits, students complete relevant reinforcement activities. The nature and scope of these activities are determined by the needs of your students and how often you meet with them.

3. Students preview the next lesson, which is usually assigned for homework.

Individual Lesson Notes

Lesson notes for each lesson appear on the following pages. These notes contain suggestions and procedures for specific items in each lesson.

The next three chapters give suggestions for preparing and teaching the lessons and selecting reinforcement activities.

LESSON 1
Review of Long and Short Vowels

Primary emphasis
- Comprehension (written questions and answers)
- Using the dictionary
- Using context clues

Secondary emphasis
- Vocabulary review (Which Word Does Not Fit?)
- Compound words
- Oral reading

Word Chart

As was mentioned in the introduction to Book 5, the word chart presents a systematic form through which the student is introduced to new words in this reading series. How much emphasis the teacher places on the word chart as a review of phonics concepts should depend exclusively on the needs of the student.

Generally, the student who has started his reading work in either Book 1 or Book 2 benefits from pronouncing the words that appear on the chart for each lesson. These students still depend on phonics rules to help them sound out new words.

All other students usually enjoy reading the words, but it is not necessary that they do so. Thus, if you find that time can be more beneficially spent on another part of the lesson or appropriate reinforcement activity, the phonics principle that underscores each word chart can be mentioned in passing rather than emphasized as a learning activity, and the reading of the words on the chart can be omitted.

Do not dwell on the definitions when doing any word chart work because students encounter troublesome words in the first exercise for all lessons and in exercises in subsequent lessons of the book. The teacher can make a note of those words that give the student continued difficulty and incorporate them in future reinforcement activities.

EXERCISE 1: WORD MEANINGS

For this exercise, students should use a dictionary to look up unfamiliar words. Students should be expected to complete these exercises with 100 percent accuracy. If a student consistently makes two or more mistakes on

word meaning exercises, spend some time helping him to pinpoint the reasons for his errors. Always encourage students to learn from their mistakes rather than to see them as signs of failure.

A major reason that students complain about having to learn definitions is that they do not understand the significance of vocabulary work. Make sure students understand that knowing the meanings of words is vital to reading comprehension.

In all exercises in which copying is involved, students should copy accurately. They should correct any words they miscopy. When this expectation of accuracy is gently but consistently encouraged, the students themselves will begin to adopt a standard of accuracy and demonstrate more patience and pride in the quality of their work.

Story

The Words for Study section contains words that appear in this lesson for the first time in this controlled-vocabulary reading series.

Tell students that the reading selections appearing in this book are adapted from well-known, critically acclaimed works. It motivates students to know that they are reading widely respected material. Introduce or review the terms *fiction* and *nonfiction*.

Generally, students should read the selections for homework, but because this is the first lesson, allot time for an oral first reading in class. Introduce the story by asking students if there are stories about family members that their families enjoy telling. Point out the title, and ask what students think the story will be about. Read the first paragraph of the story aloud. Ask students if they think this story will be serious or humorous. Discuss the humorous tone of the phrase "when brains were passed out he must have been somewhere else." Continue reading this first story aloud. Stop occasionally to ask a question, if you think it is necessary. Don't stop too often to ask questions, however, as this can be disruptive to comprehension and enjoyment.

After reading the story aloud, discuss it in a general way. This gives students a chance to get a sense of the story as a whole while giving you the opportunity to assess their comprehension skills. Begin the discussion by asking such questions as: "Did you like this story? Why or why not?" "What kind of person was Grandpa?" and "How do you think the author felt about Grandpa?"

When you have completed the general discussion of the story, preview the exercises to be done for homework. Since this is the first lesson, take plenty of time and be sure all students understand how to do each exercise. If necessary, have students complete an item in each exercise during the preview so that they have a thorough understanding of how to do the work. Discuss the importance of homework, and compare it to the daily practice that sports and music require.

EXERCISE 2: ABOUT THE STORY

During the homework preview, tell students to refer to the story when necessary in answering the questions rather than to guess or to leave an answer blank. Students should complete *all* the questions for all exercises.

If a student has trouble answering a multiple-choice question, encourage him to refer back to the reading selection. Students can also eliminate the obviously incorrect answers and then evaluate the remaining choices to select the correct one.

EXERCISE 3: WHICH WORD DOES NOT FIT?

Students who have worked in the earlier books in this series are familiar with this type of exercise. If you have students who are starting in Book 5, have them read the directions and complete the first two items during the homework preview so that they fully understand what is expected of them.

EXERCISE 4: GRANDPA CELEBRATES HIS GOOD LUCK

Review the definition for *compound word* with all students. Again, students who have worked in the earlier books are quite familiar with this type of exercise. For the student who is starting in Book 5, have him read the directions, study the example, and complete one item

during the homework preview so that he fully understands what is expected of him.

Remind students to work by process of elimination and to look for clues in the sentences themselves to help them find the right answers. It is not necessary that the student complete the items of this or any other exercise in order; it is perfectly all right to skip around. However, remind the student to check his work after having completed an exercise. Skipping around sometimes leads to skipping items.

Note: After the student has gone over the exercises and made any necessary corrections during the homework review, give him an opportunity to ask questions or make comments about what he has just accomplished. If he seems overwhelmed by the work, point out the strengths he has shown in completing the work. Remind him that this is only the first lesson and that he will get used to the work more quickly than he thinks is possible.

Activities in Writing Book 5

Review with students what a comma fault is and how to avoid this common writing error. After students have completed original writing, remind them always to review what they have written and edit for any problems such as comma faults. Explain that in writing to get ideas down, even the best and most experienced writers make errors, but then they go back and edit their work to correct them. This is an important point for students: Every writer can make mistakes.

In discussing this method for combining sentences, you might introduce the term *coordinating conjunction,* a conjunction, or connector, used to join similar or equal things, in this case, complete sentences.

Additional Writing Activities

1. Have students write a paragraph about a humorous incident involving themselves, a relative, or a friend.
2. Ask students to think about a favorite relative and why that person is so special to them. Have students list two reasons or examples about the person and then write a paragraph for each reason.

LESSON 2
Review of Consonant Blends and Digraphs: Part 1

Primary emphasis
- Comprehension (written questions and answers)
- Using the dictionary
- Using context clues

Secondary emphasis
- Vocabulary review (synonyms)
- Review of consonant blends (*ch, sh, st*)
- Oral reading

Word Chart and Word Meanings
Use the procedure suggested for Lesson 1.

WORDS FOR STUDY
1. Make sure the student can pronounce *Midas* and *Bacchus*.
2. Save your explanation of the word *synonym* for the preview of Exercise 4. All students are encountering this word for the first time in this reading series.

Story
During the preview, introduce this reading by telling students that it is a well-known myth. Explain that the main characters in myths are usually gods and heroes. The Greeks and Romans had many myths that are still familiar to us today.

Point out the title, and ask students what they think the story will be about. Explain that the two main characters are Bacchus, the god of wine, and King Midas. Ask if anyone knows the story of King Midas. If a student is familiar with this myth, have him summarize it for the class.

In the discussion during the homework review, ask students if they know any other stories about Greek or Roman gods. You might point out that the other planets in our solar system are named after Greek or Roman gods. If students are interested in reading more myths, the public library has many books containing versions of Greek and Roman myths.

EXERCISE 2: ABOUT THE STORY
For item 5, students appreciate it if you allow them to write the correct letter before each cause and then write out the causes after any necessary corrections have been made during the homework review. Item 6 provides a good starting point for a brief class discussion or a longer composition.

EXERCISE 3: STRANGE SENTENCES
Many students find it helpful if you remind them to initially read each sentence in its entirety prior to filling in the blanks. For example, sentence 1 should be read, "*Blank* first *blank* for dessert was a piece of *blank blank,* but then he *blank* his mind." If necessary, remind the student to use process of elimination to complete this exercise.

EXERCISE 4: WORKING WITH SYNONYMS
Make sure the student can correctly pronounce and verbalize the definition for *synonym* during the homework preview. Have her complete the first item so that she has a clear understanding of how this exercise is to be completed. Students often ask if they can use the dictionary for this exercise. Needless to say, the answer is, "YES!"

Oral Reading
Note that oral reading is listed as an objective in this and all subsequent lessons. Try to have the entire story, part of the story, and/or the exercises read aloud as often as time permits. When necessary, help the student to develop good oral reading habits. Some students are under the impression that good oral reading means that one reads as fast as one can. In these instances, remind the student that, in oral reading, one must always be conscious of the needs of the listeners.

Adolescents enjoy the opportunity to practice reading aloud, and many adults appreciate it. Many adult students have wanted to read to their children but have been fearful of doing so. This practice helps them to increase both their ability and confidence.

Activities in Writing Book 5
In discussing the words that can be used to combine sentences, you might wish to introduce the term *subordinating conjunction,* a conjunction used to combine complete sentences by making one of them dependent on the other. Use the example on page 7 to demonstrate this function. However, emphasize that knowing the rules and the names of grammatical constructions is not the point; the point is being able to use these rules as tools to make them better writers.

The point of the exercise on combining sentences is to have students learn and practice not only different subordinating conjunctions but also correct use of commas: Use a comma after a long introductory clause.

Additional Writing Activities

1. Ask students to write a paragraph to answer the following question: If you were King Midas, what would you have wished for?

2. Explain that myths, like fairy tales and fables, often have morals. A moral is a lesson about right and wrong or good and evil. Ask students to think about the moral that the story of King Midas tells and then write a paragraph explaining the moral. Their paragraphs should use examples from the myth to support their ideas.

LESSON 3
Review of Consonant Blends: Part 2

Primary emphasis

- Comprehension (written questions and answers)
- Using the dictionary
- Using context clues

Secondary emphasis

- Vocabulary review (synonyms; analogies)
- Review of consonant blends (*bl, br, cl, cr, fl, fr*)
- Oral reading

Word Chart and Word Meanings

Use the procedure suggested for Lesson 1.

WORDS FOR STUDY

Make sure the student understands the meaning of *panhandled* during the homework preview. The meaning of this word cannot be clearly discerned from the story. In most instances, the student should attempt to learn the meanings of confusing words from the stories and/or exercises in which they appear. Words such as *panhandled*, which are discussed during the preview, are the exception rather than the rule.

Story

Introduce this story by asking students what they think the title means. Ask "Can you think of any time when what you were wearing influenced how you behaved or how people behaved toward you?" Tell students this story is set in Paris, and have them find Paris on an atlas or world map. Explain that a character in this story undergoes an abrupt change. Tell students that as they read the story, they should try to predict what will happen.

Students may need to read this story more than once to comprehend the subtleties. Many inferences have to be made to understand the plot and to see the humor in it. Discuss the plot with students to be sure they know what took place in the story.

In the discussion during the homework review, ask: "How would you describe Tango at the beginning of the story?" Discuss how the author reveals Tango's character through the opening dialogue and actions. Have students cite lines from the story to support their descriptions.

EXERCISE 2: ABOUT THE STORY

Students' interpretation of some of these questions may vary. Accept any answer the student can justify in the context of the story. Discuss the fact that different readers will interpret a work of fiction differently because they have different backgrounds and experiences that they bring to the interpretation.

Encourage students to use the dictionary to find the answers to questions 9 and 10 if necessary.

When going over the answers during the homework review, make sure that students have used complete sentences to answer the "What do you think?" question. Initially, students may have difficulty putting their answers in sentence form, but with practice they will become increasingly proficient.

EXERCISE 3: MORE STRANGE SENTENCES

If necessary, remind the student of the appropriate procedure to use to complete this exercise.

EXERCISE 4: SYNONYMS

Review the meaning of *synonym* during the preview.

EXERCISE 5: WHICH WORD FITS BEST?

Students often have difficulty with this type of exercise. Help students get started by completing the first question during the preview. Ask them to explain the relationship between *cleat* and *football*. Then have them read the four choices and decide which word expresses a similar relationship to *gloves*. Most students will see that *boxing* is the sport in which *gloves* are used.

Activities in Writing Book 5

The grammar rule in Exercise 3 further develops knowledge of the use of commas and subordinating conjunctions. (While a comma may be used before a dependent clause if the clause is nonessential, it is not necessary to introduce that concept at this level.)

Point out the box reminding students to check their use of commas in what they have written. These reminders are the first stage in helping students to edit their work.

Additional Writing Activities

1. Have students write two paragraphs explaining how Tango changes from the beginning of the story to the end. One paragraph should describe him at the beginning of the story and the second paragraph should describe him at the end of the story.

2. Ask students to write a paragraph about a time when wearing something made a difference in how they felt about themselves.

LESSON 4
Review of Consonant Blends: Part 3

Primary emphasis
- Comprehension (written questions and answers)
- Using the dictionary
- Using context clues

Secondary emphasis
- Vocabulary review (antonyms)
- Compound words
- Review of consonant blends (*gl, gr, pl, pr, sl, str*)
- Oral reading

Word Chart and Word Meanings
Use the procedure suggested for Lesson 1.

WORDS FOR STUDY
Save your explanation of *antonym* for the preview of Exercise 4. All students are encountering this word for the first time in this reading series.

Story
During the preview, introduce this story by telling students that O. Henry is a well-known author who is famous for his surprise endings. Tell them to watch for clues to the ending as they read the story. In the discussion during the homework review, ask students to point out clues that foreshadow the ending, such as the man's scar, his expensive watch, and the fact that "Jimmy" was taller. Discuss foreshadowing as a device writers use to prepare the reader for what will come later.

EXERCISE 2: ABOUT THE STORY
During the preview, have students read the directions and study the example carefully to be sure they understand how to do this exercise. If necessary, have them complete the next one or two items in class also.

The Answer Key provides suggested revisions for the false statements. Some statements can be corrected in more than one way. Accept any correct revision.

EXERCISE 3: WORKING WITH ANTONYMS
Make sure the students can correctly pronounce and verbalize the definition for *antonym* during the homework preview. Have them complete the second item so that they have a clear understanding of how this exercise is to be completed. If necessary, remind them to work by process of elimination.

EXERCISE 4: STRANGE VERSES
During the homework review, consider using this exercise for oral reading practice. Students may need help in reading the verses with appropriate rhythm.

EXERCISE 5: COMPOUND WORDS
Have students use the same procedure they used to complete this type of exercise in Lesson 1.

Activities in Writing Book 5
Run-on sentences and comma faults vie with each other for being the most common writing error. Review with students two ways to solve both problems: Use a coordinating conjunction and a comma (Lesson 1), or use a subordinating conjunction and a comma (Lesson 2). (Ideas in one sentence may also be turned into phrases or single words, and sentences may also be split and a period used to end each one.)

Exercise 4 picks up the issue of differing interpretations of fiction that was discussed in Lesson 3.

Additional Writing Activities
1. Have students choose either Jimmy Wells or Silky Bob and write one paragraph to describe what the character is like.
2. Ask students to write a paragraph explaining what they expect to be doing in 20 years.

Review: Lessons 1–4

As was the case in the earlier books, it should be emphasized to the student that this is a review, not a test. Material is often presented in new ways to both challenge the student and, hopefully, arouse her interest.

Preview each exercise included in the review as you would a lesson. If appropriate, have the student complete an item in each exercise during the preview so that she has a better understanding of how to do the work.

An overall score of 80 percent or better on a review exercise should be considered excellent.

These reviews appear after every four lessons. The word indexes, which include the words that have been introduced in Book 5 to date, can be used as the basis for reinforcement activities such as spelling quizzes, vocabulary reviews, and word games.

EXERCISE 6: HELPING PEOPLE

If students are encountering this type of puzzle for the first time, have them complete a few of the items during the homework preview. Have them fill in the appropriate blanks in the quotation as they answer each item. In this way, they can work back and forth between the clues and the quotation, using context clues in the quotation to complete the partially filled-in words.

LESSON 5
Review of Consonant Blends: Part 4

Primary emphasis
- Comprehension (written questions and answers)
- Using the dictionary
- Using context clues

Secondary emphasis
- Vocabulary review
- Syllabication
- Review of consonant blends
- Oral reading

Word Chart and Word Meanings
Use the procedure suggested for Lesson 1.

Story
Point out that this story is in two parts. Students will be reading only the first part for this lesson. Draw students' attention to the title, and ask them what they think the story might be about. Have them describe some tricks that have been played on them. During the review, ask students to describe George's character. What clues to his character can they find in the text? Discuss students' ideas about how they would end the story.

EXERCISE 3: WORKING WITH CONSONANT BLENDS AND DIGRAPHS
During the preview, suggest that students use context clues to figure out words that make sense in each sentence. Then they should check the list of blends to make sure that the blends they selected are included. You may want to do the first sentence together as a group to be sure students understand what is expected of them.

EXERCISE 4: WHICH WORD DOES NOT FIT?
If necessary, have the student complete an item during the homework preview. Most students have little difficulty with this exercise.

EXERCISE 5: BREAKING WORDS INTO SYLLABLES
Review the definition of *syllable*. Students who have worked in earlier books have virtually no difficulty with this exercise. For the student who has started in Book 5, it may be necessary to have him or her complete a few items during the homework preview. If a student asks you if he or she can refer to the dictionary for the correct answers, tell him or her that you want to see how well he or she can do on this exercise without the aid of the dictionary. In this way, you have an opportunity to learn what the student knows about syllabication.

Because using the dictionary is a primary objective for all lessons in Book 5, the student may use this resource for any subsequent exercise pertaining to syllabication.

If the student does demonstrate some difficulty completing this exercise, plan some syllabication work as a reinforcement activity on an occasional basis. Make sure that the student understands that this type of activity contributes to overall spelling improvement.

EXERCISE 6: WHERE CAN YOU FIND IT?
Some students need to be reminded that each word in the box is to be used only once. Thus, *stench,* which is an appropriate answer for *battle*, must be matched with *trash can* in order to match *bloodshed* correctly. (Some students insist that *stench* should be matched with *sneakers.*)

Activities in Writing Book 5
You may need to review with students that a complete sentence includes a subject and a verb. The subject may be understood in an imperative sentence such as "Do it now." If either the subject or the verb is missing, the words are not a complete sentence.

Students may confuse verb parts such as words with *-ing* endings as verbs. Explain that these are not verbs (sentence predicates) unless they have a helping word such as *is, are, was,* or *were; do, does,* or *did; has, have,* or *had.*

Additional Writing Activities
1. Have students write a paragraph describing George. They need to use at least two pieces of information from the story to support their ideas about George.
2. Have students write a short piece of dialogue between George and the manager of the main jewelry store branch in which George asks for expensive rings to show a rich customer. By first reading some of the dialogue in the story, review with students the use of quotation marks, commas, and end punctuation in dialogue.

Review of Consonant Blends: Part 5

Primary emphasis
- Comprehension (written questions and answers)
- Using the dictionary
- Using context clues

Secondary emphasis
- The sound for *re-*
- Vocabulary review (antonyms)
- Review of consonant blends
- Oral reading

Word Chart and Word Meanings
Use the procedure suggested for Lesson 1.

Story
During the preview, review Part 1 of the story and some of the predictions students made about how it would end. Tell students to be alert to clues that will foreshadow the ending as they read Part 2. During the review, help students to understand the story as a whole by reviewing both parts. Then discuss how close students came to predicting the way the story would end. Did any student predict the actual ending? Were they surprised by the ending?

EXERCISE 3: MORE WORK WITH CONSONANT BLENDS AND DIGRAPHS
Students are to complete this exercise in the same manner they completed Exercise 3 in the preceding lesson.

EXERCISE 4: ANTONYMS
If necessary, remind students to use process of elimination to complete this exercise.

EXERCISE 5: WORDS BEGINNING WITH *RE-*
Keep in mind that it is the sound *re-* that is being emphasized in this lesson. No mention should be made of *re-* as a prefix. This only confuses the student.

During the homework preview, it may be necessary to review some of the definitions for the words in the box. Unless a student is exceptionally motivated, do not demand that he or she use the dictionary for the troublesome words. The dictionary practice he or she gets through completing the first exercise is sufficient. Do, however, encourage the student to write brief notes about the troublesome words in the margin so that he or she can easily recall the meanings of these words when he or she completes this exercise for homework.

Activities in Writing Book 5
Exercise 3 provides students with more practice in correcting sentence fragments. Note the use of *-ing* verb forms in the place of predicates. Remind students to check/edit their own writing for problems such as sentence fragments, comma faults, and run-on sentences.

This lesson begins formal instruction in the development of a paragraph and of longer pieces of writing. Every subsequent lesson in Level 5 provides a guide to help students gather information, plan their writing, and organize the final product.

Additional Writing Activities
1. Have students practice writing different opening and closing sentences for their paragraphs about whether George is sneaky. Suggest that they try using a question to open the paragraph. Explain that questions can hook readers' interest and make them want to read more.
2. Have students assume the role of author and write a new ending for the story. They can explain in a paragraph how they would end it and why.

LESSON 7

Review of Consonant Blends: Part 6

Primary emphasis

- Comprehension (written questions and answers)
- Using the dictionary
- Using context clues

Secondary emphasis

- The sound for *re-*
- Syllabication
- Review of consonants and consonant blends
- Oral reading

Word Chart and Word Meanings

Use the procedure suggested for Lesson 1.

Story

As students read the story, they should pay close attention to the three women. As they read, they should ask themselves, "What kind of people are they?" The unraveling of Granny's story is somewhat complicated, and students may need help in figuring out what she means at the end when she says "the child I couldn't have with James" (Granny's husband).

During the review, ask students if they guessed how the story would turn out, and if they did, when they first started to suspect the truth. Other questions to discuss are: Would students like to know any of the women? Did Kate deserve what happened to her? Is Christie believable? Is the story believable? Reintroduce the concept of different interpretations of the same piece of fiction.

EXERCISE 4: CONSONANTS AND CONSONANT BLENDS

In addition to process of elimination and context clues, the student should be encouraged to use word endings as a guide for putting the words in the right places in the sentences.

EXERCISE 5: BREAKING WORDS INTO SYLLABLES

Because of previous work with syllabication, students should have no difficulty completing this exercise with the desired accuracy (80 percent or better).

If a student wishes to use a dictionary to complete this exercise, this is perfectly acceptable. Experience indicates that students use a dictionary only for those words that stump them. Please don't worry about dictionary abuse.

EXERCISE 6: MORE WORDS BEGINNING WITH *RE-*

Again, it is the sound *re* that is being emphasized in this exercise, and no mention should be made of *re-* as a prefix. Students are to be encouraged to use a dictionary for this exercise if necessary.

Activities in Writing Book 5

Exercise 3 provides additional reinforcement of combining sentences to eliminate comma faults, sentence fragments, and run-on sentences.

Review the writing guide with students before they begin. You may need to introduce and discuss the term *point of view*. It is important for students to understand that they need to use proof or evidence to support their opinions.

Additional Writing Activities

1. Use question 10 under "About the Story" in the student reader as the basis for a writing assignment.
2. For a change of pace, have students choose sets of words from Exercise 4: Consonants and Consonant Blends and write two-, three-, or four-line poems that rhyme. Students may change the word endings, for example, *scare* instead of *scared* or *glared* instead of *glare*.

LESSON 8
Review of Vowel Combinations: Part 1

Primary emphasis

- Comprehension (written questions and answers)
- Using the dictionary
- Using context clues

Secondary emphasis

- *Pre-* and *per-* at the beginning of words
- Vocabulary review
- Review of vowel combinations
- Oral reading

Word Chart and Word Meanings

Use the procedure suggested for Lesson 1.

Story

Introduce this story by explaining that Geoffrey Chaucer (c. 1340–1400) is considered one of the greatest poets in English, and he wrote in the 1300s. This story is from his best-known work, "The Canterbury Tales," a collection of stories purportedly told by a group of pilgrims on their way to a shrine in Canterbury, England. This story was called "The Pardoner's Tale" in the original version.

As a follow-up activity, students might look up and report information on Chaucer. They might also enjoy reading some of the other Canterbury tales. There are many easy-to-read collections available.

EXERCISE 2: ABOUT THE STORY

Students' interpretation of some of these questions may vary. Accept any answer that the student can justify, and discuss differences of opinion. Discuss students' answers to questions 5 and 6 in detail.

EXERCISE 3: REVIEW OF VOWEL SOUNDS

Most students have no difficulty putting *poise* in the right place in sentence 6, but they do need additional help in understanding the meaning of this word.

EXERCISE 4: WHERE WOULD YOU FIND THIS?

Spend a few moments reviewing the meaning of words such as *galley, Huron,* and *teller.* These words have appeared in earlier books.

EXERCISE 5: WORDS BEGINNING WITH *PRE-*

It is the sound *pre* that is being emphasized, and no mention of *pre-* as a prefix should be made.

EXERCISE 6: WORDS BEGINNING WITH *PER-*

After the student has made any necessary corrections on this exercise, plan a brief spelling quiz on *pre-* and *per-* words to help the student improve his ability to distinguish between these two sounds.

Activities in Writing Book 5

Exercise 3 continues practice in combining sentences to eliminate comma faults, sentence fragments, and run-on sentences. Remind students to check/edit their own writing to make sure that their final products do not have these problems.

Additional Writing Activities

1. Have students write alternative endings to the story beginning with the two murderers drinking the wine.
2. Ask students to think about the kind of people that the three murders are. Then have them list words that describe them. Some examples are *sneaky* and *greedy.*

Review: Lessons 1–8

Use the procedure suggested for the previous review. Please note the following:

1. Exercise 2 needs to be previewed more carefully than the other exercises in this review. Use the following procedure during the preview:

   (a) After the student has silently read the directions and studied the example, ask him or her to explain why *stove* is the correct answer. Most students respond, "I don't know."

   (b) Have the student read the five words aloud in item 1. Some students now see why *stove* is the answer; others are still confused. For those who are confused, have them read the five words aloud again, and encourage them to pay attention to both the underlined letters and the sounds they are producing. At this point, most students understand why *stove* is the correct answer.

   (c) If the student still feels somewhat uncertain, have him or her complete an item or two during the preview.

   (d) Remind all students to say the words aloud and TAKE THEIR TIME when doing this exercise for homework.

   (e) During the homework review, allow some time to review the definitions of a few of the words. For example, *clove, yeast, chap,* and *artery* often need to be briefly reviewed by students.

2. Exercise 5, item 4: If the student chooses *freeway* rather than *turnpike,* which is the correct answer, spend a few moments discussing how he or she can use the components of a compound word to discern meaning. In other words, the component *free* implies that no toll would be charged. Thus, even if the student does not know the meaning of *turnpike,* he or she can easily figure out the answer because it is the only logical choice.

3. The last exercise, If You Had the Money…, is just for enjoyment. There is no one correct answer for any of the questions. For some students, this exercise provides the basis for an enjoyable composition topic.

LESSON 9
Review of Vowel Combinations: Part 2

Primary emphasis
- Comprehension (written questions and answers)
- Using the dictionary
- Using context clues

Secondary emphasis
- The ending -er meaning *person who*
- Review of common word beginnings
- Spelling/reasoning (Can You Crack the Code?)
- Oral reading

Word Chart and Word Meanings
Use the procedure suggested for Lesson 1.

Story
During the preview, ask if anyone is familiar with the legend of King Arthur. If not, explain that King Arthur is one of the great legends of English history. He is supposed to have lived in the 500s and united local British tribes against Saxon invaders from what is today Germany. You might use an atlas or world map to locate these areas. Explain that King Arthur established the Knights of the Roundtable to defend England and that the knights were supposed to be courageous, loyal, and virtuous. You may need to explain who knights were and what they did. Relate the story of Queen Guinevere and Sir Lancelot.

Students might look up and report information on King Arthur and the Knights of the Roundtable. They might also enjoy hearing some of the soundtrack from the movie musical *Camelot* as well as reading easy-to-read versions of the legend of King Arthur.

EXERCISE 3: WHO ARE THESE PEOPLE?
During the homework review, mention that -er as an ending often indicates a person.

EXERCISE 5: CAN YOU CRACK THE CODE?
Although this exercise requires quite a bit of work, students generally enjoy it. Suggest that if the student fills in the letters he or she knows to be correct from the example (onions) and thinks about the different things that can be put on sandwiches, he or she should have little difficulty completing this exercise. Students may use a dictionary to help them with spellings if they wish.

Activities in Writing Book 5
Exercise 1 is the first step in preparing students to write more descriptively. Instead of having them choose words out of context from a list, this exercise asks students to choose words and phrases by reading the actual story. They will be able to see how the author uses words and phrases to develop and enhance meaning. You may need to review what constitutes a phrase with students.

Transitions are a very important device for conveying and clarifying meaning. In Book 5, students will be working with transitions that show time order and that add information. Transitions that show time order are an excellent tool for helping students organize any writing that involves a step-by-step process. Encourage students to use transitions as they revise their writing. Make the point again, however, that knowing the name of the device is not what's important; using transitions to make their writing clearer and easier to understand is the point.

Additional Writing Activities
1. Have students think about something that must be done in steps such as changing a tire or baking a cake. The activity should not include many steps; four to six steps are sufficient. First, ask them to list the steps that must be done. It doesn't matter at this point if the steps are listed in order. Second, ask students to read over the steps and number them in order. Third, ask them to rewrite the steps in order using transitions that use time order. The transitions first, second, third, etc., are useful for this kind of step-by-step how-to process.

2. Ask students to write a paragraph about something that happened to them today. It can be as simple as getting up late and having to rush to get to work or to get children out to school. Whatever the event, it should include four to six small events within the larger happening. Students should use transitions other than first, second, third, etc., from the list on page 21.

Review of *r*-Controlled Vowels

Primary emphasis
- Comprehension (written questions and answers)
- Using the dictionary
- Using context clues

Secondary emphasis
- Compound words
- Work with word beginnings
- Syllabication (divide compound words)
- Oral reading

Word Chart and Word Meanings
Use the procedure suggested for Lesson 1.

Story
Students may have difficulty understanding the character of Eleanor. Discuss how the author creates the character by building up examples of her past actions and feelings. Ask students if how she treats her son at the end is a surprise or if her treatment is in line with the character's actions and feelings up to that point. Discuss whether it is pride, stubbornness, a lack of understanding of reality, or some other trait that motivates Eleanor to reject her son at the end. Have students consider what would happen to Eleanor if Hank, Jr., doesn't pay off her loans. How do they think Eleanor would react?

EXERCISE 4: MORE WORK WITH WORD BEGINNINGS
Students may use the dictionary to help them complete this exercise if necessary. Answers for 5, 8, and 12 are based solely on the student's judgment.

EXERCISE 5: SYLLABLES
In addition to checking the syllabication during the homework review, spend a few moments reviewing the definitions of any words that continue to confuse the students.

EXERCISE 6: COMPOUND WORDS
All students should be quite familiar with these exercises by now and should experience little difficulty completing them.

Activities in Writing Book 5
Exercise 1 continues work with using words and phrases to develop and enhance the meaning of a piece of writing.

Exercise 2 reviews the use of initial capitals to begin sentences (and questions) and end punctuation. Students should be familiar with using both periods and question marks, but may be less certain of when to use exclamation points. Explain that exclamation points are reserved for sentences that show strong emotion such as surprise, fear, and anger. (Exclamation points may also be used for imperative sentences that show strong emotion: Wash the windows now!)

Review the instruction for writing a three-paragraph essay. Constructing conclusions can be difficult for students to grasp. The conclusion is a restatement of the topic of the essay and, in a sense, a mini-summary of the body of the essay.

Additional Writing Activities
1. Have students practice writing sentences for which an exclamation point is appropriate end punctuation.
2. Ask students to imagine that they wrote this story. Then have them choose one of the questions that they wrote in Exercise 2 and answer it in a paragraph as if they were the author.

LESSON 11
The Hard and Soft c

Primary emphasis
- Comprehension (written questions and answers)
- Using the dictionary
- Using context clues

Secondary emphasis
- Vocabulary review
- The hard and soft c
- Classifying
- Oral reading

Word Chart and Word Meanings
Use the procedure suggested for Lesson 1.

Story
You might begin the preview by asking if students like science fiction. Have one or two students who like science fiction briefly relate the plot of their favorite science fiction movie or TV/cable show. Ask students who do not like science fiction why they don't; some may simply have not been exposed to such stories. Explain that students are going to read a science fiction story. They should look for clues that tell that what's happening is not real and that the story is not traditional fiction.

EXERCISE 2: ABOUT THE STORY
Remind students to go back to the story to find answers. They don't need to remember every detail; they can reread parts of the story.

EXERCISE 3: WHAT DO YOU THINK?
Question 1 requires that students cite information from the story to support their answer, whereas question 2 asks students to use their own knowledge to form an opinion.

EXERCISE 4: WHICH ANSWER FITS BEST?
If necessary, remind the student to use process of elimination to complete this exercise. Additionally, students may refer to a dictionary if they wish.

EXERCISE 5: SOUNDS FOR C
If necessary, have the student complete one or two items during the homework preview.

EXERCISE 6: CATEGORIES
Students experience little difficulty in completing this exercise accurately. A dictionary may be used if necessary.

Activities in Writing Book 5
Exercise 1 continues to build students' recognition of the use of interesting and descriptive words and phrases to develop and enhance meaning.

Exercise 2 reinforces the use of initial capitals and question marks.

In Exercise 3, students learn about and practice using transitions that add information. Point out that this type of transition connects ideas and helps to clarify meaning the same way that transitions that show time order do.

Additional Writing Activities
1. Have students write 10 lines or so of dialogue between Jim Bacchus and the leader of the shadow people. Students should first think about what Bacchus would want to know or say to the leader and what the leader might want to say to Bacchus. Remind students to use quotation marks, commas, and end punctuation.
2. Ask students to write a paragraph explaining what they think happened to the Baker family. This will give students who don't like science fiction a chance to use their imaginations.

LESSON 12
The Hard and Soft *g*

Primary emphasis
- Comprehension (written questions and answers)
- Using the dictionary
- Using context clues

Secondary emphasis
- Classifying
- The hard and soft *g*
- *Dis-* at the beginning of the word
- Oral reading

Word Chart and Word Meanings
Use the procedure suggested for Lesson 1.

Story
This story is an internal examination of a man's character. It is subtle and sophisticated and requires that students make inferences to figure out what the man is saying about himself, his wife, and their relationship. His feelings may resonate with some students.

During the preview, ask students what they know about any of the men mentioned in the story: Alexander, Napoleon, General Grant, General Hindenburg, General Pershing. All were military men who won many battles. In Alexander's and Napoleon's cases, they also conquered vast territories and numbers of people.

Ask students as they read to create a mental picture of the man, his wife, and the room where the man sits writing and thinking. Ask them to think about the man: Is he happy? Is he unhappy? Is he somewhere in between? What does he want in life? What does he want from his wife? What does he want to give her? Discuss students' ideas. Then ask them to think about the wife. What do they know about her? How do they know what they know about her? They should come to realize that all they know about her is what the man tells them. It is like hearing only one side of an argument from a friend.

EXERCISE 2: ABOUT THE STORY
Discuss students' responses to questions 7, 8, and 9. These questions require students to draw conclusions based on inferences rather than on information directly stated in the story.

EXERCISE 4: SOUNDS FOR *G*
If necessary, have the student complete one or two items during the homework preview.

EXERCISE 5: WORDS BEGINNING WITH *DIS-*
Remind the students to use the word endings to help them place the words properly in the sentences.

Activities in Writing Book 5
The instruction in Exercise 2 about the use of details formalizes what students have been practicing in Exercise 1 in Lessons 1 through 12. The use of descriptive words and phrases to develop ideas is an important writing skill. Students learn that a writer paints a picture with details. The boldfaced words and phrases in the examples describe and add information to what a writer is saying about the wife in the story.

Note that the essay prompts always ask students for three reasons, examples, or clues. Three is a good number for novice writers because it forces them to think about what they will write about. Asking for only one reason sets up a situation in which the writer will take the first thing that comes to mind whether or not it is a good or even particularly relevant reason or example.

Additional Writing Activities
1. In the second paragraph from the end, the historian says, "Why, in all our life together, have I never been able to break through the wall to my wife?" Ask students to write a paragraph to explain what they think the wall is.
2. Ask students to write a paragraph to answer the following question: Do you think that most husbands and wives communicate well with each other? Explain.

Review: Lessons 1–12

1. Use the procedure suggested for the previous reviews.
2. For Exercise 5, use the procedure outlined in the review note for Lessons 1–8. Be sure to remind students to say the words aloud and to take their time as they complete this exercise for homework.

LESSON 13
The Letter y

Primary emphasis
- Comprehension (written questions and answers)
- Using the dictionary
- Using context clues

Secondary emphasis
- Common sayings
- Adding -y to words
- Compound words

Word Chart and Word Meanings
Use the procedure suggested for Lesson 1.

Story
During the preview, tell students that a fable is a short tale that teaches a lesson or moral and that Aesop's fables are very well known. Explain that the characters in fables are often animals and that sometimes an animal is associated with a certain human trait.

During the general review, ask students to name a human trait for each animal in these fables. They might be familiar with the phrase "a sly fox." Then discuss the following sayings in relation to these fables: "Don't kill the goose that lays the golden eggs," "Cover your tracks," and "Pull your chestnuts out of the fire."

Students might enjoy reading more fables. Easy-to-read translations of Aesop's fables should be available in your public library.

EXERCISE 3: WRITE YOUR OWN MORAL
Accept all reasonable responses.

EXERCISE 4: ADDING -Y TO A WORD
Remind the students to refer to the examples when completing this exercise for homework.

EXERCISE 5: MORE COMMON WAYS OF SPEAKING
Students tend to have more difficulty with these expressions than they have with those in the preceding review. If process of elimination fails them, encourage them to make an intelligent guess for those which have them completely stumped. A score of 11 or more correct responses should be considered an excellent score.

EXERCISE 6: COMPOUND WORDS
This exercise is a bit more difficult than previous exercises pertaining to compound words. Remind students to take their time and use process of elimination.

Activities in Writing Book 5
Exercise 1 provides students with more practice in recognizing the use of description and then in using description in their own writing.

Exercise 2 again focuses on the use of descriptive details, specifically the use of sensory details, specific words, and action verbs. In Exercise 3, students have another immediate opportunity to practice writing descriptive details.

Exercise 4 provides instruction in writing a descriptive paragraph. The Prewriting section of the guide adds a step to the process in previous guides. Because the writing prompt asks students to choose a person (or thing) and then write a descriptive paragraph about the person (or thing), the Prewriting section includes thinking about someone (or something) to write about and then choosing one from the list.

Additional Writing Activities
1. Many students enjoy writing their own fables after having read these selections from Aesop's fables. Have students work in pairs to write new fables. They should first think of a moral that they wish to illustrate with a fable.
2. If any students do not wish to write their own fables, have them choose one of Aesop's fables and explain in a paragraph how the fable illustrates the moral.

Double Consonants in the Middle of Words

Primary emphasis
- Comprehension (written questions and answers)
- Using the dictionary
- Using context clues

Secondary emphasis
- Classifying
- The ending *-ment*
- Decoding words with double medial consonants
- Oral reading

Word Chart
Students need to draw a line between the double consonant only if this helps them to sound out the words.

Story
During the preview, call students' attention to the title, and ask them what they think this story will be about. Ask students to recall times or situations in which they were afraid and what it was that made them afraid. During the review, discuss students' reactions to this story. Explore the fact that people can create their own fear and that fear can spoil one's enjoyment of life. As a follow-up composition topic, have students describe a situation in which they were afraid and tell how they dealt with it.

EXERCISE 3: WHAT DO YOU THINK?
For question 2, explain that Franklin D. Roosevelt was the American president who made this statement and that he was referring to the Great Depression of the 1930s. Many students are not familiar with this period of American history. Any additional information you can provide about this decade—especially pictures—is helpful.

EXERCISE 4: THE CITY
Some students will need help understanding the meaning of *sculpture*. This word can be briefly discussed during the homework review. Pictures are helpful.

EXERCISE 5: THE ENDING *-MENT*
A brief discussion of city life vs. country life is usually an enjoyable topic. Students may enjoy having this discussion after completing the exercise.

Activities in Writing Book 5
Exercise 1 continues the work with descriptive words and phrases by asking students to choose the ones in the story that they think are best. Accept all reasonable and well-reasoned answers. Exercise 2 asks students to write their own descriptive sentences.

Exercise 3 begins to formalize the process of prewriting by explaining one method: brainstorming. Point out the importance in brainstorming of writing any and all ideas and details that come to mind on the topic. Once students have their ideas down on paper, then they can evaluate them and cross off ones they do not want to use. Criteria in deciding what to cross off might be that the idea/detail is not important, does not relate to the topic, or is covered in something else on the list.

Additional Writing Activities
1. Talk about where students live. Ask them if they live in a city or rural area. Discuss the differences. Ask students who are new to city living to write a paragraph about what they do or do not like about living in a city.
2. Ask students who have grown up in a city to write about what they do or do not like about living in a city. Ask students who live in rural areas what they like and don't like about it. Have students compare their compositions and discuss the differences.

Two Consonants in the Middle of Words

Primary emphasis

- Comprehension (written questions and answers)
- Using the dictionary
- Using context clues

Secondary emphasis

- Vocabulary review (synonyms)
- The ending -ness
- Changing the *y* to *i*
- General information (American cities)
- Oral reading

Word Chart

Students need to draw a line between the middle consonants only if this helps them to sound out the words.

Story

During the preview, tell students that "The Streets of Memphis" is part of an autobiography written by Richard Wright, a prominent black American author who wrote most of his major works in the 1940s and 1950s. Discuss the terms *autobiography* and *biography*. Discuss the meaning of the prefix *auto-*, and contrast fiction with biography and autobiography.

Tell students that this selection is another story about living in a city and being afraid, but this story really happened. During the follow-up discussion, have students compare "The Streets of Memphis" and "The Terror in the Streets" by listing as many similarities and differences between the two stories as they can think of. They should consider differences in plot and setting, but particularly the differences between the two main characters.

EXERCISE 2: ABOUT THE STORY

During the homework review, have the students speculate on the reasons Richard Wright may have chosen to write an autobiography. Review the terms *autobiography* and *biography* only if necessary.

EXERCISE 3: MORE WORK WITH SYNONYMS

If necessary, review the definition for *synonym*.

EXERCISE 6: AMERICAN CITIES

Students often need to use a dictionary to complete this exercise. If necessary, remind students to look under the cities, not the states, for the correct answer. Some students also need help in distinguishing between a city and a state.

You may also want to have students use a map or an atlas to locate the cities and states. Be willing to assist them in doing this. This activity helps some students to understand better that a city is in a state.

Activities in Writing Book 5

Exercises 1 and 2 continue work with identifying good description and writing description.

Exercise 3 asks students to practice brainstorming ideas. The ideas that they think of in this exercise form the basis of the paragraphs they will write in Exercise 4. Encourage students in the Prewriting section of the guide to add details to what they have brainstormed in order to make the details more interesting. Having these details already as part of their ideas will help them when they write their paragraphs.

Additional Writing Activities

1. Have students write a paragraph to answer the question: Was Wright's mother right in making him stand up to the gang of boys? Explain.

2. Have students write two paragraphs comparing the two main characters in "The Terror in the Streets" and "The Streets of Memphis." In the first paragraph, they should describe Margaret, and in the second paragraph, Richard Wright. The two paragraphs should describe the same information for each and in the same order of development.

LESSON 16

More Work with Two Consonants in the Middle of Words

Primary emphasis
- Comprehension (written questions and answers)
- Using the dictionary
- Using context clues

Secondary emphasis
- The endings *-ful* and *-less*
- Homonyms
- Oral reading

Word Chart
Students should draw a line between the two consonants in the middle of the word to help them sound out words.

Story
During the preview, tell students that this selection, like the one in Lesson 15, is from an autobiography. In "The Thread That Runs So True," poet and writer Jesse Stuart (1907–1984) tells about his years as a teacher. This episode takes place a week after Stuart began his first job teaching in a one-room country schoolhouse. He chose that particular school because one of the students, a large bully named Guy Hawkins, had beaten up Jesse's sister when she was the teacher there. Ask students if they have ever been in a situation where they felt forced to fight.

During the review, students might be interested to learn that after Jesse Stuart won the fight with Guy Hawkins, he became a local hero since no one else had been able to beat Guy. Stuart left Lonesome Valley at the end of that school year to continue his own education.

Students often enjoy guessing which state Jesse Stuart lived in. The answer is Kentucky.

EXERCISE 2: ABOUT THE STORY
Answers to some of these questions may vary from those in the Answer Key. Accept any answer the student can justify.

EXERCISE 4: CAN YOU HELP GUY WITH HIS ENGLISH?
Approach this exercise in the spirit of enjoyment rather than as a usage exercise. Many students are unfamiliar with the usage principles involved in the corrections. Mention these principles in passing during the homework review, but do not belabor the point. Students working in Book 5

improve their usage of standard English most effectively through composition work.

EXERCISE 5: THE ENDINGS *-FUL* AND *-LESS*
During the homework review, make sure the student understands the meanings of *-ful* and *-less* when used as suffixes. It is not necessary to introduce the term *suffix*.

EXERCISE 6: HOMONYMS
After students have read the directions during the preview, make sure that they can pronounce and define *homonym*. This is also an appropriate time to review the meanings of *synonym* and *antonym*.

Activities in Writing Book 5
Exercise 1 focuses on another common error in English: incorrect subject-verb agreement. The problem often occurs when words and phrases come between the subject and the predicate of a sentence. This is especially true if the number of the noun or pronoun closest to the predicate is different from the subject of the sentence. While instruction and exercises such as Exercise 1 can be useful in calling students' attention to the problem, recognizing and correcting errors in their own work are the best way to make the lesson real for students.

Exercise 3 provides another way to develop information for a piece of writing: answering the *who, what, when, where, why,* and *how* of a situation. Exercise 4 provides instruction on writing a summary.

Additional Writing Activities
1. Ask students to write a paragraph explaining what they think about using violence to settle differences. You might arrange for a few students who favor the use of violence and a few who do not to read their paragraphs and then have a class discussion about the pros and cons of using violence.
2. Have students imagine they are Mr. Stuart and write a letter to his sister describing the fight and how it ended. The letter should be three paragraphs in length and mirror a three-paragraph essay, that is, the first paragraph is the introduction, the second paragraph is the body, and the last paragraph is the conclusion. You may need to introduce the format for a friendly letter.

Review: Lessons 1–16

Use the same procedure as you have for previous reviews.

EXERCISE 5: FIND THE QUOTE

During the review, students enjoy swapping tricks they have developed to help them solve the puzzle. They also enjoy hearing any tricks you might have developed for problem solving.

LESSON 17
Common Word Endings

Primary emphasis
- Comprehension (written questions and answers)
- Using the dictionary
- Using context clues

Secondary emphasis
- Compound words
- Review of sounds
- Oral reading

Word Chart and Word Meanings

Use the procedure suggested for Lesson 1.

Story

During the preview, remind students that they read another O. Henry short story in Lesson 4. Ask them what is characteristic of O. Henry short stories (surprise endings). Have them read down to the line of dialogue, "'I can't refuse a call for tobacco,' he said lightly." Then ask students to predict how they think the story will end. If anyone has figured out the ending, do not acknowledge it at this point. Have students continue reading to the end of the story.

If anyone did figure out that Mr. Easton was the prisoner, now ask that student or students to explain the clues that led them to their conclusions. Remind students about foreshadowing in stories.

EXERCISE 3: COMPOUND WORDS

If the student seems ready for such an exercise based on previous writing, he often enjoys creating his own sentences in which he uses two or more compound words.

EXERCISE 4: REVIEW OF WORD SOUNDS

By now, most students can complete this type of exercise with an accuracy rate of 70 percent or better, which is an acceptable score. You may notice that some students have developed the habit of groaning in agony upon noticing that a word sound review has been included in the lesson. No matter how often they say the words aloud or how patient they are, they find this type of exercise bewildering. For these students, concentrating on reviewing the meanings of some of the words will help to alleviate their discomfort.

EXERCISE 5: MORE ABOUT THE STORY

Answering questions 3, 4, and 5 requires that the students make inferences.

Activities in Writing Book 5

Exercise 1 continues work with descriptive details, and Exercise 2 is a refresher on subject-verb agreement and the use of commas and conjunctions to combine sentences (that is, ways to avoid comma faults). Exercise 3 reinforces the use of the "Five W's and H" to help writers to gather information about their topics. Students then use the information to write three-paragraph summaries of the story.

Additional Writing Activities

1. Have students read through the story to list details that indicate that the story takes place in the past. If the story were written today, ask students to explain in a paragraph how the setting might be different.
2. The information in question 7 in Exercise 5 lists just the bare bones of events from the story. After students have completed Exercise 5, have them rewrite the sentences in order, adding details to make the information more interesting to read.

LESSON 18
Common Word Endings

Primary emphasis
- Comprehension (written questions and answers)
- Using the dictionary
- Using context clues

Secondary emphasis
- Vocabulary review
- Oral reading

Word Chart and Word Meanings
Use the procedure suggested for Lesson 1.

Words for Study
Even though one of the exercises in this lesson pertains to *banns*, briefly discuss the definition for this word during the preview.

Story
This is another story with a surprise ending, or rather two surprises: that Brently Mallard is alive and that Louise Mallard dies at the sight of him.

During the preview, ask students if they know any stories, movies, or TV/cable shows in which the wife or husband appears to others to be happy in his or her marriage but is not. The character may not even recognize his or her own unhappiness. Tell students that this is the subject of the story they will read.

After students have finished the story, ask if the ending was a surprise. Ask students if anyone ever surprised them at a birthday or anniversary party or if they ever surprised someone. What was it like? How did they or the person they surprised react? Why do they think that Louise reacted the way she did? Ask students to find details in the story to support their opinions.

EXERCISE 2: ABOUT THE STORY
Remind students to use process of elimination when they are unsure of an answer. Remind them also to reread parts of the story to find answers they do not remember or are unsure of.

EXERCISE 3: WHAT DO YOU THINK?
Question 3 requires that students infer the answer based on information in the story.

EXERCISE 4: WORD STUDY
If necessary, students are to refer to a dictionary for definitions of forgotten or unknown words.

EXERCISE 5: WHERE WOULD YOU FIND IT?
In this section, students can also refer to the dictionary if necessary.

Activities in Writing Book 5
Students continue working with descriptive details in Exercise 1. They are asked to analyze the reading for the best four details and to explain why they think they are the best. This activity will help them recognize how authors use details to build their stories.

Exercise 2 provides instruction on the correct forms of personal pronouns to use as subjects and objects.

Exercises 3 and 4 reinforce the use of the "Five W's and H" as a prewriting activity as well as the method for writing a summary of a story.

Additional Writing Activities
1. Ask each student to write a sentence describing how Louise feels about the death of her husband. Then have each student write a sentence describing how her sister thinks Louise feels. Encourage students to use details.
2. Ask each student to write a paragraph either agreeing or disagreeing with the last sentence that implies that Louise Mallard died from joy at seeing her husband alive.

LESSON 19
The Sound for *ph*

Primary emphasis

- Comprehension (written questions and answers)
- The sound for *ph*
- Using the dictionary
- Using context clues

Secondary emphasis

- Reading a circle graph
- Classifying
- Vocabulary review
- Oral reading

Word Chart

This marks the first lesson in this reading series in which the sound for *ph* is formally studied. Spend some time on the pronunciation of these words with all students.

Story

Introduce this story by pointing out that it is by O. Henry, who also wrote "After Twenty Years" (Lesson 4) and "Hearts and Hands" (Lesson 17). Remind students that O. Henry was famous for his surprise endings and that they should watch for clues that might foreshadow the ending. Note that this is the first part of a two-part story. During the general discussion, ask students about Ben Price: Who is he? How did he find out where Jimmy is and what his plans are? Discuss students' predictions about what will happen in Part 2 of the story.

EXERCISE 4: SUBJECTS FOR STUDY

During the homework review, review the definitions for *physics, geography,* and *history.* Students who have not worked in Book 4 often need a brief explanation of Adolf Hitler's role in history.

EXERCISE 5: WHICH ANSWER FITS BEST?

Remind students to take their time with this section and to work by process of elimination.

EXERCISE 6: A CIRCLE GRAPH

Because many students are not familiar with either graphs or percents, thoroughly preview this exercise. If you think it necessary, have the student complete the first two items in class after he or she has read the directions and studied the graph.

Activities in Writing Book 5

Exercise 1 works with word meanings. Exercise 2 gives students additional practice with comprehension. Exercise 3 asks students to make predictions about what they think will happen next in the story. Exercise 4 asks students to categorize words based on the area they belong in.

Additional Writing Activities

1. Introduce the term *theme,* and explain that it is the big idea that a piece of writing is about. Have students use the answer to question 9 in Exercise 2 "About the Story" as the basis for a paragraph explaining the theme of the story so far.

2. Ask students if they could question O. Henry, what would they like to know? Have them write three questions they would ask about this story, about any of O. Henry's stories they have read in this book, or about writing in general.

LESSON 20
Four-Letter Words

Primary emphasis
- Comprehension (written questions and answers)
- Using the dictionary
- Using context clues

Secondary emphasis
- Common expressions
- Pronunciation and syllabication (four-letter words)
- Compound words

Word Chart

This is a difficult word chart for many students. Spend some time on the pronunciation of these words, and consider using them as the basis for future spelling tests.

Story

During the preview, review Part 1 of this story and students' predictions about what might happen in Part 2. During the review, help students to understand the story as a whole by reviewing both parts. Discuss how close students came to predicting how the story would develop.

During the follow-up discussion, discuss how Jimmy changes in this story and the reasons for those changes. Allow students to share their ideas about how Annabel and her family would have reacted had the story continued.

EXERCISE 3: SYLLABLES

Students are to be discouraged from using a dictionary to complete this exercise in order to reinforce their ability to pronounce these words properly.

EXERCISE 4: "HEARTFELT" EXPRESSIONS

Remind the student to make an intelligent guess for any items that have him or her completely stumped.

As part of the homework review, discuss with students what the different expressions mean. Ask students if they know any other expressions that use anatomical terms such as "break a leg" and "thumbs up."

EXERCISE 5: VALENTINE'S DAY CUSTOMS OF LONG AGO

This exercise also provides the basis for many discussion topics. Many students enjoy recalling childhood memories of holidays. Additionally, many students are not aware of holidays and other days of the year that are recognized as special by other cultures. This is an appropriate time to review such days and briefly discuss their meanings and backgrounds.

EXERCISE 6: COMPOUND WORDS

For this exercise, students may refer to a dictionary if their own knowledge and process of elimination fail them.

Activities in Writing Book 5

Exercise 2 offers instruction and practice in the use of interrogative pronouns. To avoid confusion with relative pronouns, note that interrogative pronouns are used only to ask questions. Stress that the names of the different types of pronouns are not important; what is important is that the correct word is written depending on the type of sentence and use of the word in the sentence.

Additional Writing Activity

Ask students to write three-paragraph essays explaining three things that they have learned about writing in this book. Before they begin, ask them how they will go about writing their essays. (First, they need to brainstorm possible ideas. Second, they should choose the three strongest ideas. Third, they should reread their ideas and add details. Then they will be ready to write.)

Review: Lessons 1–20

The purpose of this review is to give students one more opportunity to work with many of the words and concepts emphasized in Book 5. As was recommended in the notes for previous reviews, this review should not be perceived as a test.

After any necessary corrections have been made by the student during the homework review, spend some time reviewing and evaluating the student's progress. Many students enjoy perusing the word index because it represents a concrete symbol of accomplishment.

Book 6 Introduction

The format of Book 6 corresponds to the one used in Books 2 and 4. Book 6 introduces relatively few new words and concepts in order to give students the opportunity to thoroughly review and reinforce vocabulary and reasoning skills and further develop their reading comprehension. Capitalization rules and the proper use of the apostrophe represent the major new skills emphasized in this book.

The readings for Book 6 are, for the most part, nonfiction selections that have been minimally adapted from works of widely-acclaimed writers. Experience indicates that motivation and self-esteem are bolstered when students are made aware of this fact. Adult students should also be made aware that the GED Test includes brief nonfiction passages with accompanying questions. In working with the readings in Book 6, adults often become increasingly confident of their ability to achieve this long-range educational goal.

A review appears after every five lessons. These reviews provide students with additional opportunities to review words and concepts. They also help students develop the habit of referring to previous lessons for the correct answers to some of the questions. There are no word indexes in Book 6, but a complete list of the words introduced in Book 6 is available online at newreaderspress.com.

Book 6 is generally used by students who have completed Book 5 in this series. Book 6 is also an appropriate starting place for students who score in the 6.0–7.5 range on standardized reading achievement tests. The final review in Book 5 can also be used as a diagnostic tool. An accuracy rate of 85 percent or better for this review indicates that students are ready for Book 6.

Students who start this series in Book 6 may need oral reading practice. This is because many students who begin their work at this level either lack confidence or are simply careless readers. Often their homework reflects carelessness, also. By gently calling students' attention to oral reading errors and conducting homework critiques, you can help students correct this pattern.

Book 6 builds upon procedures and practices emphasized in the earlier books in this series. Thus, you may find it worthwhile to look through the manual notes for the previous books.

Scheduling Considerations

Book 6 works well in a classroom setting. The most progress is achieved when students work with *Challenger* a minimum of 45 minutes two or three times a week. Students can work independently, in a group, or with a partner. When working with other students, they receive the support and stimulation from one another that make learning more enjoyable. Also, the more advanced students can assume much of the responsibility for giving explanations and leading reinforcement activities, which in turn reinforces their own reading skills. Experience indicates that less advanced students usually benefit from peer instruction provided that you are available to supply any necessary clarifications.

The Lesson Format

The procedure for each lesson should be as consistent as possible.
1. Students go over the writing assignment if one was given and review the work from the previous lesson first. This includes discussing the reading selection and correcting the exercises.
2. If time permits, students complete relevant reinforcement activities. The nature and scope of these activities are determined by the needs of your students and how often you meet with them.
3. Students preview the next lesson, which is usually assigned for homework.

Individual Lesson Notes

Lesson notes for each lesson appear on the following pages. These notes contain suggestions and procedures for specific items in each lesson.

LESSON 1
Healthy Food, Healthy Family

Primary emphasis

- Reading comprehension (nonfiction)
- Using context clues
- Forming a reasoned opinion

Secondary emphasis

- Vocabulary review (Which Word Does Not Fit?)
- The suffix *-ness*

Words for Study

The Words for Study section includes words that appear in this lesson that have not been introduced previously in this controlled-vocabulary reading series.

Have students pronounce the new words prior to reading the selection. Generally, students should have difficulty with no more than five of these words. When a student does have trouble sounding out a new word, remind him or her of appropriate phonics and syllabication rules he or she can use so that he or she does the sounding out rather than you. For some words, guide words provide helpful cues. For example, one student found that by jotting *California* above *calories,* she could immediately recall the correct pronunciation of *calories.* After students have pronounced the new words, have them briefly review those words with which they had difficulty.

This type of pronunciation drill is most helpful for students who have completed at least three of the preceding books in this series. Remember, this is a new book, and many students experience some degree of stage fright when beginning a new book. By having students sound out the new words and by briefly reviewing troublesome ones, you help them to see that they indeed have the skills to work in Book 6.

For some students, particularly those who scored approximately 6.0 on word recognition tests and/or are beginning in this book, it is more expedient to correct any mispronunciations by simply saying the word correctly. The primary benefit of Book 6 for these students is that it offers an opportunity to improve skills in studying, comprehension, reasoning, writing, and vocabulary. A phonics approach to troublesome words is unnecessary for these students, and it also often turns them right off.

Think of these students as you think of yourself. For example, if you ask a person for the correct pronunciation of *Jacuzzi,* you don't need to hear that the *c* is hard, the *u* has a long *oo* sound, the *i* has a long *e* sound, and the accent is on the second syllable. You simply need to hear the word and perhaps repeat it a few times. Phonics rules are like the safety ropes in a swimming pool. You only heed their presence when you need the security they offer.

There are exceptions to this rule, of course. For example, some Book 6 students consistently neglect certain word endings or confuse *per-* with *pre-*. In these cases, emphasize the trouble spot by having the student sound out the word rather than merely saying it correctly for him.

As was the case with the preceding books in this series, most of the new words appear in subsequent reading selections and exercises so that students have many opportunities to work with them. Thus, there is no need to strive for immediate mastery; mastery will come with practice.

This principle also holds true for word definitions. Students should not be expected to have mastered the meanings of the new words by the end of the lesson in which they first appear. Generally, when students ask for the meaning of a Word for Study that they are sounding out, a simple statement, such as "See if you can figure it out when you come to it in the lesson," is helpful.

Sometimes it is helpful to give an on-the-spot definition, sentence, or example of an unfamiliar word. Perhaps a student needs to know that he or she has a working relationship with you. Perhaps he or she has had a difficult day and needs a few moments to center him- or herself on the work. Whatever the reason, a few seconds of friendly conversation is more important than reminding him or her of the value of context clues.

Make your responses light-hearted and interesting. For example, a student, after having sounded out the word *gallop,* wanted to know what it meant. Knowing that the student never had a chance to eat dinner until after class, the teacher responded, "Louise was so hungry when she got home from night school that she galloped to the refrigerator as if she were a horse."

The Reading Selection

Tell students that many of the reading selections that appear in Book 6 have been adapted from the works of professional writers. It motivates students to know that they are reading material that has enjoyed critical acclaim and has been written for the general adult reading public.

Introduce the selection by asking students if they know what the term *obese* means. Discuss how Americans have become so overweight. Answers may focus on eating fast food and not getting enough exercise. Ask for suggestions about how Americans can lose weight and—better yet—not become overweight in the first place. Tell students to see how their ideas compare to those of the writer of the article as they read.

Generally, all initial readings of the selections should be done for homework. However, because this is the first lesson, allot time for an oral first reading in class. This gives you an opportunity to assess the strengths and weaknesses of students' oral reading abilities. Begin by reading the first part of the story yourself, and then ask for volunteers to continue.

Because Book 6 contains both fiction and nonfiction reading selections, it is important to introduce or review these terms for the students. Lesson 1 offers an excellent opportunity for this because both fiction and nonfiction are included in the reading passage. The best time to discuss these concepts is after students have completed reading the article in Lesson 1. Point out that it is a piece of nonfiction. Say that fiction is a story, and ask what nonfiction is. Ask how students can tell that this article is nonfiction.

Read the first part of the article yourself, and then ask students to discuss it in a general way. This gives students a chance to get a sense of the selection as a whole while giving you the opportunity to assess their comprehension skills.

When you have completed the general discussion of the reading selection, preview the exercises to be done for homework. Since this is the first lesson, take plenty of time and be sure all students understand how to do each exercise. If necessary, have students complete an item in each exercise so that they have a thorough understanding of how to do the work.

EXERCISE 1: ABOUT THE READING

During the homework preview, have students read the directions, and remind them that they are to refer to the reading selection for any answer they cannot recall. Students need to know that having to refer to the reading selection for the correct answer does *not* mean they are poor readers. Tell students who suffer from this false impression that instead it means that they are good students!

During the homework preview, you also want to encourage students to write a well-developed answer for the "What do you think?" questions. Many students find the instruction, "Use all the lines to write your answer," helpful. The goal is not wordiness; the goal is learning to support one's opinions and thoughts with sound reasons. Because this type of question appears frequently in Book 6, plan to spend quite a bit of time discussing the strengths and weaknesses of the students' writing during the homework review.

All writing mistakes should be corrected—preferably by the students with your assistance. There is no need to explain the rule for every correction. By noting the corrections, however, students gradually become accustomed to standard writing procedures. Their writing will improve, and it will become much easier.

EXERCISE 2: WHICH WORD DOES NOT FIT?

During the homework preview, encourage students to use a dictionary for any words they do not know. All answers should be spelled accurately.

EXERCISE 4: READING A NUTRITION LABEL

During the homework preview, point out that this exercise is an important tool for providing healthy meals for oneself and one's family. Students may be unfamiliar with the terms on food labels. Direct them to a dictionary to define words that they do not know. You may also need to walk students through reading the information on the labels so that they understand what each item is and how it can affect health. For example, foods high in sodium are not good for people with high blood pressure. On the other hand, people who have high blood pressure should look for foods with high amounts of potassium.

EXERCISE 5: WORDS THAT END WITH -NESS

During the homework preview, remind students that they need not complete the sentences in the order in which they appear. If necessary, teach them how to use process of elimination to complete this exercise.

Many students find it helpful if you remind them to read each sentence in its entirety prior to filling in the blanks. For example, sentence 2 should be read, "When the *blank*-ness of the car radio made Andrew's ears throb with pain, he asked his friend if he could turn it down."

For any incorrect answers, help students to identify context clues during the homework review. Granted this is time-consuming, but because this is the first lesson, you want to initiate good working patterns. All words should be spelled accurately.

Notes

1. After the students—especially any new students—have gone over the exercises and made any necessary corrections during the homework review, give them an opportunity to ask questions or make comments about what they have just accomplished. If they seem overwhelmed by the work, point out the strengths they have shown in completing the work. Remind them that this is only the first lesson and that they will get used to the work more quickly than they think possible.

2. A follow-up activity is not recommended for the first lesson. If one seems appropriate, however, consider having your students watch television for one night and jot down any commercials for food that they see. They should note if the commercial is for fast food or a restaurant. They should also note whether the meal looks "super-sized" or like a healthy portion size. This is subjective and should lead to an interesting discussion of what is a "normal" versus "healthy" portion.

Activities in Writing Book 6

Lesson 1 provides a review for students who have used Book 5 and for students new to the program, it is an easy entrée into the basic structure of the writing program in the *Challenger* series. First, students begin a lesson by working with details to learn to enhance their ideas. They then move to organizing information to write a paragraph, and later in the Book to writing an essay. In addition to working on using details, a few lessons provide review/instruction on common grammar errors that people make.

Additional Writing Activities

1. Ask students to list their five favorite foods and then to write next to each one words and phrases that describe it. This can be the basis for a class discussion about ethnic foods.

2. Ask students to write two or three sentences that tell how they felt writing their summaries. What was the hardest thing to do? What was the easiest? What else would they like to know about writing a summary? This can be a guide for you in teaching the next four lessons.

LESSON 2
An American Family Portrait

Primary emphasis
- Reading comprehension
- Forming a reasoned opinion
- Vocabulary development

Secondary emphasis
- The suffix *-ment*
- Using context clues
- Using reference materials

Words for Study
Use the procedure suggested for Lesson 1.

Reading Selection
During the preview, point out that this is another nonfiction article. The author begins the article as though it is about real people; however, the story is fictional. It is a literary device used to pull the reader into the article. That is, it sets up a situation that makes the reader curious to know what will happen next. Once into reading the article, the reader finds that the piece is really about how the American family has changed over the centuries.

Discuss how the portrait of the American family has changed since the first colonists came. Ask for facts from the article so that students get used to looking for facts. Later lessons in *Writing for Challenger 6* ask them to form reasoned opinions based on facts from the reading selections.

EXERCISE 1: ABOUT THE READING
Remind students to read the selection carefully *prior* to answering the comprehension questions. Not only will their reading improve, but also they will find Book 6 far more enjoyable.

Questions 6 through 8 require that students use their own experience and opinions to answer. There are no right or wrong answers.

EXERCISE 2: WHERE DO THEY COME FROM?
You might have students locate these countries on a world map or an atlas. If you have students from any of these countries, ask them to describe their homelands in a few sentences. They might talk about where they lived and what they did.

EXERCISE 3: WORDS THAT END WITH *-MENT*
During the homework preview, remind students that they need not complete the sentences in the order in which they appear. If necessary, teach them how to use the process of elimination to complete this exercise.

For any incorrect answers, help students to identify context clues during the homework review. This is time-consuming but worthwhile as you want to initiate good working patterns during these early lessons.

EXERCISE 4: THE CAPITOL AND CAPITALS
Tell the students to use a dictionary for any capitals they do not know. Many students are not aware of the fact that the dictionary gives this kind of information. If students ask whether they should look up the city or the state, suggest that they try both ways and see what happens.

During the homework review, review the difference between *capitol* and *capital*. Make sure students have capitalized the capitals. Because capitalization is stressed in subsequent lessons, the more practice students have, the better. Students enjoy having a map of the U.S. available so they can locate the capitals as they match them with their respective states.

Point out that each state capital has its own building.

Activities in Writing Book 6
Students again work with writing sentences using words and phrases from the article. They then focus on how to create interesting details of their own. Students may be caught up in using sensory details because they are easy to think of, so help students to understand that specific nouns and action verbs as well as adverbs are important tools in helping them develop ideas. A piece of nonfiction can be as interestingly and strongly written as any piece of fiction.

Additional Writing Activities
1. To stress the point about using adverbs, ask students to list words that end in *-ly*. Then ask them to write a phrase using a verb and each of the *-ly* words, for example, *suddenly:* fell suddenly; *furiously:* barked furiously. You could duplicate this activity with general nouns and specific nouns as well: *building:* apartment building; *bus:* M1 bus.
2. Ask students if writing a summary has gotten any easier. If not, with what part(s) are they still having trouble? For those who did find it easier, what suggestions can they make to their peers?

LESSON 3
Life with Multiples

Primary emphasis
- Reading comprehension (nonfiction)
- Vocabulary (synonyms and antonyms)
- Using context clues

Secondary emphasis
- Capitalization
- Forming the plural of words ending with *f* and *fe*

Reading Selection
Ask students if they have or know anyone who has twins or other multiple-birth children. Discuss what it is like to take care of two or more children who are exactly the same age. Lead the discussion to the personalities of the children and whether, as the children develop over time, they differ from each other.

If no one has twins or knows anyone who has twins, ask what students know about multiple births.

EXERCISE 2: SYNONYMS
Remind students to use a dictionary for unfamiliar words and to use process of elimination.

EXERCISE 3: ANTONYMS
Students are to use the same procedure as they did to complete Exercise 2. Review the terms *synonym* and *antonym* during the homework review.

EXERCISE 4: SPELLING
Students should have no trouble completing this exercise accurately.

EXERCISE 5: CAPITALIZATION RULES: PART 1
During the homework preview, go over each rule and the examples. Remind students to refer to the rules if necessary while completing the exercise. Point out in the exercise that the number in parentheses at the end of each sentence indicates how many words need to be capitalized. Review the rules during the homework review. More rules are presented in subsequent lessons, and if students have a good understanding of these rules, they will find the future rules easier.

Activities in Writing Book 6
Exercise 1 provides more practice with using words and phrases that add rich details. In Exercise 2, students are asked to come up with their own details to add to very basic, and uninteresting, sentences. In Exercises 3 and 4, students gather information, organize it, and then use it to write a summary. Exercise 3 provides experience in working with paragraphs that do not add main ideas to an article, but enlarge on details that provide depth to the discussion of the main idea in another paragraph.

Additional Writing Activities
1. Have students brainstorm words and phrases to describe what it must be like to take care of twins who are one year old. They will be introduced formally to brainstorming in Lesson 6, so you might just ask them to list whatever words and phrases come to mind about the topic.
2. Have students use some of the words and phrases that they brainstormed/listed to write a paragraph about taking care of one-year-old twins.

LESSON 4
Lunch with Grandma Janey

Primary emphasis
- Comprehension of literature (short story)
- Forming a reasoned opinion
- Vocabulary (synonyms and antonyms)
- Using context clues

Secondary emphasis
- The suffix *-ness*
- Capitalization
- Spelling (changing the *-y* to *-i* and adding *-ness*)

Reading Selection

Review the meaning of *fiction* and *nonfiction* in introducing the short story. Point out the use of dialogue, which is often, though not always, a sign that a piece is fiction.

Ask if anyone knows a person with Alzheimer's. This may be a sensitive subject for someone who has a loved one with the disease, so do not press for details. However, if a person is willing to share experiences, provide support and lead the discussion to focus on symptoms of the disease and ways to help the person perform the seven functions of daily living. It is also possible that some of the students may be professional caregivers for Alzheimer's clients for whom discussing the disease may be easier.

Note: Although we say that someone has Alzheimer's, there is no way to tell for sure until the person dies and an autopsy is performed. The other main cause of dementia, the broad medical category to which Alzheimer's belongs, is stroke, which also causes symptoms similar to those Grandma Janey exhibits in the story.

EXERCISE 1: ABOUT THE STORY

Both the content and form of the students' answers should be discussed carefully and courteously during the homework review. Responses to questions 7, 9, and 10 may vary greatly. Do not press any student who does not wish to respond to questions 7 and 10.

EXERCISE 2: SYNONYMS

Students are to use the same procedure as they did for Exercise 2 in Lesson 3.

EXERCISE 3: ANTONYMS

Students use the same procedure as they did for Exercise 3 in Lesson 3. If necessary, again review the definitions for *synonym* and *antonym*.

EXERCISE 4: MORE WORK WITH THE ENDING *-NESS*

Students use the same procedure as they did for previous exercises pertaining to suffixes.

EXERCISE 5: SPELLING

If students have trouble remembering how they completed this work in Lesson 1, have them refer to that lesson rather than showing them how to change the *y* to *i*.

EXERCISE 6: CAPITALIZATION RULES: PART 2

As in Lesson 3, preview each rule and the examples. Then review the rules in Lesson 3. Remind students to refer to these rules if necessary while completing the exercise. Point out as before that the number in parentheses at the end of each sentence indicates how many words need to be capitalized. Allot time also for reviewing both these rules and the ones presented in Lesson 3 during the homework review.

Activities in Writing Book 6

In Exercise 1, students continue working with words and phrases from a professional writer to use in writing their own sentences. Exercise 2 begins work on some of the most common errors that writers make with commas. This lesson tackles comma faults, also known as comma splices, and offers two solutions to the problem, coordinating conjunctions and subordinating conjunctions. Students learn about or review the use of the "Five W's and H" to gather information for writing their summaries.

Additional Writing Activities

1. Explain that the "Five W's and H" questions are the basis of all news reports, whether print or TV. Have students watch a TV news program or read a newspaper and choose one story to answer the "Five W's and H" questions about.

2. Armed with the information they gathered, have students write up their own news report about the incident they watched on TV or read about.

LESSON 5

How to Spend Less and Have More Fun

Primary emphasis
- Reading comprehension
- Forming a reasoned opinion
- Using context clues
- The suffix *-ment*

Secondary emphasis
- Vocabulary (compound words)
- Word families
- Capitalization

Reading Selection

During the introduction, make the point that spending wisely is a good strategy for individuals and families regardless of the strength or weakness of the economy. Ask students for ideas about how to spend less on the things they buy, such as using coupons at the grocery store or buying in bulk. Tell students to compare their ideas with what they read in the selection.

At the end of the reading, ask students what new tips they learned for saving money. Draw up a class list of money-saving tips and make copies for students, or have students copy the list. Be sure to include both ideas from the article and students' own ideas. It should be practical based on students' needs.

EXERCISE 1: ABOUT THE READING

Encourage students to use all the lines that have been provided to develop their answers. As they are correcting any writing errors during the homework review, be sure to mention the improvement they are making. Have them compare the writing they did in Lesson 1 with their writing in Lesson 5.

EXERCISE 2: WORD FAMILIES

Encourage students who have difficulty with this type of exercise to read each item aloud so they can hear which word should go where.

EXERCISE 3: CAPITALIZATION REVIEW

During the homework preview, remind students to refer to the rules they studied in Lessons 3 and 4 and to make sure they capitalize a total of 20 words.

EXERCISE 4: MORE WORK WITH THE ENDING *-MENT*

During the homework preview, remind students to read the complete sentence and to use context clues as a guide to putting the right word in each sentence. Remind students also that they need not complete the sentences in the order in which they appear.

EXERCISE 5: COMPOUND WORDS

Remind students to use a dictionary for any compound word they are not sure about.

Activities in Writing Book 6

Exercise 1 continues work with using words and phrases that add rich details. Exercise 2 provides practice in combining sentences to correct comma faults. In Exercises 3 and 4, students plan and write a summary based on a different type of article, one that presents the most important information in a list format. These points are essentially the main idea of each paragraph. Students should be able to recognize that the rest of the each paragraph provides details to explain the main idea.

For some students, writing a three-paragraph essay may be new. If they seem to be having difficulty, ask them what they are having the most trouble with, and focus on that for this lesson.

Additional Writing Activities

1. As a fun activity, have students work in pairs to write slogans to help them remember one of the money-saving tips in the article.
2. Ask students to write a paragraph telling what one thing they splurge on and why.
3. Have students choose one of the following questions to answer in a paragraph: Why do you find it hard to stick to a budget? How are you able to stick to a budget? Responses could be the basis for a helpful class discussion.

Review: Lessons 1–5

It should be emphasized to the students that this is a review, not a test. These exercises are opportunities to review words and concepts that have been introduced in previous lessons. Material is often presented in new ways both to challenge students and to arouse their interest. An overall score of 80 percent or better on a review exercise should be considered excellent.

EXERCISE 1: WORD REVIEW

For this and the other exercises, encourage students to refer to previous lessons or a dictionary for any words they cannot recall. Make sure they have spelled and capitalized words correctly.

EXERCISE 4: SUFFIXES

This is the first time the word *suffix* is formally introduced. Review the meaning of this word during the homework review. Have students identify the common suffixes in each set of answer choices.

EXERCISE 5: REVIEW OF CAPITALIZATION RULES

During the preview, review the ten rules that students studied in Lessons 3 and 4. If students have trouble thinking of examples, have them refer to these lessons for ideas, but insist that they come up with original examples.

EXERCISE 6: COMPOUND WORDS

During the homework preview, go over the directions carefully with students. Point out that they can work back and forth between the clues and the definitions. If they wish, students may use a dictionary to help them solve the puzzle. But as one student remarked, "What's the fun in solving a puzzle if you're going to use a dictionary?"

LESSON 6
Voices from the Great Depression

Primary emphasis

- Reading comprehension (nonfiction)
- Forming a reasoned opinion
- Vocabulary (synonyms)

Secondary emphasis

- Using context clues
- The suffix -*ful*
- The suffix -*less*
- A review of capitalization rules

Words for Study

If students are unfamiliar with *caseworker* and *psychiatrist,* you may want to spend some time briefly discussing these words during the preview.

Reading Selection

During the preview, briefly discuss the Great Depression so students will be aware of the conditions that are being described, and point out that Studs Terkel's book is a collection of first-person interviews. Many of the names in this reading are new words for students. If necessary, help the students to pronounce these names during the preview.

EXERCISE 1: ABOUT THE READING

After reviewing their answers to the questions, students may want to discuss the character or characters in the reading selection with whom they most sympathize.

EXERCISE 2: WHAT DO YOU THINK?

After the students have discussed their responses, it is helpful to provide some pictures of this period of American history. Many students are not familiar with the Great Depression, and pictures can help them better understand this era.

EXERCISE 4: THE SUFFIX -*FUL*

If necessary, remind students to use context clues and process of elimination to help them choose the correct answers for this and the next exercise.

EXERCISE 6: REVIEW OF CAPITALIZATION RULES

During the homework preview, review the ten rules studied in Lessons 3 and 4, and remind students to check the number of words they capitalize in each sentence against the number in parentheses.

Activities in Writing Book 6

This is a heavy lesson for students new to the series. They will learn three new concepts about writing. In Exercise 1, students formalize what constitutes strong and useful detail by reviewing/learning about sensory words and phrases, specific nouns, and action verbs. It is not necessary to introduce the term *sensory details* when discussing adjectives that refer to the five senses. Calling all details "descriptive" suffices for our purpose in helping students to get used to writing with detail.

In Exercise 2, students think about their own lives and consider how growing up would have been different if they lived during the Great Depression.

Additional Writing Activities

1. The Great Depression presents an opportunity for mini-research projects for interested students. Have them select topics for further research and present either oral or written reports. Emphasize that although an oral report does not need to be written out, the same information gathering, planning, and organizational structure apply (introduction, body to develop ideas, conclusion).

2. Ask students to think about a time that they or someone they know experienced great hardship like the Great Depression. Have them write a paragraph about it.

LESSON 7
When John Quincy Adams Lost His Job

Primary emphasis
- Reading comprehension (biography)
- Identifying symbols
- Reading classified ads

Secondary emphasis
- Word families
- Forming a reasoned opinion
- Reasoning and spelling (Can You Crack the Code?)

Words for Study
Discuss the definition of the hyphenated prefix *ex-* if students are not familiar with its meaning.

Reading Selection
This article is taken from a biography, the life of a person written by another. Explain that an autobiography, on the other hand, is written by a person about him- or herself. Ask students if they have read any autobiographies. Students who have worked through Level 5 may remember that they read "The Streets of Memphis," an excerpt from Richard Wright's autobiography *Black Boy*.

Because it does not occur to many students that prominent figures in history suffer just like others do, this concept can be the basis for a good follow-up discussion topic.

EXERCISE 1: ABOUT THE READING
The answers to several of these questions are not specifically given in the reading selection but can be inferred from the information given. If students have trouble drawing the correct conclusions, discuss the process of inferring the best choice.

EXERCISE 2: SYMBOLS
Review the definition of *symbol* during the homework preview. Remind students to use the process of elimination and intelligent guessing to complete the exercise. They may also want to ask a friend to help.

EXERCISE 3: WORD FAMILIES
Remind students who have trouble with this type of exercise to complete it aloud so they can hear which word should go where.

EXERCISE 4: LOOKING FOR A JOB
Many students wish to know if the advertisements in this exercise are examples of real ads. The answer is yes. Point out that in most newspapers ads are listed alphabetically by the first word.

Explain that some abbreviations, such as *bet* and *exper.,* are not standard in other types of writing but are commonly used in classified ads.

EXERCISE 5: CAN YOU CRACK THE CODE?
Although these puzzles require quite a bit of work, students generally enjoy them. If necessary, help students get off to a good start by having them put *J*s above all the *B*s. Once they understand the procedure for cracking the code, they have little difficulty completing this exercise correctly. It will be easier for the students who notice that numbers 9 and 10 have the same first name as the example, and that 3, 4, and 7 also share a first name.

Activities in Writing Book 6
In Exercise 1, students continue to identify words and phrases that add strong and useful details. In Exercise 2, students work with symbols, matching specific symbols with what they stand for.

In Exercise 4, students are introduced to a classified ads section of the newspaper. They will review common abbreviations used in classified ads and will answer a number of questions about the graphic.

Additional Writing Activity
Ask students if they have ever had a boss who yelled and screamed and was disagreeable to everyone all the time. Have the students write a paragraph telling the person how they think he or she should act toward employees.

Looking for a Job?

Primary emphasis
- Reading comprehension (nonfiction)
- Forming a reasoned opinion

Secondary emphasis
- Using context clues
- Vocabulary (antonyms)
- The suffix -ly
- Capitalization

Words for Study
Several of these new words are difficult. Take extra time when going over them so that students will feel comfortable when they meet them in the lesson.

Reading Selection
Ask students if anyone has recently looked for and gotten a job. Ask the person to explain the process he or she used. Where possible, connect that person's search with ideas in the article; for example, the person may have heard about a job through a friend. Point out that this is a great example of networking. During the preview, point out that the article provides sound, practical suggestions for looking for a job in the digital age.

EXERCISE 1: ABOUT THE READING
During the preview, be sure students understand that their responses should reflect their understanding of the reading and not their own opinions. Many students have their own pet theories about the job hunt, so it is important that they understand what the author is advising.

EXERCISE 3: WHO DOES WHAT?
Students may not be familiar with many of the jobs described in this exercise. In addition to using context clues, encourage students to use a dictionary to look up the words. Students also may find it interesting to search for the jobs on the Internet to find out more about them.

EXERCISE 4: THE SUFFIX -LY
It is not necessary to introduce the term *adverb* at this point. It is enough that students understand that the suffix -ly usually tells how something is done.

EXERCISE 5: CAPITALIZATION RULES: PART 3
As before, preview each rule and the examples, and then review the rules learned in Lessons 3 and 4. Remind students to refer to all the rules if necessary when they complete the exercise.

EXERCISE 6: ONLINE JOB ADVERTISEMENT
During the homework preview, go over each part of the job posting with students. Point out the various options that the posting offers: applying, saving it, e-mailing it, and printing it. Note also the buttons for returning to the search results, getting directions, and finding out about the salary. Have students read and discuss the requirements for the job.

Activities in Writing Book 6
Students continue working with details in Exercise 1, and in Exercise 2, they work on recognizing and correcting sentence fragments. In Exercise 3, students create and use a table to list information from the reading they will use in Exercise 4 to summarize strategies for the job search. The instructions in Exercise 3 point out that not all the paragraphs in the article deal with job search strategies; students should understand not to include information from these paragraphs in their summaries.

Additional Writing Activities
1. Ask students to brainstorm at least five skills they think they bring to their current jobs. Then have them choose one and write paragraphs explaining how they use that skill in their jobs.
2. Ask students to write paragraphs about the jobs they would most like to have in the world and why. They can be pure fantasy.

LESSON 9
The Job Interview

Primary emphasis
- Reading comprehension (nonfiction)
- Classifying information
- Writing positive and negative responses
- Filling out an employment application

Secondary emphasis
- Using context clues
- Abbreviations
- The suffix -ly

Words for Study
Several of these new words are difficult. Take extra time when going over them so that students will feel comfortable when they meet them in the lesson.

Reading Selection
Introduce this reading by briefly discussing job interview experiences that students may have had. Ask what students might have done differently or would have like to have known about the experience before they went to their interviews. Explain that this article will help them better prepare for future interviews.

A helpful follow-up activity to this lesson is to have interested students role-play a job interview. Role-playing is particularly useful in helping students to see that the job interview situation can be difficult for both the interviewer and the person being interviewed.

EXERCISE 2: POSITIVE AND NEGATIVE
Students enjoy reading these responses aloud. As a follow-up activity, have students choose which response they would probably make to each situation. They can then decide whether they have "positive" or "negative" outlooks.

EXERCISE 3: WORK WITH CLASSIFICATIONS
Make sure students know what each abbreviation stands for, and check for proper capitalization and periods.

EXERCISE 6: FILLING OUT AN EMPLOYMENT APPLICATION
This exercise provides an excellent opportunity to remind students during the preview of the practical benefits of accurate spelling and legibility. Also remind them to read the statement directly above the signature line carefully. Review any words students are not sure of and the term *Equal Opportunity Employer.*

Because this exercise represents a real situation for many students, spend time carefully reviewing their responses during the homework review.

Activities in Writing Book 6
In Exercise 1, students are asked to describe themselves as if they were answering questions on a job application. The purpose is to get them to apply to themselves what they have learned about using details. Exercise 2 offers more practice with sentence fragments. In Exercise 3, students practice listing information and in Exercise 4 using the list to write an expository essay. This term may be new to students, but tell them that they have been writing exposition whenever they have explained something.

Additional Writing Activities
1. As a class activity, have students make a bulleted list of the tips in each section of the article. Make copies for students, or have students copy the list.
2. Tell students that they have just completed a job interview and are going to write a thank-you note to the interviewer. The interviewer's name is Seth Johnson, and he is Human Resources Manager for the Century Company. Students can make up the job they interviewed for. Review with students the form for a formal letter: name, address, date, greeting, introduction, body, conclusion, closing, signature.

LESSON 10
How to Avoid a Job

Primary emphasis
- Comprehension of literature (fiction)
- Using context clues
- Analogies (word relationships)

Secondary emphasis
- A review of suffixes
- Spelling

Reading Selection

Introduce the selection by pointing out that this passage about whitewashing the fence is one of the best-known episodes in this popular work. Ask if students are already familiar with it. Review the meaning of fiction.

EXERCISE 1: ABOUT THE STORY

This reading selection and the comprehension questions should produce some lively discussion during the homework review.

EXERCISE 3: WORD RELATIONSHIPS

Students often have difficulty with this type of exercise. Help them get started by going over the first question during the preview. Ask them to explain the relationship between *view* and *sight*. Have them read the four choices and then decide which pair of words expresses a similar relationship. Most students will see that "food is to taste" has the same relationship as "view is to sight." If students are still confused, have them do the second one. Since *major* and *minor* are antonyms, this relationship is easier to recognize and verbalize.

Remind students that the process of elimination is often helpful in selecting the correct answer and that they may use the dictionary to look up words they have forgotten. Whether or not you choose to introduce the term *analogy* is up to you. Some students are impressed by this word.

EXERCISE 4: REVIEW OF SUFFIXES

Go over the directions and example carefully during the homework preview. Be sure students understand that dropping the final *e* of *judge* before adding the suffix is an exception to the general rule. If necessary, remind the students of the spelling rule pertaining to changing the *y* to *i*.

EXERCISE 5: SPELLING

Some students miss number 9 because they don't realize that a missing apostrophe constitutes a misspelled word. Remind them of this. Encourage students to use a dictionary when necessary.

EXERCISE 6: WHAT EXACTLY IS A JEW'S HARP?

Remind students to read the entire passage through after they have filled in the blanks.

Activities in Writing Book 6

Students continue working with details. The purpose of having students choose words and phrases from the selections is to get them attuned to how strong, informative details can make a piece of writing more interesting and clearer for the reader. Exercise 2 provides practice in recognizing and correcting the three most common errors in constructing sentences: comma faults, run-on sentences, and sentence fragments. Exercises 3 and 4 ask students to use the "Five W's and H" to gather information, plan, and organize their essays.

Additional Writing Activities
1. Ask students to brainstorm words to describe Tom and then use those words to write a paragraph describing Tom.
2. Have students choose one of the statements in Exercise 5: Spelling and write a paragraph to explain what it means.

Review: Lessons 1–10

As with the review for Unit 1, remind students that this is not a test. These exercises are additional opportunities to review words and concepts that were introduced in previous lessons. Encourage students to refer to those lessons or to a dictionary for words they cannot recall. An overall score of 80 percent or better on a review exercise should be considered excellent.

EXERCISE 3: REVIEW OF CAPITALIZATION RULES

By drawing attention to the example during the home-work preview, you can help most students to realize that this exercise isn't nearly as difficult as it appears.

EXERCISE 4: LOOKING FOR A JOB

During the preview, read aloud a few of these ads to be sure students can understand the unfamiliar abbreviations often found in classified ads. Remind them that these are often unorthodox abbreviations and are not acceptable in more formal writing.

The classified ads can be the basis for further discussion or composition topics. Students may enjoy selecting an ad and playing the roles of interviewer and applicant. Or they may select an ad and write letters of application for the position.

EXERCISE 5: FIND THE QUOTE

Students who have worked in previous books in the *Challenger* series are familiar with this type of puzzle. Remind them to fill in the appropriate blanks for the quote as they answer each item. In this way, they can work back and forth between the clues and the quote, using context clues in the quote to complete partially filled-in words.

During the review, students enjoy swapping tricks they have developed to help them solve the puzzle. They also enjoy hearing any tricks you might have developed for problem solving.

EXERCISE 6: COMPOUND WORDS

This exercise is a bit more difficult than previous exercises dealing with compound words. Remind students that they need not work in the order in which the sentences appear and that the process of elimination and a dictionary are helpful tools.

LESSON 11
Life on the Mississippi

Primary emphasis
- Reading comprehension (autobiography)
- Matching causes and effects
- Forming a reasoned opinion
- Using context clues

Secondary emphasis
- Vocabulary review (synonyms and antonyms)
- Reading a travel brochure
- Forming contractions

Words for Study
During the homework preview, make sure students understand the meanings of *accommodated* and *Jacuzzi*.

Reading Selection
Introduce the reading by pointing out that, like the selection in Lesson 10, this was also taken from a book by Mark Twain, Tell students that while *The Adventures of Tom Sawyer* is humorous fiction, *Life on the Mississippi* is autobiographical and this selection is not humorous.

Students usually enjoy reading this selection aloud during the homework review. Pictures of steamboats are helpful, since many students do not know what a steamboat is. For fun, you might point out that the title is a play on words. Ask students what the title means.

EXERCISE 1: ABOUT THE READING
During the preview, make sure students understand the concept of cause and effect.

Some students regard the "What do you think?" question as a good opportunity to discuss their own experiences with and attitudes about death; others have no inclination whatsoever to explore this topic. Use discretion in deciding whether or not to have students elaborate on this subject.

If you have students who are originally from Mexico, you might ask them to describe the significance of Dia de los Muertos (Day of the Dead), which is celebrated on All Saints Day. Discuss what people do on that day.

EXERCISE 2: IDLE THREATS
By using the process of elimination, most students, even though they may not know the definitions for all the words, are able to complete this exercise with at least 80 percent accuracy, which is acceptable. It is not necessary to make sure students know the meanings of all unfamiliar words, since they appear in subsequent lessons. Of course, if students ask for specific definitions, by all means help them to understand what the words mean.

EXERCISE 3: TRAVELING BY STEAMBOAT
A good follow-up discussion or writing topic for question ten is, "My Idea of the Perfect Vacation."

EXERCISE 4: SYNONYMS AND ANTONYMS
A suggestion that is helpful for many students is to have them first correctly match all the synonyms and then tackle the antonyms.

EXERCISE 5: CONTRACTIONS
During the homework review, make sure students understand the meaning of *contraction*. If necessary, review the term *apostrophe*.

Activities in Writing Book 6
Exercise 1 is a way to assess how well students have internalized the use of details to enhance and clarify their writing. Exercise 2 begins a review of the use of transitions. Students work with transitions that show time order, perhaps the easiest kind of transition to grasp. Exercise 3 asks students to brainstorm ideas and then add details. Exercise 4 is the first step in having students form reasoned opinions as the basis for their writing.

Additional Writing Activities
1. Have students practice writing sentences using transitions that show time order by asking them to write directions for getting from one place to another. Limit the steps to five or six.
2. Have students write an introductory statement and a conclusion to their steps and explain that they have now written a how-to paragraph. Explain that many situations in life require that people give directions about how to go someplace or do something.

LESSON 12
The Automobile Revolution

Primary emphasis
- Reading comprehension (nonfiction)
- Forming a reasoned opinion
- Using context clues

Secondary emphasis
- Analogies (word relationships)
- The prefix *un-*
- Forming contractions
- Taking a written driver's test

Words for Study
Many students associate the word *revolution* with warfare. Make sure they understand *revolution* also means "any extremely important change in a situation." Also, make sure students understand *mph* and *yield*.

Reading Selection
Use the concept of revolution as change to introduce the reading selection. After students have read the selection, discuss why the automobile did create a "revolution."

An activity that helps students to understand this more clearly is to have them list as many features of their hometown as they can think of that would not be there if it weren't for the automobile. Or you might have them list as many words as they can think of that wouldn't be in our vocabulary if it weren't for the automobile.

EXERCISE 2: WHAT DO YOU THINK?
A good follow-up writing activity topic is: "Describe the changes that would occur if your idea of the most popular form of travel 100 years from now actually happened."

EXERCISE 3: MORE WORK WITH CONTRACTIONS
If necessary, review the term *contraction*. Also, make sure students are placing their apostrophes correctly.

EXERCISE 4: WORD RELATIONSHIPS
If students still have difficulty with analogies, go over the first question during the homework preview. Remind students that process of elimination is a helpful strategy.

EXERCISE 5: THE PREFIX *UN-*
During the homework review, make sure students have capitalized the word *Unsafe* in number 10.

EXERCISE 6: TAKING A WRITTEN DRIVER'S TEST
Students who drive may want to discuss their own experiences in taking their driver's test.

Activities in Writing Book 6
Having practiced writing details of their own in Exercise 1 in Lesson 11, students have an opportunity in this lesson to again analyze how a professional writer uses details and the kinds of details that he uses. Exercise 2 introduces transitions that show cause and effect. Students can practice using these transitions in writing their essay for Exercise 4. You may need to explain that the four-paragraph essay follows the same structure as a three-paragraph essay; there is just one more paragraph in the body of the essay. In Exercise 3, students again use a table and practice classifying information as they list causes and effects. Point out that the causes and effects do not bear a one-to-one relationship.

Additional Writing Activities
1. Have students write three-paragraph essays describing how they felt taking the driver's test, both the written and road parts.
2. Ask students who have not taken a driver's test to write paragraphs to encourage someone who is going to take the test.
3. Have students focus on paragraph 3 of the expository esaay and write companion paragraphs that describe what it's like to take a drive today.

LESSON 13
Caught in Traffic

Primary emphasis
- Comprehension of literature (short story and poem)
- Forming a reasoned opinion
- Using context clues

Secondary emphasis
- Interpreting adages
- Prefixes that mean *not*
- Forming the singular possessive

Words for Study
Save any discussion of *Cupid, mythology,* and *Apollo* for the homework review. Some of the questions about these words are answered in Exercise 3.

Reading Selection
In introducing this story, mention that O. Henry is famous for his surprise endings. During the discussion, have the students state the surprise ending of this story. Ask students when they think this story took place, and discuss the clues on which they base their opinions.

EXERCISE 2: THE APOSTROPHE TO SHOW OWNERSHIP
This is the first of several exercises on using the apostrophe to show ownership. Go over the examples carefully during the preview. Be sure students recognize the signal word *of,* and point out the placement of the apostrophe.

EXERCISE 3: A FAT BOY WITHOUT ANY CLOTHES ON
Remind students to read the entire passage after filling in the blanks.

You might bring in several pictures of Cupid. (Traditional Valentine's cards are a good source.) Most students will recognize him readily.

If students seem particularly interested in this Greek myth, you might consider bringing in other myths for them to read.

EXERCISE 4: MORE PREFIXES THAT MEAN *NOT*
During the review, be sure students have capitalized *Improper, Indecent,* and *Nonsense* in numbers 10, 11, and 13.

EXERCISE 5: MONEY
During the preview, you may want to read some of these sayings aloud and ask students to put them in their own words. Explain the ones they don't understand.

If students offer sound reasons for checking adages with which you might disagree, consider their answers correct. This suggestion also applies to their interpretations of the adages about which they choose to write.

EXERCISE 6: MORE ABOUT MONEY
During the preview, read the poem aloud to the students. Be especially supportive in your critique of the students' answers during the homework review. Many students have a rather negative attitude toward poetry; any encouraging remarks you can make about their ability to interpret it will help them to approach poetry with a more positive attitude.

Activities in Writing Book 6
In Exercise 1, students can put to use what they have learned about using details. Make sure that students understand that they are not to use the phrases listed in the exercise in their sentences, but the ideas that the phrases represent. Students practice using transitions that show time order, cause, and effect in Exercise 2. Exercise 3 introduces the T-chart as a way to organize information. Exercise 4 formalizes instruction on what a reasoned opinion is and how to form one.

Additional Writing Activities
1. Have each student write a paragraph either agreeing or disagreeing with this statement: Anthony Rockwall should not have interfered with his son's romance. Students should base their opinions on what they think about the son as described in the story.
2. Have students choose one of the sayings that they believe is true in Exercise 5: Money and write paragraphs explaining why they think it is true.

LESSON 14
A Ride in Space

Primary emphasis

- Reading comprehension (article)
- Understanding a cartoon
- Distinguishing between fact and opinion
- Using context clues

Secondary emphasis

- The prefix *re-*
- Compound words
- The singular possessive

Words for Study

Because many students are unfamiliar with space flight terminology, you may want to discuss many of the new words during the homework preview. A brief discussion about how new fields bring new words into our everyday language is helpful. The automobile revolution and computer technology provide good examples with which students are already familiar.

Reading Selection

To introduce the reading, tell students that Sally Ride was the first American female astronaut. Point out that this selection is a condensation from a magazine article rather than an excerpt from a longer work. For fun, you might point out that the title is a play on words. Ask students what the title means.

EXERCISE 2: MORE WORK WITH THE APOSTROPHE

If students are still having difficulty forming the singular possessive, have them refer to Exercise 4 in the previous lesson.

EXERCISE 3: UNDERSTANDING CARTOONS

A good follow-up activity for this exercise is to have students bring in cartoons from the editorial pages of their local newspapers to analyze.

EXERCISE 4: FACTS AND OPINIONS

Most students have little difficulty with this exercise. What they do have trouble with, however, is recognizing that many of the statements they make are opinions but that they say them as if they were facts. *Of course,* it is

not just reading students who confuse fact with opinion in daily conversation. Adults especially find discussing this confusion between fact and opinion helpful.

Because *fact* and *opinion* are discussed in this lesson, you may want to consider discussing the purpose of the editorial page and reading sections from it in class.

EXERCISE 6: COMPOUND WORDS

Even though students are familiar with this type of exercise, some of these compound words may be unfamiliar. Remind them to use process of elimination and to look up the words in List A in a dictionary.

Activities in Writing Book 6

Exercise 1 affords another opportunity to review how professional writers use details. Exercise 2 is a lesson on the use of transitions that show comparison and contrast. While the instruction explains the difference between comparing and contrasting, in conversation and even in writing, most people say "compare" when they actually are contrasting differences as well as comparing similarities.

In Exercise 3, students use a T-chart to organize information and then form an opinion. T-charts are especially good for analyzing two sides of an issue: pros and cons, differences and similarities, and advantages and disadvantages. In Exercise 4, students use the information they have gathered to support their opinions. You might also point out that a T-chart is a way to classify information.

Additional Writing Activities

1. Tell students that they should imagine that they are going to write a letter to the editor of their local paper on a local issue. Provide an issue that is of importance to your town or city. Ask them to choose a side on the issue, for example, fees for parking meters should be raised because the town/city needs the money. First, students need to decide on a position, that is, make up their minds whether they agree or not. Ask students to list the kinds of information (facts) they would need to support their opinions.

2. Ask students to write paragraphs explaining why they would or would not want to be astronauts.

LESSON 15

New York to France—in a Rowboat

Primary emphasis
- Reading comprehension (article)
- Distinguishing between fact and opinion
- Finding information in reference books

Secondary emphasis
- Using context clues
- The prefix *pre-*
- Classifying information
- Vocabulary (synonyms and antonyms)

Reading Selection
To introduce this reading, have a globe or a world map available, and point out New York harbor and the coast of France so that students can get an idea of the extent of this journey they will read about.

EXERCISE 1: ABOUT THE READING
Because students have not completed this type of exercise previously in this series, spend some time during the homework preview helping them to develop a pattern for their responses.

EXERCISE 2: WHAT DO YOU THINK?
For students who say they cannot respond to the question because they would not risk their lives for any kind of fortune, encourage them to explain their point of view in detail.

EXERCISE 6: BODIES OF WATER
Make sure students note the suggestion in the directions during the homework preview. The suggestion pertains to questions 2 and 3. A dictionary with a good geographical section will probably contain all the information needed to complete this exercise, but students with smaller abridged dictionaries may need to consult an atlas or the Internet for some of the answers.

Activities in Writing Book 6
By this lesson, most students have shown considerable improvement in their writing. Be sure to acknowledge this. If students seem skeptical, refer them to their writing in earlier lessons as a comparison.

In Exercise 1, students continue to analyze how professional writers use details. Exercise 2 offers practice in using transitions that show comparison and contrast. Exercises 3 and 4 work on persuasive writing. Students choose a cause, develop reasons someone should support it, and then write a persuasive essay asking for support. You might use the term *audience* in talking about the imaginary company. Knowing one's audience is an important factor in developing a persuasive argument.

Additional Writing Activities
1. Have students revise their essays to see where they can add details or use transitions effectively.
2. Ask students to write titles for this article. The titles should reflect what they think about the two men and their trip.
3. As a fun writing activity, have students write about a great travel adventure that they would like to have. Encourage them to use imagination.

Review: Lessons 1–15

As with other reviews, students are not to consider this a test but an opportunity to review words and concepts that have been introduced in the preceding lessons. An overall score of 80 percent or better on a review exercise should be considered excellent.

EXERCISE 6: FIVE-LETTER WORDS

The only difficulty students might have in completing this review is getting started with this puzzle. You may want to help students complete a few of the items during the homework preview.

Tell students to skip around, to skim, and to use the sums as clues. For example, most students know that the answer for clue 3 is *devil.* Ask them what letter of this word is least used. Their response is usually *v,* which is correct. Tell them to skim the puzzle for a word with a *v.* Sure enough, they will spot *lived,* and they have the correct space. Remind them that the *d* is to be written on the third blank below the clues because it is the third clue. If they fill in the blanks for the largest inland sea as they go along, they may guess the answer before the puzzle is finished. This, in turn, will give them the initial letters of the remaining words.

Also point out to them that the clue numbers always add up to 34, both horizontally and vertically. This may help them to find the right answers and also to know whether or not they have the right answers.

LESSON 16
As American as Apple Pie

Primary emphasis
- Reading comprehension (nonfiction)
- Using context clues
- Words with multiple meanings

Secondary emphasis
- Reading Middle English
- The suffix *-tion*
- Forming the plural possessive

Reading Selection
During the preview, note the division marked by the asterisks, and explain to the students that this reading consists of two distinct parts. An interesting follow-up discussion can center on which of the statements about Johnny Appleseed are probably true and which are probably the product of imagination.

EXERCISE 2: A RECIPE FOR APPLE FRITTERS
During the preview, have students note the strange spellings of the words in the recipe, and explain that this is an example of English as spoken and written from the 12th to the 15th centuries. Assure them that with the help of context clues and the questions they will be able to figure out most of the words.

During the review, have students attempt to read the recipe aloud. If possible, bring in other samples of Middle English for them to see. "The Cuckoo Song," which begins "Sumer is icumen in/Lhude sing cuccu," is a good example, as is any part of Chaucer's *Canterbury Tales* in the original version.

EXERCISE 3: WORDS WITH MORE THAN ONE MEANING
Be sure students understand that all of the answer choices are correct meanings for the underlined word but that only one is correct in the context of the sentence.

EXERCISE 4: WAKE UP AND SMELL THE COFFEE!
The exercise is a fun way to teach idioms. During the preview, make sure that students understand what they are to do. You might have the class complete one or two items as a group activity. Have students think about the meaning of the individual words in the phrases and the phrases as a whole to help them figure out why the idiom means what it means. For example, a "piece of cake" means *easy;* it could be because it's easy to make or even easier to eat. This won't work for all the phrases but can lead to some humorous opinions.

Activities in Writing Book 6
Make sure that students understand that they are not to use the phrases listed in Exercise 1 in their sentences, but to write sentences about the concepts represented by the phrases. Exercise 2 provides instruction and practice in a common grammatical error, lack of agreement between subject and predicate. Note that the word *you* is always used with a plural predicate even though the speaker may be speaking to only one person.

In Exercise 3, students brainstorm reasons to use as the basis for their persuasive paragraphs in Exercise 4. In adding details, students may add words to the sentences explaining their reasons or may add additional sentences. The exercise also provides an opportunity to use transitions that add information.

Additional Writing Activities
1. Have students revise their essays to see where they can add details or use transitions effectively.
2. Johnny Appleseed is a U.S. legend. Ask students if they can think of any other legendary characters. If so, ask them to write paragraphs explaining the persons and what they did that is similar to what Johnny Appleseed is supposed to have done.
3. Have students brainstorm ideas that they could use to write a letter to persuade the state of Indiana to build a statue to honor Johnny Appleseed. Have students share their ideas, and then have the class decide on the best three.
4. Have students choose three of the idioms and write a sentence for each. Have them try to make three-sentence paragraphs as they write.

Digestive Disturbances

Primary emphasis
- Reading comprehension (nonfiction)
- Main ideas and supporting details
- Forming a reasoned opinion
- Reading a table

Secondary emphasis
- Using context clues
- Vocabulary (word review)
- The suffix *-sion*
- Forming the plural possessive

Words for Study
Several of the words are polysyllabic and may present challenges to students. Help them break them into syllables and then say them slowly at first to hear the letters.

Reading Selection
Some students may find the topic unappealing, but explain that this is important information that people should know for their own health and that of loved ones. In discussing the reading, focus on the causes of the problems and what people can do to get and maintain a healthy digestive system. Eating healthy foods and reducing stress may particularly resonate with students.

EXERCISE 1: ACCORDING TO THE AUTHOR
Since this is an unfamiliar exercise format, allow as much time during the preview as necessary to be sure students understand how to do it. Remind them to check the reading when they are unsure of where the supporting details belong.

EXERCISE 5: MORE SERIOUS PROBLEMS OF THE DIGESTIVE SYSTEM
If students are reluctant to complete "What about you?" have them skip the first set of questions and answer the second question about family health.

Activities in Writing Book 6
Exercise 1 continues the work of Lesson 16 with subject-verb agreement. Exercise 2 begins four lessons of instruction/review on the proper use of pronouns. Lesson 17 focuses on personal pronouns. Misusing subject pronouns for object pronouns is the single biggest pronoun error in both writing and speaking. There can never be too much review of the correct use of personal pronouns.

Exercise 3 asks students to reread the article to gather information and then organize that information in a table. Exercise 4 offers another opportunity to write a persuasive paragraph, based on this information from the article.

Additional Writing Activities
1. Have students revise their essays to see where they can add details or use transitions effectively.
2. Pair up students, and then assign each pair one of the six items under "Keeping Your Digestive System Healthy." Have the pairs think of three things that a person or family could do to ensure that they eat healthy foods, exercise regularly, and so on. When the pairs have finished, assemble the class by pairs, and have each group decide which are the three best tips for their topic. Have the groups share, and then have students copy the 18 tips or have copies made for each student.
3. Have students write a paragraph about how they think they have progressed with their writing and what they would like to spend more time working on. Use these as a guide for what to stress with individual students for the next four lessons in the writing workbook.

LESSON 18
A Breakfast Scene

Primary emphasis
- Comprehension of literature (drama)
- Colloquialisms
- Forming a reasoned opinion

Secondary emphasis
- Using context clues
- Vocabulary (synonyms and antonyms)
- Forming singular and plural possessives
- The suffixes *-ance* and *-ence*

Words for Study
Because this scene from *A Raisin in the Sun* could not be adapted but had to be excerpted in its entirety, the vocabulary for this lesson is a bit more difficult than usual. Preview the new words carefully, and discuss the meanings of those which are new to the students. Not all the new words have been listed. Other new words include *conspicuously, sullen, vindicated, rigidity,* and *finality.* Even if students are not familiar with the definitions for these words, they should not have too much difficulty with the pronunciations. Your assessment of students' ability to handle all this new vocabulary should determine whether to discuss these words during the preview or to help your students discern their meanings as questions arise.

The Scene
In introducing the scene, it may be wise to point out that in addition to new vocabulary, the dialogue is in the vernacular, so some of the phrasing may be unfamiliar to some students. Point out the stage directions in parentheses and italics, and explain that while these words are not spoken aloud, they should be read, since they give clues to the action of the scene and to the characters' feelings. Explain that this scene takes place near the beginning of the play.

During the homework review, students enjoy reading the dialogue aloud and sharing their answers to the comprehension questions.

As a follow-up activity, you might read Langston Hughes's poem "Harlem" and discuss its relationship to the play (the play's title comes from this poem).

EXERCISE 2: FOOD FOR THOUGHT
During the review, ask the students how many of these expressions they already knew, how many they were able to figure out by using common sense and how many required intelligent guessing and process of elimination. This type of mini-survey reminds students that there is usually more than one road to the right answer.

EXERCISE 5: THE SUFFIXES *-ANCE* AND *-ENCE*
As a reinforcement activity, plan a brief spelling quiz on *-ance* and *-ence* words to help students improve their ability to distinguish between these two spellings.

Activities in Writing Book 6
In Exercise 1, students practice writing descriptions of the characters' personalities, based on evidence from the play. Exercise 2 continues work on pronouns by having students choose the correct relative pronouns for each sentence. Here again, the correct use of the subject and object pronouns is stressed.

Exercise 3 provides additional work with using a T-chart to organize information. In order to write their essays, students need to form opinions based on information from the play. Students are reminded to use transitions that add information as they develop their essays.

Additional Writing Activities
1. Have students revise their essays to see where they can add details or use transitions effectively.
2. Ask students to imagine that they know Walter and Ruth. Have them write a paragraph addressed to either Walter or Ruth explaining how they could deal with the issue of Walter's friends in a more mature way.

LESSON 19
American Food

Primary emphasis
- Reading comprehension (nonfiction)
- Forming a reasoned opinion
- Classifying information

Secondary emphasis
- Word families
- A review of apostrophes
- Reasoning and spelling (Can You Crack the Code?)

Reading Selection

During the preview, ask students which of the foods listed under "Words for Study" are familiar to them. Are they foods that the students' families typically eat? An example might be tofu. If most students are unfamiliar with a certain food such as tofu or baklava, have students for whom it is a native dish describe it. This gives students an opportunity to discuss and share their cultures and backgrounds.

The article discusses several topics: foods that Native Americans ate, how Native Americans prepared their food, foods that colonists brought, foods that later immigrants brought, and foods that we eat today. During the reading review, ask students to decide how to divide the article into sections based on what each section is mostly about. This is a good exercise to help students developing summaries of longer pieces of writing.

To familiarize students with how time lines are set up and their usefulness, ask students a few questions that have them identify the sequence in which some foods were created (Was _____ created before or after _____? Which food came later: _____ or _____? Which food came first: _____ or _____?) and the time lapse between when some foods were created (How many years were there between when _____ and _____ were created?).

EXERCISE 2: A TASTE TEST

There may be some disagreement about how to classify some of the items. Mention that we are not born with these taste categories; they are learned, and therefore opinions may differ. Some people confuse sour and bitter, for instance.

EXERCISE 4: WHAT DO YOU THINK?

Have students read their responses aloud and discuss them.

EXERCISE 6: CAN YOU CRACK THE CODE?

Remind students that they did a similar puzzle in Lesson 7. Students enjoy seeing pictures of these jewels, if you can find them.

Activities in Writing Book 6

Exercise 1 is similar to previous exercises that ask students to write sentences describing ideas. By now, students should be using a variety of details for their sentences. Exercise 2 provides instruction/review on the use of interrogative pronouns. Observe if students have difficulty in using *who* versus *whom*. Tell students to rearrange the sentence to see whether the pronoun is the subject or object of the predicate or of a preposition (Who/Whom did he visit? He did visit whom.)

Exercise 3 has students first brainstorm foods that they like and then set up a table to classify information about the topic they chose. By now students should recognize that regardless of the type or amount of information that a writer is working with, planning and organizing are both possible and important. The more information, the more important the planning and organizing become. Exercise 4 asks students to write expository essays about their favorite foods using information from their tables.

Additional Writing Activities
1. Have students write summaries of the article, using the section headings that they developed during the reading review.
2. Have students revise their essays for this lesson to add transitions that add information.

LESSON 20
The Wizard of Alabama

Primary emphasis
- Reading comprehension (biography)
- Forming a reasoned opinion
- Using context clues
- Comprehension of literature (poem)

Secondary emphasis
- Analogies (word relationships)
- The suffix *-ize*
- Vocabulary review (puzzle)

Reading Selection

To introduce this reading, you may want to review the term *biography*. Ask if students have heard of George Washington Carver and if they know why he is remembered.

During the review, consider having this selection read aloud. Take some time to discuss Carver's life and contributions. You may want to have students create a list of adjectives such as *modest, unselfish, wise,* etc., that describe Carver.

EXERCISE 2: MORE FACTS ABOUT THE PEANUT

This is not an easy exercise. Remind students to read the entire sentence before trying to select the word that fits best and to use context clues. Also, remind them to read the entire passage after filling in the blanks. Be sure students capitalize the word *Pegs*.

EXERCISE 5: FIND THIS PEANUT PRODUCT

Remind students that they did a similar puzzle in the Review of Lessons 1–5, and refer them to that if necessary.

EXERCISE 6: TO LOOK AT ANY THING

During the preview, read the poem aloud to the students. The answers to questions 1 and 4 must be inferred from the poem and the reading. It is a good idea to review the process of making inferences during the preview.

Allow ample time to discuss the students' responses to these questions during the review. Emphasize the strengths and note the weaknesses in students' writing progress.

Activities in Writing Book 6

By now students should be confident in their ability to use details and be able to complete Exercise 1 without difficulty. Using the object form of the personal and relative pronouns may be challenging to some students in completing Exercise 2; considering that most native speakers misuse the two forms, this is not unexpected for ESL students. Encourage students to rearrange questions and sentences to identify the subject and the object.

Exercise 3 asks students to support the opinion that George Washington Carver is important. To plan their essays, students must list information from the article to support this opinion. Exercise 4 reminds them to use transitions as they add each reason to their essay.

Additional Writing Activities

1. Have students revise their essays to be sure that they used transitions and the correct form of any pronouns.
2. Ask students to think of another person they admire and why. It could be a famous person or someone they know personally. Then have them plan and write a three-paragraph essay about this person.

Review: Lessons 1–20

As with the other review lessons, remind students that this is not a test but a final opportunity to review words and concepts that were introduced in this book.

Emphasize improvement in the students' work habits, reasoning, and vocabulary development during the homework review.

Students generally experience a sense of relief and accomplishment upon completing a workbook, and they should have a few moments to enjoy and evaluate this accomplishment before continuing their studies.

Writing Activities

If you wish to use one last follow-up activity, here are two suggestions:

1. Have students write an opinion, supported with details, about how they believe completing this book has or has not helped them in their reading and writing development.

2. Have them write their own version of Exercise 6: Review of Facts and Opinions for fellow students to complete.

Book 7 Introduction

The format of Book 7 corresponds to the one used in earlier odd-numbered books in the *Challenger* series. Each lesson begins with a word chart that introduces words into this controlled-vocabulary series according to specific phonics principles.

Definitions of difficult words from the word chart appear in a matching exercise that immediately follows each word chart. All students should own or have access to a dictionary in order to complete these exercises.

Most reading selections in Book 7 are minimally adapted from well-known and well-written literary pieces, such as short stories, folk tales, drama, and myths. Take time to point out to the students that they are reading quality literature. Experience indicates that students' self-esteem and motivation are bolstered when they realize that they are studying widely-acclaimed authors.

The exercises and reviews in Book 7 help the students further develop their comprehension skills, recall, and reasoning abilities. Literary understanding is emphasized in the reading comprehension exercises. In addition, material on standard English usage is introduced.

A review appears after every four lessons. These reviews provide students with additional opportunities to review words and concepts. They also help students develop the habit of referring to previous lessons for the correct answers to some of the questions. There are no word indexes in Book 7, but a complete list of the words introduced in Book 7 is available online at newreaderspress.com.

Book 7 is the appropriate starting point for students who score in the 7.0–8.5 range on standardized reading achievement tests. The final review in Book 6 can also be used as a diagnostic tool. An accuracy rate of 85 percent or better for this review indicates that students are ready for Book 7.

Students who use this book should be given as many opportunities for oral reading practice as time permits. This practice helps to develop confidence, enjoyment, and interest in reading.

Book 7 builds upon procedures and practices emphasized in the earlier books in this series. Thus, you may find it worthwhile to look through the manual notes for some of these books.

Scheduling Considerations

Book 7 works well in a classroom setting. The most progress is achieved when students work with *Challenger* a minimum of 45 minutes two or three times a week. Students can work independently, in a group, or with a partner. When working with other students, they receive the support and stimulation from one another that make learning more enjoyable. Also, the more advanced students can assume much of the responsibility for giving explanations and leading reinforcement activities, which in turn reinforces their own reading skills. Experience indicates that less advanced students usually benefit from peer instruction provided that you are available to supply any necessary clarifications.

Other Exercises

A wide variety of exercises has been included to help students improve their recall, increase their vocabulary, and develop their reasoning abilities. As often as seems appropriate, draw students' attention to the fact that reasoning is an essential part of reading. Help them develop such patterns as using the process of elimination, making intelligent guesses, using the dictionary, and referring to previous lessons when completing these exercises.

A score of 80 percent or higher should be considered satisfactory on these exercises. If students consistently score below this figure, take some time to help them pinpoint the problem. Usually, they are trying to complete the exercises too rapidly.

Because students are encouraged to learn from their mistakes, they should not be penalized for making them. If you work in a school that gives report cards, it is strongly recommended that evaluations be based on corrected work and overall progress rather than on students' initial efforts. In no way does this practice encourage typical reading students to be careless in completing their homework. Rather, they usually become more interested in reading than in report cards, they are more relaxed and patient with themselves in completing assignments, and they develop a more realistic definition of academic progress.

Writing Assignments

Student writing is discussed in Chapter 5. It is recommended that students working in Book 7 complete weekly writing assignments of 250–500 words in addition to the writing that is required to complete the exercises in the individual lessons. Paragraphs or brief essays about discussion topics that interest students and personal and/or business letters are appropriate writing assignments. Suggestions for writing assignments are also given in the individual lesson notes.

The Lesson Format

The procedure for each lesson should be as consistent as possible.

1. Students go over the writing assignment if one was given and review the work in the previous lesson first. This includes discussing the reading selection and correcting the exercises.
2. If time permits, students complete relevant reinforcement activities. The nature and scope of these activities are determined by the needs of your students and how often you meet with them.
3. Students preview the next lesson, which is usually assigned for homework.

Individual Lesson Notes

Lesson notes for each individual lesson appear on the following pages. These notes contain suggestions and procedures for specific items in each lesson.

LESSON 1
Review of Long and Short Vowels

Primary emphasis

- Comprehension of literature (short story)
- Vocabulary development (definitions)
- Writing complete sentences
- Using context clues

Secondary emphasis

- Predicting characters' responses
- Relating fictional events to personal experience
- Vocabulary review (Which Word Does Not Fit?)
- Review of long and short vowels

Word Chart

The word chart presents a systematic form through which students are introduced to new words in this reading series. Although it is not necessary to stress phonics principles, occasional reminders are helpful. For example, many students pronounce *eke* "eck." By pointing out that the silent *e* at the end indicates that the first *e* is long and jotting down a few other examples in which this rule applies, students are reminded of a principle that they can apply to other unfamiliar words.

A good rule of thumb for all the word charts in Book 7 is to avoid mentioning phonics rules unless an explanation would be clearly helpful. Since the main purpose of the word chart is to introduce words that have not appeared previously in the *Challenger* series, intensive phonics work is neither necessary nor productive at this point in the students' reading development.

Although students usually enjoy reading the words aloud, it is not imperative that they do so. Some students especially enjoy reading the word chart as a warm-up activity; others prefer starting each class with the definitions and replacing any word chart time with oral reading.

Do not dwell on the definitions when reading chart words. Students will encounter troublesome words in the exercises.

EXERCISE 1: DEFINITIONS

For these exercises, students should use both the process of elimination and a dictionary. Students can and should be expected to complete these exercises with 100 percent accuracy. If a student consistently makes two or more mistakes on definitions exercises, spend some time helping him to pinpoint the reasons for his errors. Always encourage students to learn from their mistakes rather than to see them as signs of failure.

A major reason that students complain about having to learn definitions is that they do not understand the significance of vocabulary work. Make sure students understand that knowing the meanings of words is vital to reading comprehension.

In all exercises in which copying is involved, students should copy accurately. There should be no spelling mistakes. All misspelled words should be corrected. This pattern (cruel as it seems) is more helpful than daily or weekly spelling tests in helping students to establish good spelling habits. When this expectation of accuracy is gently but consistently encouraged, the students themselves will begin to adopt a standard of accuracy and demonstrate more patience and pride in the quality of their work.

Story

The Words for Study section contains words that appear in this lesson for the first time in this controlled-vocabulary reading series.

Tell students that the reading selections that appear in this book are adapted from well-known, critically-acclaimed works. It motivates students to know that they are reading widely-respected material rather than, as one student expressed it, "stuff for problem students."

Review the terms *fiction* and *nonfiction*. Adolescents in particular often ask, "Is this really true?" Do not expect students—adolescents or adults—to automatically be able to distinguish between fiction and nonfiction.

Introduce the story with the term *moral dilemma.* Explain that the story sets up a moral dilemma: A young man needs money, but the only way he can get enough is to accept stolen money. Does the end justify the means? Ask students to keep this idea in mind as they read. They will find that there is no easy answer for the young man's problem.

You may need to explain the job of a bursar, that is, to accept money and keep track of it for an organization, similar to the job of a treasurer.

Generally, initial readings should be done for homework, but because this is the first lesson, allot time for an oral first reading in class. Begin by reading the first part of the story yourself, and then ask for volunteers to continue.

After reading the story aloud, discuss it in a general way. This gives students a chance to get a sense of the story as a whole while giving you the opportunity to assess their comprehension skills.

When you have completed the general discussion of the story, preview the exercises to be done for homework, Since this is the first lesson, take plenty of time and be sure all students understand how to do each exercise. If necessary, have students complete an item in each exercise during the preview so that they have a thorough understanding of how to do the work. Discuss the importance of homework. As suggested earlier, you might compare it to the daily practice that sports and music require.

EXERCISE 2: UNDERSTANDING THE STORY

During the homework preview, remind students that they are to refer to the story when necessary rather than to guess or to leave an answer blank. Students are to complete *all* the questions for all exercises. Some students seem to think that having to refer to the story for an answer is a sign of poor reading. Tell them that, on the contrary, it means they are good students!

Make sure all students are familiar with the process of elimination, which will help them complete many of the exercises in this book.

EXERCISE 3: WHAT DO YOU THINK?

When going over the answers during the homework review, make sure that students have used complete sentences. Initially, students may have difficulty putting their answers in sentence form, but with practice they will become increasingly proficient. Also, make sure that their answers reflect an understanding of the story. Discuss with students what they think Kyle should have done. What do they think that most people would do?

EXERCISE 4: WHICH WORD DOES NOT FIT?

During the homework preview, tell students to use the process of elimination and, if necessary, a dictionary to complete this exercise.

EXERCISE 5: MORE ABOUT NEW YORK HARBOR

During the homework preview, tell students to read each entire sentence before attempting to find the correct answer. Tell them to pay attention to word endings and context clues in deciding which word to place in each blank. Also, they should not feel they must complete the sentences in the order in which they appear. If necessary, remind them that checking off words after they have used them is a helpful practice.

When students have finished filling in the blanks, have them read the entire passage again for comprehension.

During the homework review, discuss how suffixes provide important clues in identifying the correct answer.

Note: After students have gone over the exercises and made any necessary corrections during the homework review, give them an opportunity to ask questions or to make comments about what they have just accomplished. If they seem overwhelmed, point out strengths they have shown in completing the work. Remind them that this is only the first lesson and that they will get used to the work more quickly than they think possible.

Activities in Writing Book 7

Exercise 1 in the first six lessons asks students to analyze how professional writers use details to make their works interesting, clear, and complete. First, students review the use of descriptive or sensory details, specific nouns, and action verbs. In Exercise 2, students are asked to add or substitute more specific and interesting words in basic sentences.

The third and fourth exercises in each lesson are the same. In Exercise 3, students learn about and practice using tools for gathering information for and organizing their writing. Exercise 4 is the writing assignment. Each assignment is accompanied by a guide to help students develop each paragraph in their essays. In this lesson, the tool is the "Five W's and H" to gather information and organize a three-paragraph summary of the short story. The writing guide in Exercise 4 also begins to help students extend their conclusions beyond just restating what they wrote in the essay.

Additional Writing Activities

1. Ask students to write paragraphs answering the question: Should Kyle accept the money? Why or why not? This assignment can provide the basis for a lively discussion.
2. Have students work in pairs to think of other ways that Kyle could get money or that Maggie could get the treatment that she needs. They should be realistic in their ideas.

LESSON 2
Review of Consonant Blends: Part 1

Primary emphasis
- Comprehension of literature (short story)
- Vocabulary development (definitions)
- Writing complete sentences
- Writing brief paragraphs
- Using context clues
- Using standard English

Secondary emphasis
- Idiomatic expressions
- Using the dictionary
- Review of consonant blends

Word Chart and Definitions
Use the procedure suggested for Lesson 1. Some students are not familiar with the *Mayflower* in definition 6. If time permits, bring in some additional information and a picture.

Story
During the preview, introduce the story by pointing out that it is a series of letters between a husband and wife.

Students may need to read this story more than once before comprehending all the subtleties. A good many inferences must be made in order to understand the plot and answer the comprehension questions. In the general discussion during the homework review, point out some of the facts that are presented in subtle ways, such as the fact that Ernie is a blackmailer.

EXERCISE 2: UNDERSTANDING THE STORY
If students were unable to answer the questions correctly, you may need to review the process of using clues that the author provides to draw conclusions. Discuss "reading between the lines."

A suggested follow-up writing activity is to write a letter to a relative. Students often enjoy writing a letter in the style of Judy's first letter to Walt, describing all the terrible ordeals they're confronted with which make it impossible to keep up with personal correspondence.

EXERCISE 3: WHAT DO YOU THINK?
The answer to question 1 will reflect students' understanding of the story. If they don't recognize that Walt is very clever, although he did a "dumb" thing, they will not understand the ending. For question 2, some students may argue that Walt, not God, did most of the "providing." This offers a good opportunity to discuss the concept of irony.

EXERCISE 4: LOOK IT UP
This exercise is a good opportunity to remind students that many words have several quite different and unrelated definitions.

EXERCISE 5: STANDARD ENGLISH
During the homework preview, discuss how most people speak a variety of dialects. Discuss the fact that some of these dialects are more formal than others. People often use an informal dialect when they are talking with their family and friends. This informal way of speaking is perfectly acceptable in informal situations. But when people are talking in a more formal situation—to strangers, to supervisors at work, in school, at public meetings, and so on—it is often to their advantage to use a more formal dialect, standard English. Give students the opportunity to discuss their feelings on this issue. If appropriate, also mention that standard English usage is included on the GED Test.

Preview the exercise by discussing the meanings of each pair of words. Tell students to refer to these definitions when completing the exercise. Review the definitions during the homework review.

EXERCISE 6: COMMON EXPRESSIONS
If necessary, remind students to use the process of elimination and to check off words as they use them. Also, students need not feel that they must complete the sentences in order.

Some of these expressions may be unfamiliar to students. This can give rise to a discussion of idiomatic expressions in general. Encourage students who are interested in the origins of any of these expressions to do a mini-research project. There are many popular works on etymology available.

Activities in Writing Book 7

In Exercise 1, students analyze the letters and choose the details that they think are the best and then explain their reasons. In Exercise 2, students work on adding details to complete ideas and add information. It is important that students understand that adding details doesn't mean just inserting a word here or there, but may mean adding sentences to explain ideas.

Exercise 3 provides information on mapping as a tool for organizing certain types of information about stories.

Mapping will probably be new to students. In Exercise 4, students write expository essays.

Additional Writing Activities

1. Have students write a letter similar to Judy's first letter in which she explains why it's difficult for her to write to Walt. Students could explain in a letter to a relative why they have a difficult time keeping up their end of a correspondence. Review with students the format for a friendly letter: address, date, greeting, and closing.

2. Have students take the same information and write an e-mail. Point out that even quick e-mails require correct spelling and punctuation. Otherwise, the other person won't necessarily understand the e-mail.

LESSON 3
Review of Consonant Blends: Part 2

Primary emphasis
- Comprehension of literature (short story)
- Vocabulary development
  1. Definitions
  2. Synonyms
- Using standard English

Secondary emphasis
- Reasoning and spelling (Can You Crack the Code?)
- Review of consonant blends

Word Chart and Definitions

For number 1, you may want to point out during the homework review that although *credentials* is a plural word, its definition is singular.

Story

During the preview, note that this story is in two parts. Students will be reading only the first part for this lesson. During the review, have students speculate on how they think the plot will develop and what the conclusion will be.

EXERCISE 2: UNDERSTANDING THE STORY

When students are doing exercises, encourage them to look up the meanings of any unfamiliar words.

EXERCISE 3: WHAT DO YOU THINK?

A follow-up discussion topic that students have found interesting is the opposite side of the question: Does performing good deeds usually lead to performing more good deeds?

EXERCISE 4: SYNONYMS

Remind those students who get tired of using the dictionary "all the time" that words are reviewed frequently in this book and that learning them becomes easier with practice.

EXERCISE 5: STANDARD ENGLISH

As in Lesson 2, go over each pair of words and the examples during the homework preview. Go over them again during the review. After the students have made any necessary corrections, spend a few moments reviewing the material discussed in Lesson 2.

EXERCISE 6: CAN YOU CRACK THE CODE?

Although these puzzles require quite a bit of work, students generally enjoy them. If necessary, help them get off to a good start by having them put *S's* above the *V's* and *P's* above the *A's*. Once they understand the procedure for cracking the code, they have little difficulty completing this exercise correctly.

Activities in Writing Book 7

In Exercise 1, students analyze the story and choose three details that they think are the best and explain their reasons. Exercise 2 provides three ideas and asks students to write a sentence to describe each. Make sure students understand that they are to write about the ideas. They do not have to use the listed phrases in their sentences. Exercise 3 provides practice in using the "Five W's and H." Exercise 4 asks for a summary of the short story so far.

Additional Writing Activities

1. In addition to the class discussion about what might happen in the story, have students write paragraphs about their predictions. Remind them that even one paragraph needs a topic sentence and a conclusion.

2. Ask students to write three-paragraph essays to explain how the following saying is proven by Henry's dilemma when he sees Melwood Estates the second time: The best-laid plans often go wrong.

LESSON 4

Review of Consonant Blends and Digraphs: Part 3

Primary emphasis
- Comprehension of literature (short story)
- Vocabulary development
  1. Definitions
  2. Antonyms
- Using context clues

Secondary emphasis
- Putting events in sequence
- The suffix *-al*
- Using references to locate factual information
- Review of consonant blends and digraphs

Word Chart and Definitions
Students often find many of the words on this particular chart difficult to pronounce. You may wish to review the pronunciation of the more troublesome words, such as *strychnine*.

Story
Introduce the story by reviewing what happened in Part I, and remind students of some of their speculations about how the story will end. In the general discussion during the review, help students to understand the story as a whole by reviewing both parts. Discuss how close students came in their predictions.

EXERCISE 2: UNDERSTANDING THE STORY
With the exception of the first one, which is done for the students, all of the events in question 1 happen in the second part of the story. During the homework review, have students read the sentences aloud in the order in which they took place.

EXERCISE 4: WORDS THAT END IN *-AL*
During the preview, remind students to read the entire sentence before attempting to fill in the blank with the correct answer. Review the term *suffix*.

EXERCISE 6: LOOK IT UP
Students who have small abridged dictionaries will probably need to use an encyclopedia or the Internet to complete this exercise.

Activities in Writing Book 7
Exercise 1 again asks students to analyze the author's use of details, choose what they consider the best, and explain their reasoning. Exercise 2 begins instruction/review of transitions. In this lesson, students work with transitions that show time order. You might explain that this category of transitions is especially helpful in retelling a personal experience and in giving directions.

Students are asked in Exercise 3 to use listing as a gathering and organizing tool. They should be able to infer personality traits from Henry's behavior, and they may use Part I as well as Part II for ideas. Exercise 4 asks students to write three-paragraph essays explaining their opinions of Henry.

Note: The essays are to be based on evidence from the story, which is an important point for students to understand. Opinions need to be based on facts.

Additional Writing Activities
1. Ask students to write paragraphs explaining their own opinions of the saying in Exercise 3, "The love of money is the root of all evil."
2. Ask students to write paragraphs comparing their predictions at the end of Part I with what really happens in Part II. Were they surprised, or did they pick up on the clue in Part I that Henry had always been honest until he started gambling?

Review: Lessons 1–4

As in the earlier books in the *Challenger* series, it should be emphasized to the students that this is a review, not a test. Material is often presented in new ways to both challenge the students and arouse their interest. Preview each exercise included in the review as you do in the other lessons. An overall score of 80 percent or better on the review should be considered excellent.

EXERCISE 1: WORD REVIEW

Students may need to be told that the dates in parentheses in definitions 3 and 13 are the years in which the person was born and died.

EXERCISE 2: SYNONYMS AND ANTONYMS

A suggestion that many students find helpful for this exercise is to complete all the synonyms before tackling the antonyms.

EXERCISE 3: WORD FAMILIES

A helpful suggestion for this exercise is to encourage the students to read the sentences aloud so they can hear how the words sound in the sentences.

EXERCISE 4: WHICH WORD DOES NOT FIT?

Number 8 usually gives students difficulty. During the preview, suggest that students use a map for this one. If students wonder if looking up the location of a state or country on a map is cheating, remind them that this is not a test.

EXERCISE 5: MONEY

Students should be encouraged to use a dictionary to complete this exercise. They should be discouraged from guessing. Some students miss number 11 because they don't realize that a missing apostrophe constitutes a misspelled word. Remind them of this.

EXERCISE 6: A FINAL NOTE ON LOVE AND MONEY

During the preview, read the poem aloud to the students. Allow them an opportunity to read it aloud during the homework review. To help those who have difficulty reading poetry, have students take turns reading sentences. This practice helps students break the habit of thinking that a line of poetry is always a complete sentence.

Since many students enjoy elaborating on the theme of love versus money, question 5 makes a good follow-up discussion topic.

Writing Activity

You may wish to assign a composition to bring this unit of work to a conclusion. Here are some suggestions for composition topics relating to the theme of love and money:

1. Which Is More Important—Love or Money?
2. Love Is More Important to Me Than Money Is
3. Money Is More Important to Me Than Love Is
4. What I Would Do for Love
5. What I Wouldn't Do for Money

LESSON 5
Review of Digraphs: Part 4

Primary emphasis
- Comprehension of literature (short story)
- Vocabulary development (definitions)
- Identifying characters' feelings and reactions
- Analogies
- Using standard English

Secondary emphasis
- Predicting a character's response
- Relating the story to personal experience
- Classifying information (the *ch* sound)
- Review of consonant blends

Word Chart and Definitions
Have the students locate Chile on a world map or globe. Many students are surprised to see how "skinny" it is. Whenever a country or city is mentioned in a lesson, it is a good practice to have the students locate it on the map.

Story
To introduce this story, you may want to discuss briefly parent-child relationships and the things children do that disappoint their parents. As a follow-up writing topic, students might describe an experience that led them to see someone in a new light.

EXERCISE 2: UNDERSTANDING THE STORY
Because this comprehension exercise is quite different from previous comprehension exercises, it may be a good idea to preview it more carefully than usual. Discuss the meanings of any unfamiliar words, and have the students either give examples or use the words in sentences. A brief discussion about changes in feelings and reactions is also helpful.

EXERCISE 3: WHAT DO YOU THINK?
Students often enjoy elaborating on their responses to question 1.

EXERCISE 4: WORD RELATIONSHIPS
Students often have difficulty with this type of exercise. When necessary, help students get started by completing

the first question during the preview. Ask them to explain the relationship between *shepherd* and *flock*. Then have them read the four choices and decide which pair of words expresses a similar relationship. Most students will see that a *cowboy* tends a herd as a *shepherd* tends a *flock*.

Some students have trouble answering multiple-choice questions. Encourage them to first eliminate the obviously incorrect answers. Then have them evaluate the remaining choices to select the correct ones.

EXERCISE 5: SOUNDS FOR *CH*
Students either complete this type of exercise with no effort at all or have a great deal of difficulty matching the words with the correct sounds. Encourage those who have difficulty to complete the exercise aloud so they can hear the sounds.

EXERCISE 6: STANDARD ENGLISH
As before, preview each set of words, and go over the examples. During the homework review, the material from Lessons 2 and 3 should also be reviewed.

Activities in Writing Book 7
In Exercise 1, students will choose what they consider the best descriptive words and phrases from the story. Exercise 2 provides practice in using transitions that show time order. Exercise 3 offers practice in using the "Five W's and H" to identify important information in a narrative. Students then use this information to write a summary of the short story.

Additional Writing Activities
1. Ask students to think about a time when someone they cared about—a family member or a friend—disappointed them. Have them list words and phrases that describe how they felt. Then have each student write a paragraph to compare those feelings with how Mrs. Higgins feels in the story.
2. Have students working in pairs write one sentence for each set of words in Exercise 6: Standard English (*We were already all ready when he said to get ready.*) If students enjoy the activity, have them continue using the sets in Lessons 2 and 3 for more practice.

LESSON 6
Review of Consonant Blends: Part 5

Primary emphasis
- Comprehension of literature (short story)
- Vocabulary development
  1. Definitions
  2. Synonyms and antonyms

Secondary emphasis
- Relating fictional events to personal experience
- Comparing characters from different stories
- Spelling
- Using references to locate factual information
- Review of consonant blends

Story
Students often are unaware of the prejudice with which Jews have been confronted historically and the role of this prejudice during World War II. Any additional materials, particularly pictures that present a more comprehensive portrait of these times, can be helpful. Remind those students who worked in the earlier books in this series of the excerpts from *The Diary of Anne Frank* in Lessons 12 and 13 of Book 4.

In the general discussion during the review, help students to see the parallels between the events in the story and the events that actually occurred during the war.

The concept *point of view* provides the basis for a good follow-up discussion. Have students consider how the story might have developed had it been narrated by the father, a policeman, or any other character.

EXERCISE 3: WHAT DO YOU THINK?
Both questions 1 and 2 are good topics for further discussion. In discussing question 2, remind students that Halper wrote this story in 1938, before the start of World War II. Since he couldn't have known the extent of the persecution that the Jews of Europe were to suffer, his story was certainly prophetic.

EXERCISE 5: MARCH 1938
Two of the incorrect words in this exercise are spelled correctly. Because of the context, however, the following are incorrect:
1. Sentence 3—*then* should be *than*

2. Sentence 11—*passed* should be *past*

Some students may also miss number 10 because they forget to add the missing apostrophe.

As a reinforcement activity, you might have students copy sentences from a current newspaper in which they underline five words and intentionally misspell one. Make copies to have a student-made spelling test.

EXERCISE 6: WHO WAS GENERAL PERSHING?
Again, if time permits, bring in pictures and/or interesting articles pertaining to World War I to give students more of a sense of this period of history.

Activities in Writing Book 7
This is the last lesson in which students will be asked formally to analyze the reading for good description. However, you might continue to ask students during discussions to pick out interesting details and details that help to give them a fuller understanding of a character, event, or theme. Exercise 2 provides instruction/review in transitions that add information.

Exercise 3 has students practice brainstorming ideas. This is different from listing in that students are calling on their own experience as well as what they have read to come up with ideas. Like Exercise 4 in Lesson 4, students have a second step before they can begin writing. They have to use their brainstorming as the basis for further work in gathering and organizing information.

Additional Writing Activities
1. Ask students to think of other groups that experience racial prejudice in the United States. Have students write three-paragraph essays explaining what racial and ethnic diversity has to offer the United States. You may wish to have students participate in a class discussion to generate ideas first.
2. The "Five W's and H" is actually a device that journalists use to write news stories. The "who, what, when, and where" are all part of the lead paragraph. The "why" and "how" are explained in the rest of the article. Have students write two-paragraph news articles about the attack on the Silversteins using this formula.

LESSON 7
Review of Consonant Blends: Part 6

Primary emphasis
• Comprehension of literature (short story)
• Vocabulary development (definitions)
• Using standard English

Secondary emphasis
• Classifying
• Using references
• Chronological order
• Review of consonant blends

Word Chart
There are several unusual words in this chart, such as *squiggle, tweak, twerp,* and *twiddle,* which you may wish to draw to students' attention.

Story
To avoid giving away the point of this story too soon, introduce it by discussing the tensions involved in taking a driver's test. Students may want to briefly share their experiences in this situation.

EXERCISE 3: WHAT DO YOU THINK?
For number 2, ask students to find clues in the story that indicate that it was written a number of years ago. Refer to Lesson 6, and ask if members of other ethnic groups might find themselves in a similar situation today.

A discussion about the nature of prejudice can be launched by comparing and contrasting the prejudice in "The Test" with that in "Prelude." Some questions that may be considered are: How does prejudice create tension? How do bystanders often respond? How do prejudiced people show their hostility?

EXERCISE 5: CHRONOLOGICAL ORDER
If students don't have access to an almanac, a good dictionary or an encyclopedia will contain the necessary information in separate entries. During the preview, discuss how to go about finding this information. You may wish to have the students record additional information also. For example, for the American presidents, they could write the term of office after each president's name. For the holidays, they could write the date.

EXERCISE 6: STANDARD ENGLISH
Preview the material as before. During the review, go over the material covered in Lessons 2, 3, and 5. If students are having difficulty with this material, consider creating a worksheet with sentences based on the examples in all four of these lessons as a reinforcement activity. Have students contribute the example sentences to the worksheet. Make copies of the worksheet for students, or have them write out copies.

Activities in Writing Book 7
Exercise 1 asks students to list words or phrases to describe the three characters in "The Test." If they are unsure of what to do, refer them to Exercise 2 in Lesson 5. Students work with transitions that show cause and effect in Exercise 2. In Exercise 3, students use two steps to gather information and organize it for their essays, a brainstorming list and a chart. This information is then used as the basis for a three-paragraph essay offering an opinion on why people are prejudiced.

Additional Writing Activities
1. Have students working in pairs write ten lines of dialogue in which Marian tells Mrs. Ericson that she failed the test again and Mrs. Ericson's response.
2. Ask students to write paragraphs explaining what they think Mrs. Ericson might have said or done had she been riding in the backseat when the inspector started insulting Marian.

LESSON 8
Review of Vowel Combinations: Part 1

Primary emphasis
- Comprehension of literature (short story)
- Vocabulary development
  1. Definitions
  2. Matching things with tasks
  3. Puzzle (Find the Quote)
- Using context clues

Secondary emphasis
- The suffix -ly
- Spelling (changing the y to i)
- Review of vowel combinations

Story
To avoid giving away the surprise ending, introduce the story by briefly discussing "first days" in general. Parents might recall their feelings on sending their children to school for the first time, or students might discuss their feelings on the first day of a new job or in a new class. During the review, ask students when they first suspected that Laurie and Charles were one and the same.

EXERCISE 3: WHAT MIGHT YOU USE IF YOU WANTED TO . . .
Students may not be familiar with some of these words, such as *compost, grid, spectacles,* and *sauna.* Remind them to use their dictionaries for unfamiliar words.

EXERCISE 6: FIND THE QUOTE
If students are encountering this type of puzzle for the first time, have them complete a few of the items during the homework preview. Have them fill in the appropriate blanks in the quotation as they answer each of the items.

In this way, they can work back and forth between the clues and the quotation, using context clues in the quotation to complete the partially filled-in words.

During the review, students enjoy swapping tricks they developed to help them solve the puzzle. They also enjoy hearing any tricks you might have developed for problem solving.

Activities in Writing Book 7
Exercise 1 adds a step to the activity that students completed in the previous lesson. In this lesson, they have to list details and then write sentences using them. In Exercise 2, students learn/review transitions that show comparison and contrast. Point out that whereas people usually say that they are comparing something, they often are both comparing and contrasting.

In Exercise 3, students work for the first time in this level with a T-chart. This is a good way of organizing for looking at two sides of an issue. Exercise 4 has students writing three-paragraph essays in which they contrast the two Charleses. Beginning with this lesson, students are reminded at the end of Exercise 4 to proofread their writing for spelling and capitalization problems.

Additional Writing Activities
1. Students—particularly adults—find it helpful to discuss ways in which adults protect themselves from pressure by inventing or imagining things. A suggested composition topic is "The Charles in Me."
2. Ask students to imagine they are Laurie's teacher and are meeting his mother for the first time. Have them write out what they would say to her about Laurie's behavior.

Review: Lessons 1–8

Remind students that this is a review, not a test. These exercises give additional opportunities to review words and concepts that were introduced in previous lessons. Encourage them to refer to those lessons or a dictionary for definitions they cannot recall. An overall score of 80 percent or better on review exercises should be considered excellent.

EXERCISE 3: SOUND REVIEW

Encourage students to complete this exercise aloud so that they can hear the word in which the sound is different.

EXERCISE 4: WORD FAMILIES

Remind students that it is also helpful to read these sentences aloud to hear which word fits best in each blank.

EXERCISE 5: STANDARD ENGLISH: A REVIEW

During the preview, remind students to check the material in Lessons 2, 3, 5, and 7 when doing this review exercise. They could also review the worksheet they constructed with example sentences.

EXERCISE 6: A POET'S THOUGHTS

During the preview, read the poem aloud to the students. Give them the opportunity to read the poem aloud during the homework review. Spend some time relating the theme of "Uphill" to a few of the characters in this set of short stories.

Writing Activity

If you wish to assign a composition to conclude this unit of work, here are some suggestions for composition topics relating to the theme of struggle:
1. Putting up with Parents
2. Being a Single Parent
3. How Prejudice Holds Me Back in Life
4. Why I Am Prejudiced
5. How Fantasy Helps Me Get Through the Day
6. Life Is a Constant Struggle

LESSON 9
Review of Vowel Combinations: Part 2

Primary emphasis
- Comprehension of literature (short story)
- Vocabulary development (definitions)
- Using context clues
- Using standard English

Secondary emphasis
- Analogies
- Using references to locate information
- Review of vowel combinations

Story
You might begin by introducing the author and explaining that "Saki" was the pen name of British writer Hector Hugh Munro, who wrote fantastical short stories in the early 1900s. His genre is a clue to students that the story may not be what it seems. See if they pick up on it.

After students have read the story, ask them if they were fooled by the niece until her uncle and her aunt's brothers actually come into the room. Where there any clues in the story up until then that the niece is making up a story?

EXERCISE 3: WHAT DO YOU THINK?
Remind students of the importance of correct spelling, grammar, and punctuation in short answer responses. They need to be as careful in answering this type of question as they are in writing complete essays.

EXERCISE 4: WORD RELATIONSHIPS
Although students are familiar with this exercise format, they may have difficulty with one or two of the questions. Question 9 provides an opportunity to discuss homophones. Ask for other word pairs that sound alike. You might ask students to explain why they rejected some of the incorrect responses. Ask students to share the tricks/rules they figured out in rejecting incorrect answers.

EXERCISE 5: MORE ABOUT STANDARD USAGE
Preview each set of words and the examples, as before. If time permits, review the material in previous lessons as well. Have students continue working in pairs to write example sentences.

Activities in Writing Book 7
In Exercise 1, students will write a sentence about the characters in "The Open Window" using details from the story. Exercise 2 begins work on correcting common problems in sentence structures. This instruction/review focuses on run-on sentences. Exercise 3 introduces or reviews the purpose of persuasive writing and has students use a T-chart to gather information. In Exercise 4, students use their T-charts as the basis for their persuasive essays.

Additional Writing Activities
1. Have students imagine that the story actually takes place today. Have them imagine they are Mr. Framton sending an e-mail to his sister to describe what happened when he went to tea at Mrs. Sappleton's house.
2. Have students imagine they are the niece and have them write an e-mail that she would send to a friend about the visit from Mr. Framton.

LESSON 10
Review of *r*-Controlled Vowels

Primary emphasis

- Comprehension of literature (short story)
- Vocabulary development (definitions)
- Using context clues

Secondary emphasis

- Predicting characters' responses
- Vocabulary review (puzzle)
- Review of *r*-controlled vowels

Words for Study

If students do not know the meaning of *latitude* and *longitude,* have them look up the meanings in their dictionaries. It would also be useful to have a globe or world map handy to demonstrate the differences for them. Some people have difficulty remembering the difference between two closely related concepts, so have students think of word associations to help them remember the difference between latitude and longitude.

Story

Ask students if they know the story of *Alice in Wonderland.* Some may have seen the animated movie version. If no one is familiar with the story and can summarize it for the class, give a brief summary yourself. Tell students that they are about to read the very beginning of the story that describes how Alice's adventure starts.

EXERCISE 3: WHAT DO YOU THINK?

You might bring in a copy of *Alice in Wonderland* and read the description of how the author does solve Alice's problem in getting through the small doorway.

EXERCISE 4: ALICE IN WONDERLAND

You might remind students to cross out or check off each word as they write it in the paragraphs. This makes it easier for them to see what they have left to work with. It also means that if they skip a blank because they aren't sure of the answer, they will know what is left when they have filled in all the blanks that they know.

During the homework review, have students read the paragraphs aloud as a continuous article.

EXERCISE 5: SPELLING CHECK

Students not familiar with this type of puzzle may need to complete an answer or two during the homework preview. Remind students to check off the syllables as they use them. They need not work in the order in which the clues appear.

Activities in Writing Book 7

In Exercise 1, students write sentences based on ideas from the excerpt. Explain that they do not need to use these clauses in their sentences, only the ideas. Exercise 2 continues work in correcting run-on sentences. The directions also remind students to use italics for the titles of books and how to indicate italics in handwriting and in computer-generated text.

Exercise 3 provides more practice in using the "Five W's and H." Exercise 4 asks students to write three-paragraph expository essays.

Additional Writing Activities

1. Have students put themselves in the persons of the Liddell sisters and write thank-you notes to Charles Dodgson for writing *Alice in Wonderland* for them. The body of the note can be one paragraph. Have them follow the format for a friendly letter: address, date, greeting, and closing.
2. As a fun activity, have students in pairs think up headlines that a tabloid might publish about Alice's adventure.

Review of *r*-Controlled Vowel Combinations

Primary emphasis
- Comprehension of literature (short story)
- Vocabulary development
  1. Definitions
  2. Words that describe and don't describe
- Using context clues

Secondary emphasis
- Vocabulary review
- Review of *r*-controlled vowel combinations

Story
In the preview for the lesson, ask students if they have ever experienced a dream that seemed so real that they didn't want it to end. Ask two or three students to describe the dream and why they liked it so much. Then ask if they have ever awakened from a deep sleep and wondered where they were and what they were doing because the dream was so real. Explain that this reading is like that. They will finish the story and wonder what's real and what's a dream in the story.

After students have finished the story, have a discussion about which parts of the story are a dream and which parts are real. Students will not be able to come to a consensus.

EXERCISE 4: WORD REVIEW
During the preview, tell students that both words in a set must make sense in the sentence. They should use the process of elimination and context clues to select the correct set. Remind them to take their time and use dictionaries when necessary.

EXERCISE 6: WORDS THAT *DON'T* DESCRIBE
Finding a negative match is a bit harder than the matching in Exercise 5. During the preview, be sure students understand how to complete this exercise.

Activities in Writing Book 7
In Exercise 1, students write sentences based on ideas from the short story. Explain that they do not need to use these words and phrases in their sentences, only the ideas. Exercise 2 offers instruction/review on recognizing and correcting sentence fragments. You may need to explain that a word ending in *-ing* requires a form of the verb *to be* in order to be a verb. The example sentences also provide an opportunity to review the parts of the verbs *lie* and *lay* and their meanings and uses.

A T-chart is the information-gathering tool in Exercise 3. In Exercise 4, students use this information to write three-paragraph expository essays about what is real and what is fantasy in the short story. Exercise 4 also continues offering suggestions about how to tie up ideas and move students' conclusions beyond a simple restating of what they wrote in their essays.

Additional Writing Activities
1. Have students work in pairs to brainstorm at least six ideas that they could use to write a story about a nightmare. If students are interested, they could then choose one idea apiece and write a paragraph describing the nightmare. Before they write their nightmares, they should brainstorm words and phrases to use in their descriptions.
2. The theme of the short story is what is real and what is fantasy. Ask students to write three-paragraph essays comparing (contrasting) the excerpt from *Alice in Wonderland* with this short story. They should answer the question: Why is it easier to recognize that Alice's adventure is fantasy?

LESSON 12
Vowels Followed by the Letters *w* and *i*

Primary emphasis
- Comprehension of literature (short story)
- Vocabulary development (definitions)
- Proverbs
- Using standard English

Secondary emphasis
- Word families
- Using context clues
- Review of vowels followed by *w* and *i*
- The suffix *-ness*

Story
This short story builds in a gruesome way on the unit's theme that things are not always what they seem. By now students should be aware of the supernatural or surreal elements in these stories. Some students may be appalled at the ending, whereas others may think it is a great scary story. Help students to get past their reactions and analyze how the author Ambrose Bierce uses details and organization to build to the ending. Ask students if they guessed the ending before they finished the story. What clues alerted them to what was happening?

EXERCISE 4: PROVERBS
This exercise is particularly difficult for students who are unfamiliar with these proverbs. Encourage these students to get help from those who are familiar with some of the proverbs. During the homework preview, a brief discussion about the value and durability of proverbs is recommended. During the review, discuss the meanings of any proverbs the students don't understand.

EXERCISE 5: THE SUFFIX *–NESS*
Remind students that they do not have to do the sentences in order and can skip ones they don't immediately know. They should cross out or check off each word as they use it in a sentence. This will help them figure out answers to the questions that are more difficult for them.

EXERCISE 6: MORE ABOUT STANDARD ENGLISH
This is the last material about standard English formally introduced in this book. Preview it as before. Allot time during the review to go over the material studied in Lessons 2, 3, 5, 7, and 9. If students continue to have difficulty with some of this material, appropriate reinforcement activities should be used.

Have students add example sentences to their worksheets of standard English. You might have students read the corrected sentences as a continuous biographical sketch of Bierce.

Activities in Writing Book 7
In Exercise 1, students write sentences based on ideas from the story. Explain that they do not need to use these clauses and phrases in their sentences, only the ideas. Exercise 2 continues work in correcting sentence fragments. Exercise 3 guides students through gathering information from the story to support their opinion of the story. This information becomes the evidence for the essay that they write in Exercise 4. Remind students to proofread their essays, the most basic step in editing.

Additional Writing Activities
1. Ask students to write a paragraph answering the question: Do you like science fiction movies? Why or why not?
2. Any of the proverbs in Exercise 4 make excellent topics for writing. Have students explore the truth of the proverb in terms of their own experience.

Review: Lessons 1–12

As before, remind students that this review is not a test but an additional opportunity to practice words and concepts introduced in previous lessons. An overall score of 80 percent should be considered excellent.

EXERCISE 3: A REVIEW OF SOUNDS

Encourage students to complete this exercise aloud so that they can hear the word in which the sound is different.

EXERCISE 4: SPEAKING IN IDIOMS

Some of these expressions may not be familiar to all students, and a dictionary may not be much help. Suggest that they use the process of elimination or seek the help of a friend. During the review, discuss any expressions that students do not understand.

EXERCISE 5: A REVIEW OF STANDARD USAGE

Remind students to review the usage material they studied in Lessons 2, 3, 5, 7, 9, and 12 in completing this exercise. Have students use their worksheets of example sentences also.

EXERCISE 6: "LIFE IS REAL"

Read the poem aloud during the homework preview. Students will probably have less difficulty understanding the poem than they will remembering the relevant details about the characters in Unit 3's stories. Remind students to skim the stories for details they may have forgotten. During the review, have students read the poem aloud and share their responses to the following prompts.

1. The Most Courageous Event I Have Ever Witnessed
2. What I Fear the Most
3. My Most Courageous Moment
4. The Time Courage Failed Me
5. The Bravest Person I Know
6. How I Overcame My Worst Fear

Writing Activity

If you wish to assign a final writing assignment for this unit, here are some suggestions for three-paragraph essays:

1. What to Do When Awakening from a Frightening Dream
2. Get a Life If Dreams Are the Most Exciting Things That Happen to You
3. My Worst Nightmare
4. My Favorite Science Fiction Movie
5. If I Wrote a Science Fiction Movie, It Would Be About _____
6. When Things Aren't What They Seem

LESSON 13
The Hard and Soft *g*

Primary emphasis
- Comprehension of literature (drama)
- Vocabulary development
  1. Definitions
  2. Synonyms and antonyms
- Understanding tone of voice
- Using context clues

Secondary emphasis
- Using references to locate factual information
- Review of the hard and soft *g*

Play
In introducing the scene, point out the characters' names, and note the stage directions in italics. Explain that while these words are not spoken aloud, they should be read, because they give clues to the action of the play and to the characters' feelings. Explain also that this scene takes place near the end of the play. During the homework review, have students read the play aloud.

EXERCISE 2: UNDERSTANDING THE PLAY
In discussing these questions, help students to see that in reading a play, the meanings are communicated primarily through dialogue, unlike short stories, which have descriptive passages as well.

EXERCISE 3: WHAT DO YOU THINK?
Allow students to share their answers during the review. A follow-up discussion topic might be based on students' personal brushes with death.

EXERCISE 4: TONE OF VOICE
This exercise is good for oral reading practice because students can practice tone of voice. Have them take turns reading innocently, mysteriously, and so on.

EXERCISE 5: VACATIONS AROUND THE WORLD
Have students locate at least some of these places on a map or globe. If time permits, have them list the words according to city, state, or country (exclude the two seas). Some students have difficulty distinguishing among these three divisions, and this type of exercise is helpful.

Activities in Writing Book 7
In Exercise 1, students are to write two connected sentences to describe the characters in the scene. Exercise 2 deals with the third common error in using commas, the comma fault. Three different ways to solve the problem by combining sentences are given. Two other ways to handle comma faults are to split the two parts into two sentences or to use a semicolon to separate them.

Exercise 3 provides further practice in brainstorming, and Exercise 4 asks students to write three-paragraph letters. You may need to remind students of the form for a friendly letter.

Additional Writing Activities
1. Ask students if they know any elderly couples. Have them write paragraphs to compare an elderly couple with Norman and Ethel. They should focus on the way that Norman and Ethel joke with each other and how comfortable they seem to be with each other.
2. Have students choose one of the following topics as the basis of a three-paragraph essay: My Dream Vacation, The Place I Would Most Like to Visit, or My Favorite Trip.

LESSON 14
The Hard and Soft c

Primary emphasis

- Comprehension of literature (biography)
- Vocabulary development
  1. Definitions
  2. Identifying words that do not fit
  3. Matching people with things they know about

Secondary emphasis

- The suffix -ist
- Using references to locate factual information
- Puzzle (anagrams)
- Review of the hard and soft c

Words for Study

This set of words tends to be particularly difficult for students and should definitely be previewed in order that the reading can be better understood and appreciated.

Reading

During the homework preview, mention that this selection is taken from a biography about the famous Russian novelist Fyodor Dostoyevsky. Be sure students understand what a biography is. Mention one or two of Dostoyevsky's best-known works, such as *Crime and Punishment* and *The Brothers Karamazov*. During the review, it is helpful to discuss tzars and their role prior to the Russian Revolution and the significance of the Russian Revolution in general. Pictures from this period in Russian history are also very helpful.

EXERCISE 2: UNDERSTANDING THE READING

After reviewing the comprehension questions, discuss in detail Dostoyevsky's reactions throughout this ordeal. You may want to contrast his brush with death with that of Norman in *On Golden Pond.*

EXERCISE 4: LOOK IT UP

If students are interested in learning more about Russia or Russian history, encourage them to select a topic for a mini-research project.

EXERCISE 6: THE MYSTERY TZAR

If students are not familiar with this type of puzzle, have them complete a few of the items during the homework preview. Tell them to skip around, to skim, and to use the sums as clues. For example, most students immediately know that the answer for clue 7 is *angel.* If they skim the puzzle, they will usually spot *angle* without any trouble. Have them write *angel* on the line and put 7 in the circle. Remind them to write *a* on the blank numbered 7 at the bottom. If they fill in these blanks as they go along, they may guess the answer before the puzzle is finished. This, in turn, will give them the initial letters of the remaining words. Also point out that the clue numbers always add up to 34, both horizontally and vertically. This may help students to find the right answers and also to know whether or not they have the right answers.

Activities in Writing Book 7

In Exercise 1, students write two connected sentences about the listed ideas. Exercise 2 provides practice and reinforcement of ways to correct comma faults. Exercise 3 has students complete two steps to gather information for their essays. Exercise 4 asks students to write three-paragraph expository essays that use examples from the excerpt to support their opinions. Since Lesson 4, the writing guides have reminded students to use some type of transitions. In this guide, students are given the choice of transitions to use depending on how they organize their ideas.

Additional Writing Activities

1. Have students write at least three questions that they would like to ask Dostoyevsky based on their reading of this excerpt. Be sure that they invert the verb and subject and use a question mark as the end punctuation.
2. Have students summarize the excerpt using the "Five W's and H" to gather information from the excerpt.
3. Ask students if they know anyone who has had a near-death experience. Ask them to write paragraphs explaining whether and how that person was changed by the experience.

LESSON 15
The Letter y

Primary emphasis
- Comprehension of literature (short story)
- Vocabulary development
  1. Definitions
  2. Words with multiple meanings
- Using context clues

Secondary emphasis
- Analogies
- Using a dictionary to locate factual information
- Homonyms
- Review of the letter *y*

Story

In introducing this story, mention that Ernest Hemingway is a very well-known author. Several of his works have been made into movies including *A Farewell to Arms, The Sun Also Rises, The Old Man and the Sea,* and *The Snows of Mount Kilimanjaro.* Hemingway himself led a life of adventure. In the general discussion, you may want to draw attention to Hemingway's straightforward style.

EXERCISE 2: UNDERSTANDING THE STORY

During the homework preview, tell students that they will probably need to refer to the dictionary to answer questions 1 and 3. These questions are asking about the boiling point of water. You may want to mention that other substances boil at different temperatures.

EXERCISE 3: WORKING WITH MEASUREMENTS

Answers to question 1 will vary slightly depending on how students arrive at the answer. Accept any figure that is approximately 80 miles. Again, questions 4 and 5 refer to the freezing point of water.

EXERCISE 4: MULTIPLE MEANINGS

During the preview, review the fact that a word can have more than one meaning.

EXERCISE 6: HOMONYMS

Homonyms are often a source of spelling difficulty for students. You may wish to follow up this exercise with a spelling quiz in which you say a homonym, use it in a sentence, and have the students write the correct spelling. This exercise is more effective if students discuss each correct answer immediately after writing it.

Activities in Writing Book 7

Remind students that in Exercise 1 they do not need to use the phrases listed, only the ideas. They are, however, to write two connected sentences about each idea. In Exercise 2, students have to recognize the sentence structure problem in each sentence and correct it accordingly. Students have additional practice in using the "Five W's and H" in Exercise 3, which will provide the information for the summary they write in Exercise 4. The guide reminds students that transitions that show time order are a good way to connect ideas and ensure the flow of ideas in retelling a narrative.

Additional Writing Activities

1. Hemingway is known for his terse dialogue. Have students write ten-line dialogues that take place the next day between father and son. It might be a breakfast-table conversation about something trivial, but it should show how weak Schatz still is.

2. Ask students to write about a time when they had the flu and how they felt. What did they want most during that time—company, silence, a special kind of food, etc.?

LESSON 16
The Sound for *ph*

Primary emphasis
- Comprehension of literature (short story)
- Vocabulary development (definitions)
- Contrasting characters' reactions
- Using context clues

Secondary emphasis
- Hyphenated words
- Review of the *ph* sound

Story

To introduce this story, you might compare and contrast it with "A Day's Wait," mentioning that a central character is ill in both stories, but while Schatz only believed that he was dying, in this story the character really does face death.

In addition to discussing the story as a whole during the review, you may want to discuss contrasts between O. Henry's writing style and that of Hemingway.

EXERCISE 3: WHAT DO YOU THINK?

Questions 2 and 3 in this exercise call for the students to contrast the reactions of characters from two different stories. For many students, this is not an easy activity. For this reason, the questions say, "Describe the difference . . ." rather than using the term *contrast.*

If you sense students are going to have difficulty with the concept of *contrast,* spend a few moments during the homework preview discussing this. Many students, for example, have found it easier to think about the difference between characters' reactions if they discuss briefly the difference between how they usually feel on a Monday morning and on a Friday afternoon. During this discussion, it is helpful if students also perceive how people often respond differently to the same situation. (Not all students hate Monday mornings!) By having a clear idea of what is expected of them for questions 2

and 3, students are more apt to take their time in sorting out the differences between Schatz's and Johnsy's reactions.

EXERCISE 4: HYPHENATED WORDS

Make sure students do not forget the hyphens. Some students do not recognize that including hyphens in their answers is part of accurate spelling.

EXERCISE 5: THE $24 SWINDLE

Remind students to read the entire passage through after filling in the blanks.

Manhattan in the 18th, 19th, and 20th centuries and today will help students to visualize the changes that have taken place.

Activities in Writing Book 7

In Exercise 1, students continue to write connected sentences to describe and explain ideas that are given. Exercise 2 instructs/reviews rules on personal pronouns, relative pronouns, and interrogative pronouns, with emphasis on the correct use of the subject and object forms of pronouns.

Exercise 3 provides a tool, the cause-and-effect chain, for gathering and organizing information that deals with causes and their effects. Students should recognize that the effect of a cause can become the cause of another effect that, in turn, becomes a cause. The cause-and-effect chain provides the information for the three-paragraph expository essays that students write in Exercise 4.

Additional Writing Activities

1. Ask students to write paragraphs describing what they would paint as their masterpiece if they could paint.
2. Have students develop 20-line dialogues between Peter Minuit and the chief of the Wappinger group of Native Americans who sold Manhattan to the Dutch.

Review: Lessons 1–16

As with other reviews, remind students that this is not a test but an additional opportunity to practice words and concepts introduced previously. Encourage them to look back to previous lessons if necessary. An overall score of 80 percent should be considered excellent.

EXERCISE 2: FIND THE HOMONYM

During the preview, go over the example and make sure students understand what is expected of them. Point out that the numbered definitions are for the homonyms they fill in rather than for the ones that appear on the page. They do not have to do these in order.

EXERCISE 5: A POET'S VIEW OF DYING

During the preview, read the poem aloud, and explain that this is an excerpt from a longer poem. Have the students read it aloud during the review. Allot plenty of time to discuss the poem and their responses to the questions.

Writing Activity

To conclude this unit of work about brushes with death, you may wish to consider one or more of the following:

1. A writing assignment in which students discuss their feelings about death.

2. A writing assignment in which students relate an experience in which they felt close to death and the *meaning* this experience had for them.

3. A writing assignment in which the student writes his or her own obituary, using examples from newspapers as models. This may sound morbid, but some students have found that this activity has helped them to focus on what they truly wish to accomplish in life.

LESSON 17
Silent Letters

Primary emphasis
- Comprehension of literature (short story)
- Vocabulary development
  1. Definitions
  2. Matching adjectives with character descriptions to read

Secondary emphasis
- Using context clues
- Classifying
- Review of silent letters

Story

In introducing the short story, mention that James Joyce is considered one of the greatest writers in English for his use of language. Reading masters of fiction such as Joyce should help students realize how far they have come in their reading. Tell students to think about their own first crushes as they read the story. Does the narrator's awkwardness around the young woman ring true to them? Follow up on this question in the discussion after students have read the story. Ask students if they think that the essence of Joyce's story is universal. If not, why not? Are there cultural differences? Ask students to elaborate on any.

EXERCISE 2: UNDERSTANDING THE STORY

Remind students to reread parts of the story to find answers that they are unsure of. If this were a test, they could not do that for every question because of time constraints, but they should get in the habit of checking answers they are unsure of rather than guessing or omitting an answer.

EXERCISE 3: CHARACTER DESCRIPTIONS

Have students choose one of the numbered items and the adjective that they assigned to it and write a paragraph further describing the character.

EXERCISE 6: MORE ABOUT IRELAND

Remind students to read the entire passage through after filling in the blanks.

Activities in Writing Book 7

In Exercise 1, students write at least two connected sentences about the listed ideas. Exercise 2 provides practice and reinforcement on the correct use of pronouns. Exercise 3 takes students through a two-step process for gathering and organizing information for writing their three-paragraph essays, the task in Exercise 4.

Additional Writing Activities

1. Misuse of the subject personal pronoun as object of a preposition is not only a common writing error, but also one often made in speaking. Have students work in pairs to write four lines of dialogue that correctly use the personal pronouns *I* and *me*.
2. A secondary theme of this short story is missed opportunity. Have students write three-paragraph essays that explain a missed opportunity.

LESSON 18
Double Consonants

Primary emphasis

- Reading comprehension (nonfiction)
- Vocabulary development (definitions)
- Using context clues

Secondary emphasis

- Analogies
- Spelling (puzzle; state search)
- Review of double consonants

Reading

The concepts discussed by Erich Fromm in this selection are difficult for some students to grasp. In introducing the reading, help students to understand the contrast between *having* and *being* by pointing out that what a person *has* is not the same as what a person *is*. During the general discussion, be sure that students understand what Fromm means by "modes of existence." Have students summarize this selection as a group. Be sure they include all the major points.

EXERCISE 2: UNDERSTANDING THE READING

Review the differences between the terms *story*, *auto-biography*, *biography*, and *essay* during the homework review.

EXERCISE 3: WHAT DO YOU THINK?

Allow ample time to discuss students' responses to questions 2 and 3. A debate on these questions can help to further clarify the concepts Fromm discusses.

EXERCISE 4: WORD RELATIONSHIPS

Although not specified in the directions, students should be instructed to write the answers out on the lines provided.

EXERCISE 5: ON LATIN AND LANGUAGE

During the preview, make sure students understand that they do not use all the words listed at the left. As a follow-up activity, students might look up the derivations of the Words for Study to see how many have Latin roots.

EXERCISE 6: STATE SEARCH

If students are not familiar with this type of puzzle, point out the example, and have them find one or two more states during the class period. When comparing answers during the review, you should note that while *Kansas* is listed separately, it is also contained in *Arkansas*. Either answer should be counted as correct.

Activities in Writing Book 7

Exercise 1 takes three ideas presented in the reading and asks students to write two connected sentences about each one. This exercise can be used as a check on how well students understand the reading. Untangling confusing sentences is the subject of Exercise 3 for this lesson and the next two. In this lesson, students focus on misplaced modifying phrases, which are often the result of trying to get ideas down on paper quickly. Students may recognize the problem when they reread to revise their work, and they may not because they are so certain of what they mean that they don't see the problem. Encourage students to reread carefully for sense as they revise. Having students read one another's work can also help students to identify this problem.

Exercises 3 and 4 ask students to use their own experience in supporting their opinions, a phrase that students will see on GED writing questions. Students use brainstorming to generate ideas for the essays they will write in Exercise 4.

Additional Writing Activities

1. This reading may prove difficult for students. Have them write out definitions of Fromm's ideas of *having* and *being* with an example to explain each concept. Then have pairs exchange papers and discuss whether they agree with their partner's definitions and examples, and if not, how they should be changed.

2. Have students work in pairs and refer to the reading to list characteristics that a *being* person and that a *having* person would exhibit. Have the class as a whole agree on a single list for each type.

LESSON 19

More Work with Two Consonants in the Middle of Words

Primary emphasis

- Comprehension of literature (drama)
- Vocabulary development
  1. Definitions
  2. Synonyms and antonyms
- Using context clues

Secondary emphasis

- Word families
- Using the dictionary
- Classifying
- Review of two consonants in the middle of words

Play

To introduce this play, compare it with the scene from *On Golden Pond* in Lesson 13. While that was written for the stage, *The Woman Who Willed a Miracle* was written for TV. Point out some of the differences, such as the use of a narrator and the very short scenes. Remind students that the stage directions give clues to the characters' actions and reactions and are not spoken aloud. Point out that this play is concluded in Lesson 20.

During the review, ask students to predict what will happen in the conclusion of the play. The title should give them some ideas. You may want to postpone an oral reading of the play until the review of Lesson 20, when it can be read from beginning to end.

A general discussion on the difficulties of living with a disability may be appropriate. Students can share examples from their own experience or discuss famous people with disabilities. A simple activity that helps students become more aware of how a disability can make even easy things difficult is to have them blindfold themselves and then try to do a simple task, such as walk across the room, draw a simple picture, or write a sentence or two of dictation.

EXERCISE 5: USING THE DICTIONARY

A good dictionary is needed to complete this exercise correctly. If students have small abridged dictionaries,

you may decide to have them complete this exercise in class.

EXERCISE 6: WORD FAMILIES

Unlike previous Word Families exercises, students select only one of the three word choices for each question.

Activities in Writing Book 7

Students continue working with details in Exercise 1. Omitting words when writing is another problem that may result from writing quickly to capture ideas. Again, careful proofreading is needed to identify this common problem. It can be even more difficult to catch, however, than misplaced phrases (and words) because the brain will often fill in the missing words.

By this lesson, students should have recognized that gathering information for a piece of writing may require more than one step. Exercise 3 takes students through three steps. In Exercise 4, students write their first five-paragraph essays in this level. If they are concerned about how much they have to write, explain that this structure allows them to use more details to develop their ideas. They should feel confident in their ability to do this because they have been practicing building details in Exercise 1 of this level since the first lesson.

Additional Writing Activities

1. Have students list words that describe what they think and how they feel when they see someone with a disability like Leslie's. Then have them write what it must be like for that person to deal with "normal" people.

2. Students interested in learning more about cerebral palsy could look up the topic and prepare a short oral presentation on what it is, its causes, and treatments. The presentation should follow the same introduction, body, and conclusion format as an expository essay.

LESSON 20
Four-Letter Words

Primary emphasis
* Comprehension of literature (drama and poetry)
* Vocabulary development
  1. Definitions
  2. Finding the word that doesn't fit
  3. Matching people and problems

Secondary emphasis
* The prefixes *uni-, bi-,* and *tri-*
* Four-letter words

Play
Briefly review what took place in the first three scenes of the play, and remind students of their predictions about how it would end. During the homework review, have students read the play aloud. Discuss their predictions in relation to the outcome of the plot. Ask if they were surprised to find that the play was based on actual people.

EXERCISE 5: A LITTLE LATIN
During the preview, make sure students understand how to do this exercise.

EXERCISE 6: ON LIVING AND LOVING: A POET'S POINT OF VIEW
As you did in previous lessons, read the poems aloud during the preview, and have the students read them aloud during the homework review. During the general discussion of the poems and the questions, have students give reasons why the Lemkes would agree with Johnson's point of view.

Activities in Writing Book 7
In Exercise 1, students continue working with details. Exercise 2 tackles personal pronouns from another angle: unclear antecedents. Like the previous two lessons, item 4 asks students to check their latest essays for confusing sentences. Remind students that they need to read carefully to find this type of problem. Exercise 3 takes students through another three-step information-gathering and organizing process. In Exercise 4, each student writes another five-paragraph essay.

Additional Writing Activities
1. Have students review their lists of descriptors for how they feel when they see someone like Leslie. Now that they have read this play, ask students if their ideas have changed and how. Have them write paragraphs comparing what they thought before about people with disabilities and what they think now.
2. As a follow-up activity to Exercise 6, have students select one of the two poems and explain why they agree or disagree with the poet's point of view.

Review: Lessons 1–20

As with the other reviews, this last review is not to be perceived as a test but rather as a final opportunity to work with many of the words and concepts introduced in Book 7.

EXERCISE 3: WORLD CAPITALS

Have students locate the countries and their capitals on a map or globe.

EXERCISE 5: MORE WORK WITH EXPRESSIONS AND PROVERBS

During the homework review, discuss the meanings of any expressions or proverbs that are unfamiliar to the students.

EXERCISE 6: FIND THE QUOTE

Remind students to refer to Exercise 6 in Lesson 8 if they have forgotten how to do this type of puzzle.

After any necessary corrections have been made by the students during the homework review, spend some time reviewing and evaluating the students' progress. Compare the writing activities that they did in the early lessons with writing they have done recently. Many students, particularly those who began their work in the early books of the *Challenger* series, enjoy perusing the word index at the back of this manual, because it is a concrete representation of their accomplishment.

Writing Activity

Exercises 3 and 4 in the Review section of this writing book ask students to reflect on what they have learned about gathering information and organizing it as prewriting activities. They may not be aware that they have been learning a process, and these two exercises offer the opportunity to formalize this instruction.

Book 8 Introduction

The format of Book 8 corresponds to the one used in earlier even-numbered books in the *Challenger* series. Book 8 introduces relatively few new words and concepts in order to give students the opportunity to thoroughly review and reinforce vocabulary and reasoning skills and further develop their reading comprehension.

The readings for Book 8 are, for the most part, nonfiction selections that have been minimally adapted from works of widely-acclaimed writers. Experience indicates that motivation and self-esteem are bolstered when students are made aware of this fact. Adult students should also be made aware that the GED Test includes brief nonfiction passages with accompanying questions. In working with the readings in Book 8, adults often become increasingly confident of their ability to achieve this long-range educational goal.

A review appears after every five lessons. These reviews provide students with additional opportunities to review words and concepts. They also help students develop the habit of referring to previous lessons for the correct answers to some of the questions. There are no word indexes in Book 8, but a complete list of the words introduced in Book 8 is available online at newreaderspress.com.

Book 8 is generally used by students who have completed Book 7 in this series. Book 8 is also appropriate for use with students who score in the range of 8.0 and above on standardized reading achievement tests. The final review in Book 7 can also be used as a diagnostic tool. An accuracy rate of 85 percent or better for this review indicates that students are ready for Book 8.

Students who use this book should be given as many opportunities for oral reading practice as time permits. This practice helps to develop confidence, enjoyment, and interest in reading.

Book 8 builds upon procedures and practices emphasized in the earlier books in this series. Thus, you may find it worthwhile to look through the manual notes for some of these books.

Scheduling Considerations

Book 8 works well in a classroom setting. The most progress is achieved when students work with *Challenger* for a minimum of 45 minutes two or three times a week. Students can work independently, in a group, or with partners. When working with other students, they receive the support and stimulation from one another that make learning more enjoyable. Also, the more advanced students can assume much of the responsibility for giving explanations and leading reinforcement activities, which in turn reinforces their own reading skills. Experience indicates that less advanced students usually benefit from peer instruction provided that you are available to supply any necessary clarifications.

Other Exercises

A wide variety of exercises has been included to help students improve recall, increase vocabulary, and develop reasoning abilities. As often as seems appropriate, draw the students' attention to the fact that reasoning is an essential part of reading. Help them develop such patterns as using the process of elimination, making intelligent guesses, using the dictionary, and referring to previous lessons when completing these exercises.

A score of 80 percent or higher should be considered satisfactory on these exercises. If students consistently score below this figure, take some time to help them pinpoint the problem. Usually, they are trying to complete the exercises too rapidly.

Because students are encouraged to learn from their mistakes, they should not be penalized for making them. If you work in a school that gives report cards, it is strongly recommended that evaluations be based on corrected work and overall progress rather than on students' initial efforts. In no way does this practice encourage typical reading students to be careless in completing their homework. Rather, they usually become more interested in reading than in report cards, they are more relaxed and patient with themselves in completing assignments, and they develop a more realistic definition of academic progress.

Reinforcement Activities

Suggestions and procedures for reinforcement activities for those words and concepts that give students difficulty are discussed in Chapter 4.

Writing Assignments

Student writing is discussed in Chapter 5. It is recommended that students working in Book 8 complete weekly writing assignments of 350–600 words in addition to the writing that is required to complete the exercises in the individual lessons. Suggestions for writing assignments are given in the individual lesson notes. It is also recommended that students working in Book 8 keep a journal in which they briefly record their responses to the readings or class discussions.

The Lesson Format

The procedure for each lesson should be as consistent as possible.

1. Students go over the writing assignment if one was given and review the work from the previous lesson first. This includes discussing the reading selection and correcting the exercises.

2. If time permits, students complete relevant reinforcement activities. The nature and scope of these activities are determined by the needs of your students and how often you meet with them.

3. Students preview the next lesson, which is usually assigned for homework.

Individual Lesson Notes

Lesson notes for each lesson appear on the following pages. These notes contain suggestions and procedures for specific items in each lesson.

LESSON 1
Houdini: His Legend and His Magic

Primary emphasis

- Reading comprehension (biography)
- Forming a reasoned opinion
- Vocabulary development (synonyms)
- Putting statements in proper sequence

Secondary emphasis

- Using context clues
- Using the dictionary
- Learning word origins

Words for Study

The Words for Study section includes words that appear in this lesson that have not appeared previously in this controlled-vocabulary series. As was the case with the preceding books in this series, most of the new words appear in subsequent reading selections and exercises so that students have many opportunities to work with them. Thus, there is no need to strive for immediate mastery; mastery will come with practice.

It is recommended that the words be pronounced and briefly discussed prior to the students completing the reading independently. If done in a brief and informal manner, this practice increases students' confidence in their ability to complete the lesson. Also, it often arouses their curiosity about the reading.

Not all words need to be defined during this brief discussion. For example, if a student asks what the word *shackles* means, tell him that the word will appear in the lesson and that the context in which it appears will help him to understand the meaning of the word. If necessary, review the meaning of *context*.

Sometimes it is helpful to give an on-the-spot definition, sentence, or example of an unfamiliar word. Perhaps a student needs to know that he has a working relationship with you. Perhaps he has had a difficult day and needs a few moments to center himself on the work. Whatever the reason, a friendly conversation for a few seconds is more important than reminding him of the value of context clues.

The Words for Study section provides an excellent resource for spelling quizzes, brief writing assignments, and classroom games. Suggestions regarding these activities are found in Chapter 4 of this manual.

Reading Selection

Tell students that all the readings in Book 8 have been taken from the works of professional writers. Knowing this fact has proved to be an excellent source of motivation for many students.

Introduce this reading selection by pointing out that it was taken from *Houdini: His Legend and His Magic* by Doug Henning. You may want to get this book or another book on Houdini from the library so students can look at the illustrations. Review the meaning of the term *biography*. Because some students have difficulty distinguishing between nonfiction and fiction, it may be helpful to review these terms also.

Generally, all initial readings of the selections should be done for homework. However, because this is the first lesson, allot time for an oral first reading in class. This gives you an opportunity to assess the strengths and weaknesses of students' oral reading abilities. Begin by reading the first part of the story yourself, and then ask for volunteers to continue.

Good oral reading skills often foster not only more proficient reading but also a greater appreciation of reading. Oral reading practice is especially welcomed by adults who would like to read with more confidence to their children or, occasionally, to their peers.

After reading the selection aloud, discuss it in a general way. This gives students a chance to get a sense of the selection as a whole while giving you the opportunity to assess their comprehension skills. Because the comprehension exercises often address specific reading skills, the general discussion can be focused on personal thoughts about or reactions to the reading. Otherwise, students are likely to develop the habit of thinking that reading comprehension merely consists of recalling as much as they can about what they have read and nothing more.

When you have completed the general discussion of the reading selection, preview the exercises to be done for homework. Since this is the first lesson, take plenty of time and be sure all students understand how to do each exercise. If necessary, have students complete an item in each exercise so that they have a thorough understanding of how to do the work.

During the homework review, allot some time to help students analyze the dictionary entry for *Houdini*. Have them look up the entry for *Houdini* in a current dictionary. Briefly discuss the entry formats, and remind students that they will find the dictionary an excellent resource in completing many of the exercises in *Challenger 8*.

EXERCISE 1: UNDERSTANDING THE READING

During the homework preview, remind students that they are to refer to the story for any answer they cannot recall. If students seem to think that having to go back to the story for an answer is a sign of poor reading, tell them that this simply isn't so. If anything, it is a sign of good scholarship.

Tell students to complete *all* the questions for this and all other exercises in Book 8. If you establish this pattern of completing all the work at the outset, students will more quickly develop a habit of thoroughness about their work.

Some students have the misconception that they should skip a question if they are not completely certain that their answer is correct. Remind these students that a blank is marked as an incorrect answer on many tests and that these questions give them an opportunity to practice the art of "intelligent guessing."

A score of 80 percent or better should be considered good on comprehension questions of this type. During the homework review, help students who had difficulty with the last three questions to find clues in the reading that indicate the correct answer. Students often need to be reminded that having some understanding of the author's motives or attitude is a valuable reading skill because it helps them to form a more reasoned judgment of what they read.

EXERCISE 2: WHAT DO YOU THINK?

During the homework preview, encourage students to write well-developed answers for these questions. Point out that the directions require them to support their thoughts and opinions with sound reasons.

When going over this section with the students during the homework review, make sure the answers are written in complete sentences. Initially, students may have difficulty putting their answers in sentence form, but with practice they will become increasingly proficient.

Also, help students make any necessary spelling and grammatical corrections. It may be helpful to remind them that writing is a form of communication, and spelling and grammar rules have been designed to make this communication clearer. When students begin to see that their writing improves with this attention to corrections and that there is no penalty for having made an error in the first place, they tend to progress more rapidly.

EXERCISE 3: SYNONYMS

During the homework preview, suggest that students use the process of elimination and a dictionary to complete this exercise. Review the process of elimination if students are unsure of what you mean. This is a useful tool that will help students complete many of the exercises in this book. During the homework review, review the meaning of *synonym*. Again, 80 percent or better should be considered a good score for exercises of this type.

EXERCISE 4: NAMES THAT HAVE MADE THE DICTIONARY

During the homework preview, point out that in addition to correct spellings and word definitions, dictionaries contain other interesting information, including the origins of many words. Students may not be aware that people's names are one source of words in our language. During the review, you might ask if students know any other words that come from people's names. *Boycott, cardigan, dunce, Pullman, valentine,* and *silhouette* are some other examples.

EXERCISE 5: CHALLENGES

During the homework preview, point out that there may be more than one possible way to order these sets of sentences. Students are asked to put them into a *sensible* order. You might discuss what is meant by the phrase "sensible order" and how students would decide what is sensible.

During the homework review, you may wish to have students act out these challenges in class. They can then see if the order they selected is a sensible one.

Note: After students have gone over the exercises and made any necessary corrections during the homework review, give them an opportunity to ask questions or make comments about what they have just accomplished. Students who are not familiar with the format of *Challenger* workbooks may feel overwhelmed by the work. Point out strengths they have shown in completing the work. Remind them that this is only the first lesson and that they will get used to the work more quickly than they think possible.

Activities in Writing Book 8

By focusing on composing five-paragraph essays, the writing activities in this book will help prepare students for the writing section of the GED. Most assignments require expository essays. Attention is also given to revising and editing essays by highlighting these steps at the end of the two-page writing lessons. To help students recognize common writing problems, each lesson begins with exercises on untangling confusing sentences, adding details, or correcting sentence structure. Instruction is also provided in using transitions to help the flow of ideas within paragraphs and between paragraphs.

In Lesson 1, Exercise 1 asks students to supply the missing words in sentences and to clarify antecedents. Exercise 2 provides the writing prompt for the lesson and guides students through mapping Houdini's life in order to gather information to use in their essays. You might point out that mapping is a good way to gather information about a story, including the story of a person's life. The instruction also defines a *summary*.

Exercise 3 explains how and why to use chronological order as the organizing principle for a summary of a person's life. Point out that chronological order is a good way to organize any sequenced activity. Exercise 4 is the writing activity itself and provides a step-by-step writing guide for students to follow. The lesson ends with a reminder to revise and edit the first draft of the essay.

Additional Writing Activities

1. Have students choose an event in their own lives and write five-paragraph narrative essays describing it. They should include details to make them interesting and complete.

2. Have students write one-paragraph summaries of their five-paragraph essays. Then have them compare the two essays in a class discussion. They should recognize that their summaries have just the main points of what happened and that the five-paragraph essays have many more details.

LESSON 2
Mirror, Mirror, on the Wall...

Primary emphasis

- Reading comprehension (nonfiction)
- Forming a reasoned opinion
- Comparing points of view
- Reading a map

Secondary emphasis

- Vocabulary development (antonyms)
- The suffix -logy
- Using the dictionary

Reading Selection

During the homework preview, read aloud the two paragraphs that introduce this selection, and briefly discuss students' views on the use of cosmetics and the concepts *primitive* and *civilized*.

During the homework review, discuss the author's thoughts about our use of the words *primitive* and *civilized*. One activity that has helped students to understand the author's point more clearly is to make two columns marked *primitive* and *civilized* on the chalkboard. Then have the students list words we use to label people and record them in the appropriate column. For example, they may list *simple* for primitive people and *sophisticated* for civilized people. Students also find it helpful to explore questions such as "What is the difference between our use of these terms and that of an anthropologist?" and "Is one use better than another?"

Because the theme of Unit 1 is appearances, another discussion topic or writing activity is to have students more fully explore the author's view that cosmetics are related to our sense of personal identity. This concept can be extended to include clothing styles and jewelry as well. Suggested questions include "What are we trying to tell others by the way we dress?" and "Does this message reveal our true selves?"

EXERCISE 1: UNDERSTANDING THE READING

Remind students to read the selection carefully *prior* to answering the comprehension questions. Not only will their reading improve, but also they will find *Challenger 8* far more enjoyable.

The answer to question 1 cannot be found in the reading selection. Mention this during the homework preview and tell students to make an intelligent guess.

EXERCISE 2: MORE ABOUT *WE* AND *THEY*

During the homework preview, have the students study the directions and examples carefully. Be sure they understand what is expected of them. Many students have the tendency to skim directions, skip examples, and then wonder why a particular section of work is so confusing.

During the review, give students a chance to discuss and debate any differences they may have in their responses to question 1 for Situation 1. Follow this up with discussions for Situations 2 and 3.

EXERCISE 3: ANTONYMS

During the homework preview, remind students to use a dictionary and the process of elimination to complete this exercise. Review the terms *synonym* and *antonym* during the homework review.

EXERCISE 4: THE SUFFIX *-LOGY*

Students should also use the process of elimination and a dictionary to complete this exercise. They need not complete the exercise in order but should be encouraged to start with what they consider the easiest items. It may be helpful to review the pronunciation of the words in the box. In this type of exercise, students should strive to have all answers correct—including the spelling.

EXERCISE 5: MORE ABOUT MELANESIA

During the homework preview, have students find Melanesia on a globe or map of the world. This will give them a better sense of the location and size of Melanesia. Most students have no idea that this part of the world even exists.

It is helpful to have pictures of Melanesian life available during the homework review.

Activities in Writing Book 8

In Exercise 1, students practice revising sentences to move misplaced modifiers closer to the words they modify. The last item asks students to look at their own writing and check for misplaced modifiers. Exercise 2 sets up the writing assignment and takes students through the decision-making process and information-gathering step, which consists of both brainstorming and listing.

Exercise 3 explains organizing an essay using a pattern of most important to least important point. To minimize confusion, the reverse pattern (least important to most important point/evidence) in order to end the body of an essay with the most important point or piece of evidence is not included in Writing Book 8. However, as students approach the end of the book, you might suggest this as an alternate organizing pattern.

Exercise 4 provides a writing guide for the essay and ends with a reminder to revise the draft and to look especially for confusing sentences.

Additional Writing Activities

1. Before students revise their essays, ask them what kinds of problems writing can quickly lead to. Explain that even the best professional writers will write quickly to get ideas down before they forget them. That's why the writing process has an editing step.

2. Have students collect some print ads for cosmetics—for both men and women. Then as a class, have students compare the wording on the ads and make a list of words that appear often. Have pairs write their own ad copy for cosmetics using some of these words or even more fantastic claims for cosmetics.

LESSON 3
Celebrity vs. Reality

Primary emphasis
- Reading comprehension (nonfiction)
- Forming a reasoned opinion
- Vocabulary (synonyms and antonyms)

Secondary emphasis
- The suffix *-ist*
- Using context clues
- Classifying information

Reading Selection
During the lesson introduction, ask students if they ever read the supermarket tabloids or watch reality shows. What are their favorites? What do they like about the tabloids? Do they think the stories are true and the pictures are real? Ask similar questions about reality shows. What would students think if both tabloid stories and reality shows were faked? Would they feel cheated? What would they think of the contestants on reality shows?

EXERCISE 2: REALITY CHECK
During the homework preview, ask students how they might feel if they were the title character in *The Truman Show* and found out that their lives were not real. You might point out that the character had grown up, married, and had a child on the show—and everyone was an actor and knew it except him. In the end, when the character discovers the truth, he escapes from the TV soundstage.

EXERCISE 3: SYNONYMS AND ANTONYMS
Remind students to use a dictionary if necessary to complete this exercise.

EXERCISE 4: THE SUFFIX *-IST*
If you sense students will have difficulty with this exercise, complete the first item with them during the preview. After they have read the first sentence, ask them to identify what they consider a key word. Most students will respond *trance*. Then ask them to locate the word in the box that they associate with *trance*. Generally, they

have no trouble finding the correct answer, and they better understand how to complete the exercise. Mention that this is an example of using context clues, a valuable reading skill, and review the meaning of *context*.

Review the pronunciation of the words in the box during the homework review.

EXERCISE 5: WORKING WITH HEADINGS
The typical classification exercise has students going from the general to the specific. This exercise reverses the process by having students determine the categories for each group. You may need to explain the term *sitcom* for students before they begin.

The Extra Credit exercise should be viewed as a fun activity and the source for a classroom discussion.

Activities in Writing Book 8
In Exercise 1, students work with subject-verb agreement, another common writing error. Often the problem results from a phrase or clause that comes between the subject and verb and confuses students, the subject of Exercise 1 in Lesson 4. Exercise 2 takes students through another series of decision-making and information-gathering steps. The instruction/review is about brainstorming, and students use charts to record their information.

Exercise 3 takes them through organizing their essays from the most important to least important reason. Exercise 4 provides a writing guide. The focus is on adding details to make the reasons interestingly worded and complete. The special revision feature asks students to check for subject-verb agreement issues.

Additional Writing Activities
1. Ask students to keep charts of their TV/cable viewing for a week and then write five-paragraph essays explaining what they watched and why.
2. Have students brainstorm what they could do besides watch TV/cable in their spare time. Ask them to choose one idea and write about it.

LESSON 4
Keeping up with the Joneses

Primary emphasis
- Reading comprehension (nonfiction)
- Forming a reasoned opinion
- Analogies

Secondary emphasis
- The suffix -ism
- Using context clues
- Spelling

Reading Selection

This selection is not easy to read or to comprehend. In introducing it, you might mention that Veblen's book is required reading for many college courses. You may wish to consider having the students read and discuss the selection in class rather than assigning it for homework. Or you may decide to review their answers to Exercise 1 prior to the general discussion to make sure they have understood the basic points. During the general discussion, allow time for students to discuss their reactions to the points Veblen raises.

EXERCISE 2: WHAT DO YOU THINK?

For question 3, suggest that students phrase their objections in the form of quoted statements. For example, a student may list his or her MP3 player as the first item and write, "I can't concentrate or fall asleep at night unless my favorite songs are playing."

A discussion topic that students have found interesting is whether or not consumerism is the problem that Veblen suggests it is. Encourage students to relate the theme of appearances to consumerism, if possible (because this type of discussion can turn into a heated debate in spite of your best efforts).

EXERCISE 3: WORD RELATIONSHIPS

Students often have difficulty with this type of exercise. Help them get started by going over the first question during the preview. Ask them to explain the relationship between *Houdini* and *illusionist*. Then have them read the four choices and decide which pair of words expresses a similar relationship. Most students will have no trouble selecting *Edison is to inventor*.

Remind students that the process of elimination is often helpful in selecting the correct answer and that they may use the dictionary to look up unfamiliar words. Whether or not you choose to introduce the term *analogy* is up to you. Some students are impressed by this word.

EXERCISE 4: THE SUFFIX -ISM

During the preview, remind students that context clues and the process of elimination are helpful tools in completing this type of exercise.

Review the meanings of the suffixes *-logy, -ist,* and *-ism* during the homework review.

EXERCISE 5: SPELLING CHECK

During the preview, draw students' attention to the fact that in some sentences all the words may be spelled correctly. During the review, you may want to discuss the meaning of *et cetera*.

Activities in Writing Book 8

In Exercise 1, students continue working with subject-verb agreement. The lesson focuses on the most common reason for a problem, an interrupting phrase or clause. Exercise 2 has students state their opinion and then list evidence to support it. Some students may need to reverse the order because they have no opinion. You might explain that which step they choose to do first depends on what they think about a topic. Sometimes they have an opinion, and sometimes they may not. Gathering information first will help them decide what they think.

Exercise 3 guides students through deciding the order of importance for their examples. Exercise 4 offers a writer's guide to developing an essay. The final feature reminds them to check for subject-verb agreement issues as they revise and edit their writing.

Additional Writing Activities

1. As a follow-up essay, have students write two paragraphs describing a time when they bought something simply because someone else had it or because they wanted to impress someone. The first paragraph should describe the reason for buying the item, and the second paragraph should explain how they feel about the purchase now.

2. The current interest in anticonsumerism reflects a concern for the environment. Have students in pairs write one-sentence slogans to remind people that buying things for the sake of buying things is bad for the environment. (This actually provides practice in writing topic sentences.)

Book 8 Lesson 4 TEACHER'S MANUAL **137**

L E S S O N 5
While the Auto Waits

Primary emphasis
- Comprehension of literature (short story)
- Forming a reasoned opinion
- Vocabulary review
  1. Which word does not fit?
  2. Word associations

Secondary emphasis
- Review of suffixes
- Using context clues

Story
During the homework preview, mention that, unlike the readings in the previous lessons, this is a work of fiction. Review the meanings of *fiction* and *nonfiction*. To introduce the story, you might mention that O. Henry is known for his surprise endings. Students who have used earlier books in the *Challenger* series are familiar with O. Henry's work. Point out that this story was originally published in 1908. Ask students to think about the story as they read and decide whether a situation like that could happen today.

EXERCISE 1: UNDERSTANDING THE STORY
The answers to several of these questions are not specifically given in the reading selection but can be inferred from the information given. If students have trouble drawing the correct conclusions, discuss the process of inferring the best choice.

EXERCISE 2: WHAT DO YOU THINK?
During the review, discuss the concept of pretenses and its relationship to the theme of appearances.

EXERCISE 3: WHICH WORD DOES NOT FIT?
Remind students that a dictionary and the process of elimination will be helpful in completing this exercise.

EXERCISE 4: MORE ABOUT O. HENRY
During the homework preview, tell students to read each entire sentence before attempting to find the correct response. Tell them to pay attention to word endings and context clues in deciding which word to place in each blank.

When students have finished filling in the blanks, have them read the entire exercise again for comprehension.

Review the various suffixes in the groups of words on the left during the homework review.

EXERCISE 5: PRETENSES IN THE PARK
During the homework preview, have students study the example. Stress that they are to match the people listed above with statements they would make if they were *pretending*. Therefore, they are to look for the opposite of what the people would say if they were telling the truth.

As a follow-up activity, students enjoy selecting their own "people" words and creating their own bits of pretentious dialogue to go with them.

Activities in Writing Book 8
Exercise 1 begins a series of instructions/reviews about the use of transitions. A great deal of coverage is given to transitions in the writing series because of their importance in creating flow. Their use is also a mark of a more polished writer. This lesson discusses transitions that show time order. Exercise 2 introduces the use of the "Five W's and H" as a method for gathering information in the prewriting step.

Exercise 3 guides students through the use of chronological order to organize essays about events. Exercise 4 guides students through writing three-paragraph summaries. The feature at the end reminds them to use transitions as they write.

Additional Writing Activities
1. Ask students to write paragraphs predicting what might have happened if Mr. Parkenstacker had returned the book to the young woman.
2. Have students write paragraphs explaining why they think the young woman acts as she does and then additional paragraphs explaining why they think Mr. Parkenstacker assumes another identity, too.
3. As a culminating writing activity, have students summarize briefly the theme of appearances as it relates to the five different readings in this unit.

Review: Lessons 1–5

It should be emphasized to the students that this is a review, not a test. These exercises are opportunities to review words and concepts that have been introduced in previous lessons. Material is often presented in new ways both to challenge the students and to arouse their interest. Preview each exercise included in the review as you do in other lessons. An overall score of 80 percent or better on the review should be considered excellent.

EXERCISE 2: WORD REVIEW

Remind students to read the entire statement before selecting the correct response. Both context clues and the process of elimination are helpful tools.

EXERCISE 3: SYNONYMS AND ANTONYMS

Many students find this exercise more manageable if they first complete all the synonyms and then complete the antonyms.

EXERCISE 4: A POEM ABOUT APPEARANCES

During the homework preview, begin reading the poem aloud to the class. After two or three stanzas, ask for volunteers to continue the reading. Expression, especially with the blind men's observations, should be encouraged.

After discussing students' responses to the comprehension questions, discuss the relationship of this poem to the theme of Unit 1, appearances.

EXERCISE 5: FARAWAY PLACES

An encyclopedia is recommended for this exercise, although most of the answers may be found in a good dictionary. You may want to have students complete this exercise during class time if they don't have access to other references outside of class.

Writing Activity

If you wish to assign a composition to bring the unit of work to a conclusion, the following are some suggestions relating to the theme of appearance:

- When I Was Deceived by Appearances
- Why I Think It Is (or Is Not) All Right for a Person to Create an Illusion
- When I Pretended to Be What I Wasn't
- Why I Think It Is (or Is Not) All Right for Children to Watch TV
- Television Has (or Doesn't Have) Too Much Influence on Our Lives

LESSON 6
Marco Polo

Primary emphasis
- Reading comprehension (nonfiction)
- Forming a reasoned opinion
- Using context clues

Words for Study
During the homework preview, discuss any of the Words for Study that are not familiar to students.

Reading Selection
Introduce the selection by discussing briefly what students think of when they hear the word *explorer*. What historical explorers can they name? What did they do? What modern-day explorers do they know about?

Ask students if they know the children's tag game called "Marco Polo." Ask them if they have any idea what the name means or why the game got that name. Tell them that they may be able to figure it out from the historical Marco Polo's exploits.

Ask any students who are of Chinese heritage to describe something about China that they know. It could be something about Chinese culture, the city or area that relatives lived in, the educational system, or the work someone did. Tell students that they are going to read about China as it was almost 800 years ago seen through the eyes of an Italian named Marco Polo.

EXERCISE 1: UNDERSTANDING THE READING
In the homework review, you might point out the signals for cause and effect in questions 7 and 9 and the time order signal in question 8.

EXERCISE 2: WHAT DO YOU THINK?
These answers require students to use inference and their outside knowledge. For example, they may not know how big the Lop Nor Desert is, but they should recognize that there were no cars, trains, or planes in the 1200s so travel by foot, horseback, or camel might well have taken a very long time.

In question 4, be sure that students take into account the work of the experts noted in the article. Remind them that opinions are to be based on facts.

EXERCISE 3: ANCIENT CHINA
Students will need intelligent guessing, the process of elimination, and context clues to complete this exercise. Encourage them to use the dictionary for unfamiliar words.

EXERCISE 4: EARLY EXPLORERS
During the preview, remind students to read each entire sentence before deciding on the correct responses. Remind them to read the entire exercise through for comprehension after they have filled in all the blanks.

Review the meaning of the term *prefix* during the homework review. Then review the meanings of the prefixes used in this exercise.

EXERCISE 5: ANIMALS OF MYTH
During the homework preview, you might ask students if they know the game "Gossip." Either they as children or their children will probably have played this game. Tell them that this may be the process by which real creatures became exaggerated beasts.

Activities in Writing Book 8
Exercise 1 begins by ensuring that there are enough details to explain and describe main points in an essay. The instruction/review focuses on descriptive (sensory) words and phrases, the use of specific nouns, and action verbs. Exercise 2 takes students through a three-step process for brainstorming ideas, choosing ones to use for their essays, and adding details. The final step in prewriting often involves creating charts similar to the one in this lesson because charts are a neat and organized way to enter data for easy reference later. If students balk at the time or trouble it takes to create charts or even to think about details before they begin to write (it is work), explain that creating charts means that the information is easy to find when they begin to write. They don't have to stop and start as they try to decipher the notes they may have written all over a page or to think of details as they write.

Students work through organizing the information on their charts from most important to least important in Exercise 3. In Exercise 4, students follow a writing guide to develop their essays. The final feature reminds them to evaluate whether they need more details for their essays.

Additional Writing Activities
1. Have students imagine that it is 1300 and they have just read Marco Polo's book. Have them write paragraphs to answer the question: Do you believe Marco Polo? Why or why not?
2. A few people don't believe that the astronauts walked on the moon. Ask students to write paragraphs comparing and contrasting Marco Polo's journey with the moonwalk.

LESSON 7
The Journals of Lewis and Clark

Primary emphasis
- Reading comprehension (nonfiction)
- Using context clues
- Distinguishing fact and opinion

Secondary emphasis
- Vocabulary
- Spelling
- Reading a picture

Words for Study
It is helpful to discuss briefly the meanings of difficult words during the preview.

Reading Selection
The Journals of Lewis and Clark contains amazing firsthand accounts of what the plains and western mountains were like before white Americans began to settle the regions. Their reports to President Thomas Jefferson as well as the specimens that they sent back opened up the West to settlement by white Americans. They also doomed the Shoshones' way of life and that of other nations of the plains and mountains, California, and the Pacific Northwest.

When you introduce the selection, ask students to list facts that they know about Lewis and Clark, the Louisiana Purchase, and Native Americans of the Plains, mountains, and Pacific coast. Ask them to consider whether Lewis and Clark could have predicted what happened to the Native Americans as a result of their journey to the Pacific and back. You might introduce the concept of unintended consequences.

EXERCISE 1: UNDERSTANDING THE READING
Some of the questions require that students infer the answers. You might review the process of making inferences during the homework preview.

EXERCISE 2: WHAT DO YOU THINK?
This exercise asks students to look for facts to support or reject Lewis's opinions as expressed in the excerpts.

Point out that being able to distinguish facts from opinions is an important skill, for example, in weighing the claims of opposing politicians. Also point out that a person's own opinions are stronger when they are based on facts. You might discuss with students how to find out the facts about an issue in order to make an informed decision, a responsibility of citizenship.

EXERCISE 3: WORDS IN CONTEXT
During the homework review, point out that while a dictionary can be very useful, in many circumstances students won't have access to dictionaries—or dictionary sites on the Internet. Then they will need to rely on their ability to use context to decipher the meanings of unfamiliar words.

EXERCISE 4: SPELLING CHECK
During the preview, tell students that in some sentences all the underlined words may be spelled correctly. (Note that *defence* is the accepted British spelling of *defense*.)

EXERCISE 5: POWERS OF OBSERVATION
This exercise will help students with their descriptive writing. In the homework preview, you might point out that students don't need to know the names of animals and plants in order to describe them.

Activities in Writing Book 8
Students work with transitions that add information in Exercise 1. In Exercise 2, students complete prewriting for their essays by listing examples from the excerpt, choosing three to use, and then creating a chart to add details to the examples. Exercise 3 guides students through deciding the order of importance for their examples, and in Exercise 4, they write their essays following a writer's guide. The feature reminds them to use transitions that add information.

Additional Writing Activity
Ask students to find pictures from a magazine or newspaper and write paragraphs about them.

LESSON 8
Endurance

Primary emphasis
- Reading comprehension (nonfiction)
- Forming a reasoned opinion
- Using context clues
- Comparing and contrasting information

Secondary emphasis
- Vocabulary
- Using the dictionary
- Sequencing information

Reading Selection

In introducing the selection, you might point out that the excerpt is a special kind of nonfiction, a first-person account, also known as a primary source. Ask students if they know anything about Shackleton and the search for the South Pole. If not, save the following information as the wrap-up to the lesson. The ordeal that Shackleton describes in this excerpt took place on his third expedition to Antarctica. In the end, he and five of his crew made an 800-mile journey overland to bring help to the crew. Shackleton died on his fourth expedition in 1922.

Ask students to describe how they might feel if they were trapped on ice in the Antarctic with no means of communicating with the outside world. How do they think that they would pass the time day after day for months? How would they feel?

EXERCISE 1: UNDERSTANDING THE READING

Question 7 requires that students infer their answers. Question 8 is the basis for the writing assignment in Writing Book 8. You might mention that the factors suggested are broad categories, not the answers.

EXERCISE 2: COMPREHENSION CHECK

Students should try to complete the exercise using just context clues and what they read in the lesson's reading selection. However, if they can't figure out some of the answers even through the process of elimination, they should use a dictionary. Encourage students to cross off each word as they use it in an answer.

EXERCISE 3: SHADES OF MEANING

This exercise is an excellent way for students to understand the concept of words with multiple meanings.

Discuss the more familiar meanings of the words during the homework review.

EXERCISE 5: LABELING A STORYBOARD

This activity is both educational and fun. You might have students create their own storyboards of events that happened to them. Some students may complain that they can't draw, but encourage them to try at least drawing stick figures. Explain that the artwork is less important than getting their ideas across to an audience.

Activities in Writing Book 8

Exercise 1 provides instruction/review on transitions that show comparison and contrast. The instructional information notes that often people say they are comparing something when they mean they are considering both similarities and differences. You might point out that in weighing pros and cons or advantages and disadvantages, people are also comparing and contrasting information.

Exercise 2 expands on question 8 under Exercise 1 in the Student Book. It also provides instruction/review on creating a Venn diagram to compare and contrast information. If students find drawing lines out from the information in the circles and adding details too messy, they could create a chart for similarities and one for the differences and add details to the chart.

Exercise 3 guides students through organizing the ideas for their essays. The writing guide in Exercise 4 takes students through developing their essays and reminds them in the revision stage to be sure that they have included transitions to show the connections between their ideas.

Additional Writing Activities

1. Ask students in a class discussion to pick out words, phrases, or clauses that they think are especially good in helping them visualize what happened to Shackleton and his crew. Talk about why the description is so good. Use the phrases "paint a picture in the mind's eye" and "makes the ordeal come alive for readers."

2. Ask students to write stories of one or two paragraphs that describe something scary that happened to them. They should use descriptions and comparisons the way that Shackleton does to make their writing "come alive" for readers.

LESSON 9
Exploring the Deep

Primary emphasis
- Reading comprehension (nonfiction)
- Forming a reasoned opinion
- Interpreting poetry

Secondary emphasis
- Learning common prefixes
- Using context clues

Reading Selection

During the preview, introduce the selection by discussing any unfamiliar words in the Words for Study section. Ask students what they know about submarines and oceanography. Perhaps some of them may know the novel *Twenty Thousand Leagues Under the Sea* by Jules Verne. Tell them that the article that they will read is about exploration of the ocean depths and that we know more about the stars and planets than we do about the oceans.

EXERCISE 1: UNDERSTANDING THE READING

Remind students that they may look back at the reading to find an answer or to check an answer they are unsure of. Instead of reading the entire selection each time, they should skim the reading to find a key word from the question. For example, for number 2, they would look for paragraphs that include the names *Beebe* and *Barton*.

EXERCISE 3: WORD RELATIONSHIPS

Remind students to first recognize the relationship between the given words and then to use the process of elimination to find a similar relationship among the answer choices.

EXERCISE 4: STILL MORE PREFIXES

Some students think that if they know the meaning of a prefix, they should automatically know the meaning

of the word. Remind them that it doesn't always work this way and to use a dictionary if necessary. During the review, after going over the students' responses, review the meanings of these prefixes.

EXERCISE 5: A LOOK BACK

Read the poem aloud during the homework preview, and have students read the poem aloud during the review. Discuss with students Coleridge's language and his use of descriptive words and phrases.

Activities in Writing Book 8

Exercise 1 continues instruction/review on transitions by introducing transitions that indicate causes and effects. Exercise 2 provides students the option either to state their opinions first if they have them already and then find information to support those opinions, or to gather information and then make up their minds. Students should add the best three pieces of evidence to their charts and add details for each.

By now students should realize that order of importance is the typical method of organizing information for an essay. Exercise 3 takes students through this pattern to arrange their essays. In Exercise 4, students follow a guide to develop their essays. The revision and editing feature reminds them about the use of transitions.

Additional Writing Activities

1. Have students use their answers in Exercise 2 in the Student Book as the basis for essays or short narratives titled "When I Became an Explorer."
2. Interested students could do additional research on ocean explorations and prepare written or oral reports on the subject. Remind them to narrow their topics so that their research is manageable.

A Brief History of Space Exploration

Primary emphasis
- Comprehension of literature (nonfiction)
- Forming a reasoned opinion
- Vocabulary review (synonyms)
- Reading and creating time lines

Secondary emphasis
- Using context clues

Words for Study
A brief discussion of difficult words during the preview is recommended.

Reading Selection
In introducing the selection, point out that exploration of the heavens began centuries before investigation of the oceans. Ask students to speculate why this may be true. Why do they think it was easier for people to think about and investigate the stars and planets from Earth than the oceans on Earth?

Have students talk about what they know about the space programs of different countries. Point out that China has now launched a satellite into space.

EXERCISE 1: UNDERSTAND THE READING
Many of these answers require that students make inferences. Remind students to use what they have read and their own knowledge to make informed guesses.

EXERCISE 3: SYNONYM REVIEW
Remind students to use the dictionary for unfamiliar words and to use the process of elimination. You might point out that using synonyms adds variety to writing.

EXERCISE 4: PUT EVENTS IN ORDER
This exercise provides practice in sequencing. Remind students that they may and should consult the time line in order to complete this exercise.

EXERCISE 5: MAKE YOUR OWN TIME LINE
This exercise provides practice not only in sequencing but also in evaluation and decision making. During the homework review, discuss what criteria students used in making their decisions. See if the class can agree on criteria.

Activities in Writing Book 8
Students may think that details mean descriptive details. The instruction in Exercise 1 focuses on adding details to complete thoughts and bring clarity to one's writing. Exercise 2 has students brainstorming their own ideas, listing ideas from the reading selection, choosing the best, and adding details to enhance them. Exercise 3 takes students through organizing their information, and Exercise 4 guides them through writing a persuasive essay, the first such essay in this level. The revision feature reminds them to use transitions to connect ideas.

Additional Writing Activities
1. Have students write five-paragraph essays to persuade NASA to accept them into the astronaut program. They should be able to recognize the usefulness of applying Exercise 4's writing guide to the essays.
2. Have interested students write reports or prepare oral reports on space exploration. Remind them to narrow their topics so their research is manageable.
3. Question 4 under Exercise 2 in the Student Book would make a good extended writing assignment.

Review: Lessons 1–10

As with the review for Unit 1, remind students that this is not a test. These exercises are additional opportunities to review words and concepts that were introduced in previous lessons. Encourage students to refer to those lessons or to a dictionary for words they cannot recall. An overall score of 80 percent or better on a review exercise should be considered excellent.

EXERCISE 1: DEFINITIONS

Suggest that students try to complete the exercise without using a dictionary and then consult a dictionary for the words they do not know. As they write a word on a line, they should cross it off in the chart. This will help them to see what words they still have to use.

EXERCISE 4: TODAY'S EXPLORERS

After the homework review, go over with students the meanings of the different prefixes. Remind them that although they may know the meaning of a prefix, that doesn't necessarily mean that they will be able to figure out the meaning of a word with that prefix. However, they often will be able to; when they can't, they should consult their dictionaries.

During the homework review, you may want to have students summarize the theme for Unit 2, Explorers, as it relates to the readings in these five lessons.

Writing Activity

If you wish to assign a writing project to conclude this unit of work, the following are some suggestions relating to the theme of explorations:

- I Would Have (Not Have) Joined Marco Polo
- I Would Like to Travel to _____ Because . . .
- I Would Have (Not Have) Joined Shackleton's Search for the South Pole
- I Would Like (Not Like) to Be a Submariner
- I Would Like (Not Like) to Be an Astronaut

LESSON 11
A Fable for Tomorrow

Primary emphasis
- Reading comprehension (nonfiction)
- Forming a reasoned opinion
- Reading a table

Secondary emphasis
- Using context clues
- Learning word origins
- Using the dictionary

Reading Selection

This reading introduces the theme for Unit 3, the Good Earth. Introduce the reading by explaining that it is comprised of two excerpts from different sources. Mention that the first part of the reading is taken from Rachel Carson's well-known book *Silent Spring* and that the second excerpt is about Rachel Carson herself. Review the terms *fable* and *biography*.

A follow-up discussion is recommended about substances and practices that are currently considered harmful to the environment, including those that may increase global warming.

You may want to develop a class or group project for this unit. Have students collect items from newspapers, magazines, and other sources that pertain to environmental pollution and protection issues as well as global warming. Students could create classroom or bulletin board displays, or a scrapbook with the materials they gather. Groups of students might give presentations on specific issues when the unit comes to an end.

EXERCISE 2: WHAT DO YOU THINK?

Have Chief Seattle's statement read aloud during the homework preview, and briefly discuss what it means. Allow time during the homework review for a general discussion of students' reactions to the questions and to the statement.

EXERCISE 3: WHAT IS THE NOBEL PRIZE?

During the preview, remind students to read the entire exercise through for comprehension after they have filled in all the blanks. Like DDT, dynamite has proved to be a mixed blessing. Although it is not included in the exercise, you may wish to mention that Nobel was despondent over the consequences of his invention.

EXERCISE 4: GLOBAL WARMING

After the homework review, you might discuss with students what things ordinary people can do to decrease global warming. If students are unaware of steps they can take, this could become a research project resulting in either a brief written report or an oral report.

EXERCISE 5: NAMES IN NATURE

Encourage students to use a dictionary in completing this exercise, but warn them that not all references agree on the origins of all words. Etymology is an inexact science, and some dictionaries may differ about the origins of the words included in this exercise. For some words, there may be no source given in the dictionary. Remind students to use the process of elimination if they have doubts about which answer choice is best. Review the term *etymology* during the homework review, and discuss various ways that words enter our language.

Activities in Writing Book 8

Exercise 1 provides further practice on using details that complete and clarify ideas. In Exercise 2, students prewrite for another persuasive essay. Exercise 3 takes them through the organizing step, and Exercise 4 provides a writing guide. Note that the last sentence asks the reader to do something. This is the call to action and an important part of a persuasive letter (or speech) that urges the reader (or audience) to act.

Additional Writing Activities

1. Although the writing activity is set up as an essay, you could change the directions in Exercise 4 to a persuasive letter and have students write business letters. As practice, you could also have students research the contact information for their state legislators and U.S. Representative and Senator on the Internet.

2. Have students use the chart in Exercise 4 in the Student Book as the basis for five-paragraph essays explaining the projected impact of global warming. First, students need to choose what they think are the three best examples and then organize them. Second, they need to write a brief writing guide for themselves. It doesn't have to have complete sentences, but it needs to provide a structure for their essays (intro: topic sentence, three impacts; body: example 1; body: example 2: body: example 3; conclusion: restatement of topic sentence, three examples, final statement).

LESSON 12
No Way to Treat a Forest

Primary emphasis
- Reading comprehension (nonfiction)
- Forming a reasoned opinion
- Vocabulary (synonyms and antonyms)

Words for Study
This list is both longer and more difficult than most of the Words for Study lists. Briefly discuss the meanings of the more difficult words during the homework preview. Use these words and concepts to introduce the reading selection.

Reading Selection
During the general discussion of the reading selection, you might remind students of the fable by Rachel Carson in the previous lesson, and ask them how the concepts in this reading relate to Ms. Carson's ideas.

If your students have begun a class project on environmental issues, have them look specifically for materials on the rainforest. If there is a current local environmental issue, such as a movement to clean up a polluted river or lake, the location of a trash-burning plant, or the disposal of toxic wastes, you might invite one or two people who are knowledgeable about the details to discuss or debate the issue in your class.

EXERCISE 2: UNDERSTANDING THE READING: PART 2
During the review, allow time for students to share their views on the questions, especially the "What do you think?" question. Ask students if they were surprised to learn about the rainforest, how valuable it is, and how it is being deforested. What surprised them the most?

EXERCISE 3: SYNONYMS AND ANTONYMS
Students may find it easier to complete the synonyms first and then go back and fill in the antonyms. To make it easier to see the words that are available for use, students should cross off each word as they use it.

EXERCISE 4: TWO ENVIRONMENTALISTS
This exercise offers students practice in comparing and contrasting information as well as providing information for a class discussion about how two people with similar views can approach an issue differently. Remind students to read the exercise through once they have completed it.

Activities in Writing Book 8
In Exercise 1, students begin working with correcting faulty sentence structure. The exercise focuses on recognizing and correcting run-on sentences. Exercise 2 guides students through gathering information for a summary. The organizing pattern for the summary (Exercise 3) follows the author's pattern, which in this case is order of importance. Exercise 4 provides a writer's guide and notes that a summary should not include the writer's opinions of the original article. The revision feature reminds students to correct any run-on sentences in their essays.

Additional Writing Activities
1. Ask students to write five-paragraph essays about one thing that ordinary people can do to improve their local environment. First, students will need to brainstorm problems and solutions and then choose one to write about.
2. Have students work in pairs to write two-line (one-sentence) headlines that might accompany the article "No Way to Treat a Forest."

The Good Earth: Two Points of View

Primary emphasis
- Reading comprehension (nonfiction)
- Forming a reasoned opinion
- Interpreting a cartoon
- Using context clues
- Comparing and contrasting points of view

Secondary emphasis
- Word families
- Using reference materials
- Solving a puzzle (cryptogram)

Reading Selection

Introduce this selection by having students read the three introductory paragraphs aloud during the homework preview. Find the Cascade Range on a map of the United States. (It extends from northern California through Oregon and Washington into British Columbia. Both Mount Rainier and Mount Saint Helens are in this range.)

Perhaps the most startling piece of information in this selection is the fact that it took ten million tons of rock to make a hundred thousand tons of copper, which, in turn, is the amount of copper used to wire a city the size of Kansas City. You may want to have students try to estimate how much rock and copper are required to provide electrical wiring for the major cities in your state, using recent population figures as the basis for comparison with Kansas City.

EXERCISE 1: UNDERSTANDING THE READING

Allow time during the review for students to exchange their views about the uses of natural resources. Students can continue their work on a class project by collecting information on the use and misuse of natural resources.

EXERCISE 2: THE EARTH: A CARTOONIST'S POINT OF VIEW

Students with artistic ability may want to try drawing other cartoons that illustrate different aspects of environmental problems.

EXERCISE 3: WORD FAMILIES

It is helpful to review the meanings of the words in the left column during the homework review and to discuss the meanings of the various prefixes and suffixes.

EXERCISE 4: AMERICA'S RESOURCES

Students may be unfamiliar with many of the places mentioned in this exercise. Remind them to use key words in the sentences as their guides for finding the correct answers. During the homework review, locate the various places on a map of the United States. Pictures also enable students to gain a better sense of these places.

EXERCISE 5: CAN YOU CRACK THE CODE?

If necessary, help students get off to a good start by having them put *C*'s above all the *A*'s. A dictionary or other reference work may be helpful for finding the names of the less familiar metals.

Activities in Writing Book 8

Exercise 1 continues work on sentence structure by providing instruction/review on correcting sentence fragments. Exercise 2 guides students through creating and using T-charts to track differing opinions. Point out that if students were being asked to compare as well as contrast information, Venn diagrams would be better organizing tools.

Exercise 3 guides students through using charts to add details to the three differences that they will write about. In Exercise 4, students will follow guides to write their essays. The final help suggests that they state their own opinions of the men's ideas. The revision and editing feature reminds students to use transitions that contrast information.

Additional Writing Activities

1. Ask students working in pairs to think of ways that people can reduce what they buy and use. Have the class assemble a list of the top five, ten, or whatever number of tips while valuing contributions from everyone.
2. Ask students to think about the two men and decide which one they would like to meet in real life. Have them write paragraphs to explain why they would want to meet the person.
3. Explain that John McPhee is a prize-winning nature writer. Have them choose three examples of details from the excerpt that they like and wish they had written, and explain in a sentence or two what they like about each detail.

LESSON 14
Antaeus: Part I

Primary emphasis
- Comprehension of literature (short story)
- Forming a reasoned opinion
- Analogies

Secondary emphasis
- Compound words
- Using reference materials
- Vocabulary (mythological figures)

Story

Inform students during the homework preview that "Antaeus" is a short story in two parts and that it will be concluded in Lesson 15. Tell them Antaeus is the name of a figure in Greek mythology but that this is a modern story. The meaning of the title will be discussed during the homework review.

EXERCISE 1: UNDERSTANDING THE STORY

During the homework review, try to have resources such as Internet access or Bulfinch's *Mythology* available so that students can look up information on Antaeus. Ask them why they think Borden Deal titled his story "Antaeus."

EXERCISE 2: WHAT DO YOU THINK?

Students working on class projects can collect information on national and worldwide farming problems.

EXERCISE 4: FROM THE EARTH

If students have trouble forming the names of the plants, tell them to use a dictionary to look up the words in List A. However, a dictionary will not give them all the information they need to complete this exercise. An online or print encyclopedia is another good source for this information.

Activities in Writing Book 8

Exercise 1 continues instruction/review on sentence structure issues by focusing on comma faults. Students practice using four different solutions to the common writing problem. Exercise 2 asks students for personal essays about goals they achieved. The exercise takes them through brainstorming, making decisions, and charting information.

Exercise 3 introduces chronological order as an organizing tool. Students follow a writer's guide in Exercise 4 to develop their ideas. The revision and editing feature reminds them to look at spelling, punctuation, and grammar problems when they edit their writing. This means that they need to keep in mind everything they have learned so far when they revise and edit.

Additional Writing Activities

1. Have students write paragraphs predicting what will happen in the second part of the story. Ask students to read their paragraphs aloud during the homework review.

2. If any students are or were once farmers or like to garden, ask them to write paragraphs describing some aspect of what they like about farming or gardening and what they don't like about it.

LESSON 15
Antaeus: Part II

Primary emphasis
- Comprehension of literature (short story)
- Forming a reasoned opinion
- Homonym review

Secondary emphasis
- Vocabulary (Which Word Does Not Fit?)
- Solving a logic puzzle

Words for Study
Both the pronunciation and meanings of many of these words are difficult. Briefly discuss them during the homework preview.

Story
Since this story is in two parts, it is helpful to begin the general discussion by having students briefly summarize the entire story. Remind them of the predictions they made about what would happen in the second part of the story. Discuss how close they came to the real ending.

EXERCISE 2: WHAT DO YOU THINK?
During the preview, suggest that students might want to write their answers to question 1 in the form of a dialogue. After discussing students' responses to the two questions during the review, ask if they have any further ideas about why Borden Deal titled this story "Antaeus."

EXERCISE 3: WHICH WORD DOES NOT FIT?
If students are confused by the five choices in number 1, remind them that Atlas was a Titan in Greek mythology, while the rest are Roman gods, and Atlas is also the only one for whom no planet is named.

EXERCISE 4: HOMONYM REVIEW
During the preview, review the term *homonym*. Make sure students understand how to complete this exercise.

EXERCISE 5: LOGIC PROBLEM
This is not an easy puzzle. During the homework preview, make sure students understand how to go about solving this logic problem. Go over the directions and the example carefully with them. If they still seem confused, you may want to have them fill in information from clue 2 in class. Remind them to reread the clues as often as

necessary to complete the puzzle. Be sure they understand that for each *Y* they fill in, they can add six *N*'s to the chart (three up and down and three across). Students will find it helpful if you mention that the key to the solution is using the process of elimination.

Activities in Writing Book 8
Exercise 1 provides practice in identifying and correcting run-on sentences, sentence fragments, and comma faults. Exercise 2 offers students a choice of whom they write about and takes them through steps for both options.

Exercise 3 gives students an option for how they want to organize their essays. The purpose of providing options is to help students see that there are different ways to organize their essays. Some ways are more appropriate than others depending on the topic; for example, the best way to organize a summary is to follow the order of the original piece, the most appropriate way for a narrative is to use chronological order, and the most appropriate way for essays explaining reasons, ideas, causes and effects, or evidence is to use order of importance.

Exercise 4 offers a writing guide to help students develop their essays. The revision and editing feature reminds students to check specifically for run-on sentences, comma faults, and sentence fragments.

Additional Writing Activities
1. Ask students to draw two-column charts and in one column list words and phrases that they could use to describe how T.J. felt while he was building his rooftop garden. In the other column, they should include words and phrases to describe how he feels after he loses it. (You might point out that rooftop gardens in cities are now the new "green" thing to do.)
2. If students were going to build a garden from scratch, what would they need to do? Have students write step-by-step lists of things that they would need to do. Then have them turn these into essays, preferably of five paragraphs. In terms of organizing the information, point out that they are writing how-to essays and that sequencing—the order in which the steps need to be taken—is the best way to organize them. This sets up Exercise 4: Save the Earth: Go Green! in the unit review.

Review: Lessons 1–15

As with the previous reviews, remind students that this is not a test. These exercises are additional opportunities to review words and concepts that were introduced in previous lessons. Encourage students to refer to those lessons or to a dictionary for words they cannot recall. An overall score of 80 percent or better on a review exercise should be considered excellent.

EXERCISE 1: DEFINITIONS

Because much of the vocabulary in this unit has been difficult, you may want to develop one or more reinforcement activities to review words that are not included in this exercise or in Exercise 3. The Word Index available online will help you select additional words.

EXERCISE 4: SAVE THE EARTH: GO GREEN!

You may wish to use this as a discussion topic and ask students which ideas are practical for them and why.

EXERCISE 5: A POET'S POINT OF VIEW

During the homework preview, read the poem aloud to the class. Give students the opportunity to read it aloud during the review. Have them take turns reading complete sentences. This practice helps students break the habit of thinking that a line of poetry is always a complete sentence. After discussing their responses to questions 1 and 2, give students an opportunity to share their responses to number 3.

Because this review concludes this unit on environmental issues, allow students time during the homework review to discuss their concern or, perhaps, their lack of concern for the environment. They should be finishing up work on their class project. You may also want to make a written assignment based on any of the topics covered by their project.

Writing Activity

If your class did not participate in a class project, you may wish to conclude this unit of work with an essay relating to the theme The Good Earth. The following are some suggestions:

- What Surprised Me the Most in This Unit Was _____
- I Feel Close to Nature When _____
- The Most Urgent Environmental Problem
- The World's Natural Resources Are Being Poorly Managed
- How We Can Help Planet Earth

Life without Furnace, Pipe, or Wire

Primary emphasis
- Reading comprehension (nonfiction)
- Forming a reasoned opinion
- Outlining
- Vocabulary

Secondary emphasis
- Using context clues
- Using reference materials

Reading Selection
During the preview, tell students that the theme of this unit is Change. Introduce this reading by having the three introductory paragraphs read aloud. Ask students to name some things in their homes that would not have been found in nineteenth-century homes. During the review, students might discuss our modern concepts of comfort, leisure time, and basic necessities in relation to the description of nineteenth-century life in the reading.

EXERCISE 1: UNDERSTANDING THE READING
During the preview, discuss the value of outlining as a means of ordering information so that it can be better understood and remembered. Describe the process for students who are unfamiliar with building an outline. If students have trouble with this exercise, you may want to have them outline one or two more readings or short articles as reinforcement activities. Be sure to select readings or articles that are organized in a logical, straightforward way.

EXERCISE 2: WHAT DO YOU THINK?
Students often ask if they should answer these questions in terms of their own lives or of society in general. Encourage them to think in terms of society in general.

EXERCISE 3: USING CONTEXT CLUES
Remind students to read each quotation through for comprehension after filling in the blanks.

EXERCISE 5: INVENTORS AND THEIR INVENTIONS
Many dictionaries note only that these men were inventors, so access to an online or print encyclopedia is recommended for this exercise. If necessary, allow time for students to complete it in class.

Activities in Writing Book 8
Exercise 1 provides more practice with identifying and correcting run-on sentences, sentence fragments, and comma faults. To complete Exercise 2, students must first identify a topic and then list information from the reading as well as brainstorm their own ideas. Students should recognize that the information about what life was like in the nineteenth century without the particular convenience is only background for why the student would miss it. The latter is the focus. This is made clear in the writer's guide.

Exercise 3 takes students through organizing both sets of information for their essays. Exercise 4 offers a writing guide to help students develop their essays. The revision and editing step reminds students to check for run-on sentences, comma faults, and sentence fragments in particular.

Additional Writing Activities
1. Ask students working in pairs to list at least ten things that hadn't been invented by 1850. For the most part, they will be able to figure out items based on the reading, for example, cars, trucks, light bulbs, computers, and MP3 players. If they are unsure, make access to the Internet or a print encyclopedia available.
2. Have students imagine they are meeting time travelers from the nineteenth century and need to explain to them how to do something with one of the devices that was not around in the 1800s. Have students write how-to essays about how to operate the device.

LESSON 17
A Marriage Proposal

Primary emphasis
- Comprehension of literature (drama)
- Forming a reasoned opinion
- Predicting an ending
- Vocabulary
  1. Synonyms
  2. Monetary terms

Secondary emphasis
- Word families
- Using context clues
- Using the dictionary

The Play

In introducing this play, tell students that it is set in Russia toward the end of the 19th century. Help them to pronounce the Russian names. Have students act out the scene during the homework review. Encourage them to play the parts as broadly as they wish. If your students enjoy reading plays, you may want to bring in copies of this play and have students act out the entire play. It can be found in various anthologies.

EXERCISE 2: YOU BE THE PLAYWRIGHT

Allow students to read aloud or act out as many of their responses as they wish. Then briefly discuss how close their endings came to the actual ending of the play (see the Answer Key for a brief summary).

EXERCISE 3: MORE ABOUT ANTON CHEKHOV

Remind students to read the entire exercise through for comprehension after filling in all the blanks.

EXERCISE 4: FOREIGN CURRENCY

If you or any of your students have examples of foreign coins or paper money, it is interesting to bring these to class for the others to see.

Activities in Writing Book 8

In Exercise 1, students continue identifying and correcting run-on sentences, sentence fragments, and comma faults. Exercise 2 reviews the use of a T-chart to gather information about two sides of a problem or issue. Prewriting is a multistep process that also includes decision making and charting details.

Rather than telling students how to organize their essays, Exercise 3 asks students to identify the process by which they will organize their essays. Exercise 4 guides students through the development of their essays and reminds them to check for spelling, punctuation, and grammar problems. They should be able to apply to the task what they have learned so far.

Additional Writing Activities

1. Ask students working in pairs to create lists of at least five words or phrases to describe each of the following: Ivan, Stepan, Natalia, and Anton Chekhov (after they have complete Exercise 3).
2. Ask students to write essays to answer the question: Would you have liked to meet Anton Chekhov? Why or why not?

LESSON 18
Digital Activism: The New Change Agent

Primary emphasis
- Reading comprehension (nonfiction)
- Forming a reasoned opinion
- Writing optimistic and pessimistic responses

Secondary emphasis
- Vocabulary
- Antonyms
- Word associations
- Solving a puzzle (anagrams)

Reading Selection
The reading is about a new trend called *digital activism*. Digital activism involves using the latest technology such as the Internet and cell phones to publicize and support social or environmental causes.

Ask students if they have ever supported a cause. List some common causes that students might be familiar with such as breast cancer research, nonviolence, hunger, or global warming. Find out if any students have participated in events to support a cause. Ask them if they know of any events that have happened or are going to happen in your area. Discuss how these events (walks, fund-raising auctions, bake sales, etc.) might help to support a cause and/or spread the word about the cause.

EXERCISE 2: OPTIMISTS AND PESSIMISTS
During the preview, discuss the example and the differences between optimistic and pessimistic thinking to be sure students understand how to do this exercise. Students enjoy reading their statements aloud during the homework review. They also enjoy discussing which were easier to write—the optimists' or the pessimists' statements. If students are interested in exploring more about optimism and pessimism, ask them if they think that activists are usually optimists or pessimists? Ask them to explain their opinions.

EXERCISE 5: AN INVENTOR'S ADVICE
Remind students to fill in Franklin's words of advice as they go along and that the numbers will add up to 65 both horizontally and vertically.

Activities in Writing Book 8
Exercise 1 continues work with adding details to make writing complete, clear, and interesting. Explain to students that adding more details can also help readers to better understand the opinions or positions students are writing about. Exercise 2 takes students through the prewriting steps to gather ideas for a personal essay based on students' own causes. The organizing tools are an idea map and a detail chart. As in Lesson 17, students are not given a detail chart as a guide, but must figure one out on their own. The purpose is to get students to think on their own about what information they need to gather, organize, and plan their essays. They may need to research their causes by talking to others who are involved in them or searching the Internet to find out what can be done to support the cause.

Exercise 3 asks students to explain how they will organize their essays. Exercise 4 provides a writer's guide, and the revision and editing feature reminds students to be sure that their essays have enough details to make them clear, complete, and interesting.

Additional Writing Activities
1. Have students write about something they have done or something someone they know has done to support a particular cause.
2. Have students write paragraphs about why they chose their particular causes and what it would mean to them to see the positive change take place.

LESSON 19
The Face of Change

Primary emphasis

- Reading comprehension (autobiography and speech)
- Forming a reasoned opinion
- Create a diagram (family tree)

Secondary emphasis

- Using context clues
- Vocabulary

Reading Selection

This lesson contains excerpts from three of President Barack Obama's speeches, the first before the Democratic National Convention in 2004, which brought him to national attention; his acceptance speech at the same convention in 2008; and his speech on election night acknowledging his election as the nation's first African American president.

Introduce this selection by having the introductory paragraphs read aloud. Review the term *autobiography*. Point out that Barack Obama wrote an autobiography titled *Dreams of My Father* and that the first speech draws on his life story to illustrate how diverse the U.S. population has become over the centuries. His story is like that of many Americans.

During the homework review, you might ask students how Obama uses the life story of another African American in one of the other excerpted speeches to illustrate the continuing change in the United States. You might introduce the concept of continuity and ask students what Obama says has not changed in the last 200 years.

EXERCISE 2: WHAT DO YOU THINK?

The quotation in question 1 refers to political and social changes, though students may read it as being about or including physical or material changes.

EXERCISE 3: HISTORY IN THE MAKING

You might ask students to tell what they know about the various people, places, and events. This can give them confidence for the GED if they are taking the test.

EXERCISE 4: COMPREHENSION CHECK

Remind students that they can refer back to the reading if they are unsure of an answer. They should also use the process of elimination and intelligent guessing for questions such as number 5 that require prior knowledge or inference.

EXERCISE 5: BIOGRAPHIES AND FAMILY TREES

Be sensitive to the life stories of the students in your class. Not all students may be able to complete the family tree aspect of this exercise.

Activities in Writing Book 8

In Exercise 1, students are asked to choose what they consider the five best phrases and clauses and then explain their choices based on criteria given in the exercise. The goal is to have students reflect on what makes details interesting and how they add clarity and completeness to one's writing. Exercise 2 asks students to gather their ideas for their essays using Venn diagrams.

Exercise 3 sets up a slightly different pattern for students' essays. Instead of discussing three similarities and three differences in six separate paragraphs, students will choose one similarity or difference to highlight in a paragraph of its own. Then they will combine the remaining two or three similarities and two or three differences in one paragraph each. If you think this is too complex for your students, change the assignment to choosing one similarity or one difference and writing a five-paragraph essay about it. Students would then sketch out their own writer's guides to develop their essays.

Exercise 4 provides a writer's guide for the essay on similarities and differences. The revision and editing feature is a general reminder to check for spelling, punctuation, and grammar problems.

Additional Writing Activities

1. Have students imagine they are Ann Nixon Cooper and write letters to Barack Obama thanking him for honoring her and her life story. They should format them as business letters.
2. Have interested students complete research reports on one of the events Barack Obama mentions in his speech during which Ann Nixon Cooper was alive.

LESSON 20
Heir to Tradition

Primary emphasis
- Reading comprehension (nonfiction)
- Forming a reasoned opinion
- Interpreting poetry

Secondary emphasis
- Using references
- Vocabulary (synonyms and antonyms)
- Spelling

Reading Selection

During the homework preview, make sure that students have a sense of what the title means. This will help them to better understand the ideas presented in the reading. These ideas may be difficult for students to comprehend. Allot enough time during the general discussion and the review of the comprehension questions to be sure that students grasp the fundamental points that Overstreet makes.

EXERCISE 2: REACTING TO THE READING

As a follow-up activity to question 3, students might follow through on one or more of the ways to establish a link with the past that they have listed in their responses. For instance, if a student listed reading some of the classics, he or she could develop a reading list and give reasons for his or her selections. A student who listed visiting a museum could do so and give a report on his or her or visit. Or someone who chose to talk with older people might interview a senior citizen and write a report on the interview.

EXERCISE 3: A POEM BY LANGSTON HUGHES

As before, read the poem aloud during the preview, and give students the opportunity to read it aloud during the review. Have an atlas or world map available so students can locate the various rivers. Discuss how this poem and the reading selection relate to the theme of this unit, Change.

EXERCISE 5: SPELLING CHECK

Two of the incorrect words in this exercise are spelled correctly. Because of the context, however, the following are incorrect:
1. Sentence 5—*foul* should be *fowl*
2. Sentence 10—*forth* should be *fourth*

A suggested follow-up activity is to have students gather information about other holiday traditions to present to the class.

Activities in Writing Book 8

Exercise 1 continues work with details. Exercise 2 focuses on a personal topic and takes students through gathering information by brainstorming and then creating a detail chart. Exercise 4 provides a writer's guide, and the revision and editing feature is a general reminder about what to look for.

Additional Writing Activity

It would be useful as a concluding activity to have students create their own general writer's guides that they could follow for any five-paragraph essays that they have to write.

Review: Lessons 1–20

As with the previous reviews, this last review is not to be perceived as a test but rather as a final opportunity to work with many of the words and concepts introduced in Book 8.

After any necessary corrections have been made by the students during the homework review, spend some time reviewing and evaluating the students' progress. In keeping with the theme of this unit, try to focus on the concept of change. Have students noticed a change in their reading ability? Have they experienced any changes in their thoughts about reading or about learning in general? How have they seen their writing improve over time? What do they think was the single biggest help in improving their writing? What writing tools will they take with them from these activities?

This is also an opportunity for you to share your perceptions. Needless to say, the emphasis should be placed on growth, for it is hoped that at least some of the readings in this workbook will have aroused the students' curiosity to learn more—to see that they are far more than "the powers and limitations they were born with" (Overstreet).

Writing Activity

The Review section of the Writing Book asks students to reflect on what they have learned about gathering information and organizing it in prewriting and drafting activities. Students may not be aware that they have been learning a process, and these exercises offer the opportunity to formalize this instruction and create takeaways.

Challenger Writing 5

Lesson 1

1 USE THESE WORDS IN SENTENCES.
Answers may vary.

2 WHAT DO YOU THINK?
Answers may vary.

3 COMBINE THE SENTENCES.
Answers may vary. Some possible answers are:

1. Grandmother was happy to see Grandpa, but then she got angry.
2. Grandpa never earned much, but (yet) the family always had food on the table, and they also had clothes to wear. *Or* Grandpa never earned much, but (yet) the family always had food on the table and clothes to wear. *Or* Although Grandpa never earned much, the family always had food on the table and clothes to wear.

4 WRITE PARAGRAPHS.
Answers may vary.

Lesson 2

1 USE THESE WORDS IN SENTENCES.
Answers may vary.

2 WHAT DO YOU THINK?
Answers may vary.

3 COMBINE THE SENTENCES.
Answers may vary. Ask students for the rule about using commas after introductory clauses. Some possible answers are:

1. When King Midas touched the roses, they lost their red color and (they) turned to gold. *Or* Because King Midas touched the roses, they lost their red color and (they) turned to gold.
2. Although Bacchus thought that Midas's wish was strange, he granted it anyway. *Or* Bacchus granted Midas's wish anyway, although he thought it was strange.
3. Before Midas got his wish, he had always wanted more and more gold.

4 WRITE THREE PARAGRAPHS.
Answers may vary.

Lesson 3

1 USE THESE WORDS IN SENTENCES.
Answers may vary.

2 WHAT DO YOU THINK?
Answers may vary.

3 COMBINE THE SENTENCES.
Answers may vary. Some possible answers are:

1. As the officer walks closer to Tango, he does not move and (he) salutes the officer. *Or* Tango does not move and salutes as the officer walks closer.
2. The Boss and the Eel rob the house while Tango walks slowly up and down the street. *Or* While the Boss and the Eel rob the house, Tango walks slowly up and down the street.

4 WRITE PARAGRAPHS.
Answers may vary.

Lesson 4

1 USE THESE WORDS AND PHRASES IN SENTENCES.
Answers may vary.

2 WHAT DO YOU THINK?
Answers may vary.

3 COMBINE THE SENTENCES.
Answers may vary. Some possible answers are:

1. The officer was checking doors on the dark street, and a man was standing in one doorway.
2. After the officer moved on, the man stood for another ten minutes before he looked at his watch again.
3. The West had treated the man well, and he wished his friend had gone with him because they would have been great together.

4 WRITE PARAGRAPHS.
Answers may vary.

Lesson 5

1 USE THESE WORDS AND PHRASES IN SENTENCES.
Answers may vary.

2 WHAT DO YOU THINK?
Answers may vary.

3 COMBINE THE SENTENCES.
Answers may vary. Some possible answers are:

1. George unlocks the case and (he) brings out rings with different prices.
2. The cowboy pays by check, and George cashes the check the next morning.
3. George thinks of a plan, but first he needs to make sure the check is good.

4 WRITE PARAGRAPHS.
Answers may vary.

Lesson 6

1 USE THESE WORDS AND PHRASES IN SENTENCES.
Answers may vary.

2 WHAT DO YOU THINK?
Answers may vary.

3 COMBINE THE SENTENCES.
Answers may vary. Some possible answers are:
1. Mr. Green pushed in front of George to meet Mr. James, who was dressed differently.
2. Looking like she would faint, Miss Barns moved to the door and locked (it) the door. *Or* Miss Barns, looking like she would faint, moved to the door and locked it. *Or* Miss Barns looked like she would faint, but she moved to the door and locked it.

4 WRITE A PARAGRAPH.
Answers may vary.

Lesson 7

1 USE THESE WORDS AND PHRASES IN SENTENCES.
Answers may vary.

2 WHAT DO YOU THINK?
Answers may vary.

3 COMBINE THE SENTENCES.
Answers may vary. Some possible answers are:
1. Granny and Christie had a special relationship that was based on love and respect. *Or* Granny and Christie had a special relationship, and it was based on love and respect.
2. Granny, talking very softly, told her story, and everyone listened quietly. *Or* Granny talked very softly and told her story while everyone listened quietly.
3. Kate's father got sick, and they couldn't afford to take care of the baby, so they gave the baby away. *Or* When Kate's father got sick, they couldn't take care of the baby, so they gave the baby away. *Or* Because Kate's father got sick and they couldn't afford to take care of the baby, they gave the baby away.

4 WRITE A PARAGRAPH.
Answers may vary.

Lesson 8

1 USE THESE WORDS AND PHRASES IN SENTENCES.
Answers may vary.

2 WHAT DO YOU THINK?
Answers may vary.

3 COMBINE THE SENTENCES.
Answers may vary. Some possible answers are:
1. As the men raced to the eight baskets of golden coins, they never wondered how the coins got there. *Or* The men raced to the eight baskets of golden coins, but they never wondered how they got there.
2. The boy said that Death had killed the drunk and (he) called Death a "sneak thief," but the young men laughed and said they would kill Death.
3. One man tricks the youngest into going for food and drink and gets the third man to agree to kill the youngest, but the youngest decides to poison the other two. *Or* Tricking the youngest into going for food and drink, one man gets the third man to agree to kill the youngest, and the youngest decides to poison the other two.

4 WRITE A PARAGRAPH.
Answers may vary.

Lesson 9

1 LIST WORDS AND PHRASES TO USE IN SENTENCES.
1. Answers may vary.
2. Answers may vary.

2 What Do You Think?
Answers may vary.

3 PUT THESE SENTENCES IN ORDER.
Answers vary for the inclusion of transitions. The following correct order of events in the story also indicates some possible uses of transitions:
First, Arthur and his forces fought Mordred and his men.
Arthur was wounded, and his knights carried him to a chapel.
Soon Arthur heard cries from the battlefield.
Sir Lucan ran to the battlefield to see who was crying out.
Robbers were taking rings and gold from the knights.
Next, to save the king, Sir Lucan and Sir Bedivere lifted the king to carry him away.
Then Sir Lucan fell back and died.
At last, Arthur felt that he was dying and asked Sir Bedivere to throw Excalibur into the lake.

4 WRITE A PARAGRAPH.
Answers may vary.

Lesson 10

1 LIST WORDS AND PHRASES TO USE IN SENTENCES.
1. Answers may vary.
2. Answers may vary.

2 WHAT WOULD YOU LIKE TO KNOW?
Answers may vary.

3 PUT THESE SENTENCES IN ORDER.
Answers vary for the inclusion of transitions. The following correct order of events in the story also indicates some possible uses of transitions:
The ranch prospered with Hank's hard work.
Then Hank got cancer and died.

Eleanor would tell Hank Jr. to do chores around the ranch, but he wasn't much help.

After a while, Hank Jr. enlisted in the army.

Eleanor borrowed money from the bank, a little bit at a time.

Later Eleanor began borrowing money to pay the interest on what she had borrowed.

The bank manager came to talk to Eleanor about past-due notices on her payments.

Then the bank manager said that Eleanor would lose her ranch and have to move.

Now Eleanor saw a car coming toward the ranch.

4 WRITE AN ESSAY.

Answers may vary.

Lesson 11

1 LIST WORDS AND PHRASES TO USE IN SENTENCES.

1. Answers may vary.
2. Answers may vary.

2 WHAT WOULD YOU LIKE TO KNOW?

Answers may vary.

3 UNSCRAMBLE THE SENTENCES.

The boldface terms indicate placement of the transitions that add information.

1. **In addition** to the loud knocking on the door, they heard something moving on the roof.
2. Breakfast dishes covered the table, and the coffeepot **as well as** the television was still turned on.
3. **Another** reason I'm scared is that I can see them out of the corner of my eye.

4 WRITE AN ESSAY.

Answers may vary.

Lesson 12

1 USE THESE WORDS AND PHRASES IN SENTENCES.

Answers may vary.

2 ADD DETAILS.

Answers may vary. Some possible answers are:
1. The shy historian sits among his many books in his quiet room silently writing. *Or* The shy historian sits silently writing among his many books in his quiet room.
2. General Grant, tired from battle, slid off his dusty gray horse and walked alone into the cool green wood. *Or* Tired from battle, General Grant slid off his dusty gray horse and walked alone into the cool green wood.

3 UNSCRAMBLE THE SENTENCES.

The boldface terms indicate placement of the transitions that add information.

1. The historian says that his wife is quiet **as well as shy** and has black hair turning gray.
2. **Besides** writing his books, the historian thinks about why he cannot connect with his wife who **also** is shy and quiet.

4 WRITE AN ESSAY.

Answers may vary.

Lesson 13

1 LIST WORDS AND PHRASES TO USE IN SENTENCES.

Answers may vary.

2 ADD DETAILS.

Answers may vary. Some possible answers are:
1. The black crow spied dirty water inside the cracked green pitcher. *Or* The black crow spied water inside the dirty cracked green pitcher.
2. The skinny gray wolf leaped over the wooden fence and met face to face with a fat brown collie.

3 WRITE A DESCRIPTIVE PARAGRAPH.

Answers may vary.

Lesson 14

1 CHOOSE THE BEST DESCRIPTIVE WORDS AND PHRASES.

Answers may vary.

2 TRY YOUR HAND AT USING DETAILS.

Answers may vary.

3 WHAT WILL YOU WRITE ABOUT?

Answers may vary.

4 WRITE A DESCRIPTIVE PARAGRAPH.

Answers may vary.

Lesson 15

1 CHOOSE THE BEST DESCRIPTIVE WORDS AND PHRASES.

Answers may vary.

2 TRY YOUR HAND AT USING DETAILS.

Answers may vary.

3 WHAT WILL YOU WRITE ABOUT?

Answers may vary.

4 WRITE A DESCRIPTIVE PARAGRAPH.

Answers may vary.

Lesson 16

1 IS IT ONE OR MORE THAN ONE?

1. starts, jump
2. is, seems
3. see, learns, wonder

2 USE THESE WORDS AND PHRASES IN SENTENCES.

Answers may vary. Be sure students use correct subject-verb agreement.

3 WHAT WILL YOU WRITE ABOUT?

1. A teacher and a student are fighting.

2. Mr. Stuart, the teacher; Guy, the student
3. schoolroom
4. at the end of a school day
5. Answers may vary. Some possible answers are: Guy doesn't like Mr. Stuart, but the reason is unclear. He beat up Mr. Stuart's sister when she tried to teach in the school. Mr. Stuart says that he has to fight Guy. He has to prove that he has a right to be the teacher.
6. Mr. Stuart defeats Guy, and Guy accepts his defeat in a fair fight.

4 WRITE A SUMMARY PARAGRAPH.

Answers may vary.

Lesson 17

1 LIST WORDS AND PHRASES TO USE IN SENTENCES.

Answers may vary.

2 COMBINE THE SENTENCES.

Answers may vary. Some possible answers are:

1. The real marshal was a nice guy to pretend he was the prisoner and save Mr. Easton from being embarrassed. *Or* The real marshal was a nice guy to pretend he was the prisoner to save Mr. Easton from embarrassment.
2. Once Miss Fairchild recognized Mr. Easton, she became confused. *Or* When Miss Fairchild recognized Mr. Easton, she became confused. *Or* At first, when Miss Fairchild recognized Mr. Easton, she became confused.
3. Mr. Easton probably counterfeited money in Washington because he was living there among rich people, but he wasn't rich. *Or* Mr. Easton probably counterfeited money when he lived in Washington because he wasn't rich, but he was living among rich people.

3 WHAT WILL YOU WRITE ABOUT?

Answers may vary.

4 WRITE A THREE-PARAGRAPH SUMMARY.

Answers may vary.

Lesson 18

1 CHOOSE THE BEST DESCRIPTIVE WORDS AND PHRASES.

Answers may vary.

2 USE PRONOUNS IN SENTENCES.

1. him, me, us
2. he, her, him
3. she, I

3 WHAT WILL YOU WRITE ABOUT?

Answers may vary.

4 WRITE A THREE-PARAGRAPH SUMMARY.

Answers may vary.

Lesson 19

1 CHOOSE THE BEST DESCRIPTIVE WORDS AND PHRASES.

Answers may vary.

2 USE PRONOUNS IN SENTENCES.

1. who
2. which
3. whom

3 WHAT WILL YOU WRITE ABOUT?

Answers may vary.

4 WRITE A THREE-PARAGRAPH ESSAY.

Answers may vary.

Lesson 20

1 CHOOSE THE BEST DESCRIPTIVE WORDS AND PHRASES.

Answers may vary.

2 USE PRONOUNS IN SENTENCES.

1. whose
2. which
3. whom
4. what

3 WHAT WILL YOU WRITE ABOUT?

Answers may vary.

4 WRITE A THREE-PARAGRAPH ESSAY.

Answers may vary.

Review

1 LIST DESCRIPTIVE WORDS AND PHRASES TO WRITE ABOUT.

Answers may vary.

2 USE DESCRIPTIVE WORDS AND PHRASES IN SENTENCES.

Answers may vary.

3 WHAT WILL YOU WRITE ABOUT?

Answers may vary.

4 PUT SENTENCES IN CORRECT TIME ORDER.

Answers may vary.

5 WRITE A THREE-PARAGRAPH SUMMARY.

Answers may vary.

6 WRITE A THREE-PARAGRAPH ESSAY.

Answers may vary.

7 WRITE A DESCRIPTIVE PARAGRAPH.

Answers may vary.

Challenger Writing 6

Lesson 1

1 USE THESE WORDS AND PHRASES IN SENTENCES.

Answers may vary.

2 ADD DETAILS.

Answers may vary. Some possible answers are:

1. Being obese can lead to health problems such as diabetes, high blood pressure, and high cholesterol.
2. A hundred years ago, people had to go from the butcher to the baker to the outdoor vegetable and fruit market to buy food.
3. Reading food labels is important because they tell you about calories, fats, sugars, carbohydrates, and serving sizes.

3 WHAT WILL YOU WRITE ABOUT?

The main idea of the list of healthy tips is provided because the paragraph is unusual in that it is a list itself.

Paragraph 1: Reading food labels is one way to check if a person is getting good nutrition.

Paragraph 2: How much a person eats, how slowly, and how often make a difference in healthy eating.

Paragraph 3: Exercise is good for everyone, whether or not they are trying to lose weight.

Paragraph 4: A person can get exercise in a variety of ways.

Paragraph 5: The article also offers some other tips including eating and drinking foods that are low in fat and calories, packing lunch, comparing labels, and not skipping meals.

Paragraph 6: Working together, a whole family can make good choices for a healthier family life.

4 WRITE A ONE-PARAGRAPH SUMMARY.

Answers may vary.

Lesson 2

1 USE THESE WORDS AND PHRASES IN SENTENCES.

Answers may vary.

2 ADD DETAILS.

Answers may vary. Some possible answers are:

1. Immigrants in the 1800s came from many countries such as Ireland, Germany, Italy, Romania, and Hungary.
2. The Census counts the nation's population and tells us how many people we are, who we are, and what we do.
3. Immigrants have come for many reasons. Some have come because of crop failures or poverty, and some were forced to come as slaves.

3 WHAT WILL YOU WRITE ABOUT?

Answers may vary. Some possible answers are:

Paragraph 7: Since the early 1900s, most Americans are from somewhere else. They have come from other countries, including Italy, England, Ireland, and Germany.

Paragraph 8: Starting in 1620, settlers from Europe and Africa have come to America for a number of reasons. This includes coming because of poverty, coming to start over, coming due to famine, or coming because they were forced.

Paragraph 9: Today immigrants are still coming to America. They are coming from countries such as Mexico, China, and Vietnam. Several states, including California, New York, and Texas, have high immigrant populations.

Paragraph 10: New immigrants join their communities and get involved. This helps the "new family picture" to form.

4 WRITE A ONE-PARAGRAPH SUMMARY.

Answers may vary.

Lesson 3

1 USE THESE WORDS AND PHRASES IN SENTENCES.

Answers may vary.

2 ADD DETAILS.

Answers may vary. Some possible answers are:

1. Genes carry important information in cells. They determine a person's hair and skin color, height, and the way the person will look.
2. Even identical twins can be different in their interests and what they are good at.
3. It is expensive to have twins because you need two of everything.

3 WHAT WILL YOU WRITE ABOUT?

Main Idea: The article is about what causes multiple babies and what life is like for parents who have two or more children born at once.

Paragraph 2: Superstitious beliefs about twins have persisted for centuries.

Paragraph 3: Identical twins come from one egg that splits into two embryos.

Paragraph 4: Fraternal twins are created when separate eggs form into embryos at the same time.

Paragraph 5: The overall rate of multiple births has been increasing.

Paragraph 6: In general, the chance of giving birth to twins in the 21st century is about three percent.

Paragraph 9: People who don't have multiples have no idea about the work involved.

Paragraph 10: Parents must decide which ways of coping with their multiples work best.

Paragraph 11: Having multiples is expensive.

Paragraph 13: Twins may grow up in the same house and be treated the same, but they can turn out very differently.

4 WRITE A ONE-PARAGRAPH SUMMARY.

Answers may vary.

Lesson 4

1 USE THESE WORDS AND PHRASES IN SENTENCES.

Answers may vary.

2 COMBINE THE SENTENCES.

Answers may vary. Some possible answers are:

1. Grandma Janey was forgetful, and she always complained about the food.
2. Alzheimer's disease attacks nerve cells, so people begin to forget things. *Or* Because Alzheimer's disease attacks nerve cells, people begin to forget things.
3. When Grandma Janey began forgetting her lines and acting confused, she stopped acting. *Or* Because Grandma Janey began forgetting her lines and acting confused, she stopped acting.

3 WHAT WILL YOU WRITE ABOUT?

1. Lisa, Grandma Janey, and Marcia, Lisa's mother
2. Lisa and her mother are fixing lunch for Grandma Janey. Then they stop at the drugstore to get a prescription filled for Grandma Janey. Lisa and her mother talk about Alzheimer's disease and other diseases that affect older people. Lisa worries that her mother will get sick and she will have to take care of her.
3. probably now
4. where Grandma Janey lives and at a drugstore
5. Lisa and her mother visit Grandma Janey every week to make lunch, and this is one of those times.
6. Lisa's mother reassures her that she takes good care of herself and also that there may not be so many illnesses when Lisa's mother is Grandma Janey's age.

4 WRITE A ONE-PARAGRAPH SUMMARY.

Answers may vary.

Lessons 5

1 USE THESE WORDS AND PHRASES IN SENTENCES.

Answers may vary.

2 COMBINE THE SENTENCES.

Answers may vary. Some possible answers are:

1. Saving money can be hard, but there are ways to save, and you have to be willing to try. *Or* Saving money can be hard, but there are ways to save if you are willing to try.
2. When you use a grocery list, you save money because you don't buy things you don't need for the week's meals. *Or*

When you use a grocery list, you don't buy things you don't need for the week's meals, and you save money.

3. Although people try not to overspend, they can still get into trouble with debt when they buy on impulse.

3 WHAT WILL YOU WRITE ABOUT?

Answers for the important details may vary. While students may copy the main ideas word for word from the article, they should reword the ideas when they write their summaries.

Main Idea: There are some practical things that people can do to change their buying behavior and save money.

Paragraph 1: Use what you have more efficiently.

Paragraph 2: Don't waste food.

Paragraph 3: Redecorate on a budget.

Paragraph 4: Sell unwanted items.

Paragraph 5: Say "no" to things you can't pay for.

Paragraph 6: Make a list before you shop.

Paragraph 7: Say "yes" to things you can do for free.

Paragraph 8: Hold a family meeting.

4 WRITE A THREE-PARAGRAPH SUMMARY.

Answers may vary.

Lesson 6

1 CHOOSE THE BEST DESCRIPTIVE WORDS AND PHRASES.

Answers may vary.

2 COMBINE THE SENTENCES.

Answers may vary. Some possible answers are:

1. "You're fired" is a TV joke today, but in the Great Depression, it was very serious.
2. An empty milk bottle had value because you could turn it in for a nickel, and a nickel got you a ride on the subway.

3 WHAT WILL YOU WRITE ABOUT?

Answers may vary.

4 WRITE A DESCRIPTIVE PARAGRAPH.

Answers may vary.

Lesson 7

1 CHOOSE THE BEST DESCRIPTIVE WORDS AND PHRASES.

Answers may vary.

2 COMBINE THE SENTENCES.

Answers may vary. Some possible answers are:

1. When John Quincy Adams was defeated for president in 1828, he became depressed and (he) shut himself off from others.
2. After Adams ran for president and was defeated, he ran for Congress in 1830 and (he) won.
3. Because Adams had fought slavery, many people paid their respects.

3 WHAT WILL YOU WRITE ABOUT?

Answers may vary. Students will find details about his looks in the article but will need to infer personal qualities such as dedicated, moral, and courageous.

4 WRITE A DESCRIPTIVE PARAGRAPH.

Answers may vary.

Lesson 8

1 CHOOSE THE BEST DESCRIPTIVE WORDS AND PHRASES.

Answers may vary.

2 COMBINE THE SENTENCES.

Answers may vary. Some possible answers are:

1. A job search is hard, can feel impossible, and can take what seems like forever. *Or* A job search is hard and can feel impossible and seem to take forever.
2. Telecommuters work from home, reducing their daily drives, saving money on gas, and helping the environment. *Or* By working from home, telecommuters reduce their daily drives, save money on gas, and help the environment.

3 WHAT WILL YOU WRITE ABOUT?

Strategies are listed below, but the details chosen may vary.

1. Trust the experts.
2. Learn new skills, if necessary, to apply online.
3. Network online.
4. Learn and use new strategies for online searching.
5. Learn and benefit from changes in the traditional job search and the job market.

4 WRITE A THREE-PARAGRAPH SUMMARY.

Answers may vary.

Lesson 9

1 TRY YOUR HAND AT USING DETAILS.

Answers may vary.

2 COMBINE THE SENTENCES.

Answers may vary. Some possible answers are:

1. Selection interviews take several forms including one-on-one or group interviews and a work sample.
2. I always find that a thank-you note is a good idea because it shows that you are still interested in the job and (you) realize the time that people took with you.
3. Benefits like health care, life insurance, holidays, and sick days are important, and you should consider their value along with salary. *Or* Consider the value of important benefits like health care, life insurance, and paid holidays and sick days along with the value of the salary.

3 WHAT WILL YOU WRITE ABOUT?

Answers may vary.

4 WRITE A THREE-PARAGRAPH EXPOSITORY ESSAY.

Answers may vary.

Lesson 10

1 CHOOSE THE BEST DESCRIPTIVE WORDS AND PHRASES.

Answers may vary.

2 COMBINE THE SENTENCES.

Answers may vary. Some possible answers are:

1. Tom laughed to himself and couldn't believe his good luck that there were so many silly boys to trick. *Or* Laughing to himself, Tom couldn't believe his good luck that there were so many silly boys to trick.
2. Ben Rogers was the first boy to fall for Tom's trick, and giving up his apple, he couldn't wait to whitewash. *Or* Ben Rogers was the first boy to fall for Tom's trick, and he couldn't wait to whitewash, so he gave up his apple.
3. The boys gave up marbles, a piece of glass, a useless key, a doorknob, and many other things that seemed like junk to me, but they were important to them.

3 WHAT WILL YOU WRITE ABOUT?

Answers may vary. Some possible answers are:

1. Tom Sawyer, Ben Rogers, other boys
2. Tom is supposed to whitewash his Aunt Polly's 30-yard-long by 9-foot-high fence. He doesn't want to and figures out how to trick other boys into doing the work for him—and paying him for being allowed to paint the fence.
3. Saturday morning in summer
4. on the street in front of Aunt Polly's house
5. Tom doesn't want to paint the fence. He wants to have fun.
6. Tom makes it seem that whitewashing the fence is something special—important and fun.

4 WRITE A THREE-PARAGRAPH EXPOSITORY ESSAY.

Answers may vary.

Lesson 11

1 TRY YOUR HAND AT USING DETAILS.

Answers may vary.

2 ADD TRANSITIONS.

The words in bold below are possible uses of transitions.

1. **Most** people were asleep.
2. George rang to signal that full steam was needed.
3. **Right away** four of the boilers exploded with a terrible noise.
4. **Soon** fire broke out.
5. **Then** passengers began fighting for the safety of a wood boat.
6. **Next**, Henry fell in the river.
7. **Then** Henry swam back to the boat to help others.

3 WHAT WILL YOU WRITE ABOUT?

Answers may vary.

4 WRITE AN EXPOSITORY PARAGRAPH.

Answers may vary.

Lesson 12

1 CHOOSE THE BEST DESCRIPTIVE WORDS AND PHRASES.

Answers may vary.

2 ADD TRANSITIONS.

Answers may vary. Some possible answers are:

1. Because the first cars were very noisy, horses were frightened of them. *Or* The first cars were very noisy, so horses were frightened of them.
2. Tires could blow out miles from help. Consequently, motorists carried blowout patches, French chalk, and tire irons. *Or* Because tires could blow out miles from help, motorists carried blowout patches, French chalk, and tire irons.
3. More cars on the road resulted in more accidents, so getting a driver's license became harder and car inspections began. *Or* Because there were more cars and more accidents, getting a driver's license became harder and car inspections began.

3 WHAT WILL YOU WRITE ABOUT?

Causes: 1. A car had to be made that the average American could afford, depend on, and take care of without too much difficulty. 2. Good roads had to be built. 3. Garages and filling stations had to be plentiful.

Effects: Answers may vary.

4 WRITE A FOUR-PARAGRAPH EXPOSITORY ESSAY.

Answers may vary.

Lesson 13

1 TRY YOUR HAND AT USING DETAILS.

Answers may vary.

2 ADD TRANSITIONS.

Answers may vary. Some possible answers are:

1. Before he left to meet the young woman he loved, his aunt gave Richard a ring that had been his mother's. *Or* When he was leaving to meet the young woman he loved, his aunt gave Richard a ring that had been his mother's.
2. Because the traffic jam kept Richard and the young woman in the cab for two hours, he was able to tell her how much he loved her. *Or* As a result of the traffic jam that lasted two hours, Richard was able to tell the young woman how much he loved her. *Or* The traffic jam kept Richard and the young woman in the cab for two hours. Consequently, Richard was able to tell her how much he loved her.
3. Anthony Rockwall paid the drivers to create a traffic jam because he loved his son.

3 WHAT WILL YOU WRITE ABOUT?

Answers may vary.

4 WRITE A THREE-PARAGRAPH EXPOSITORY ESSAY.

Answers may vary.

Lesson 14

1 CHOOSE THE BEST DESCRIPTIVE WORDS AND PHRASES.

Answers may vary.

2 ADD TRANSITIONS.

Answers may vary. Some possible answers are:

1. Unlike the first Russian woman in space who had little training, Ride had years of training. *Or* In contrast to the first Russian woman in space who had little training, Ride had years of training.
2. Just like male astronauts, Ride spent many years training for space.
3. Ride's family ate meals whenever they wanted, unlike many families who eat dinner together. *Or* Although many families eat dinner together, Ride's family ate meals whenever they wanted.

3 WHAT WILL YOU WRITE ABOUT?

Answers may vary.

4 WRITE A THREE-PARAGRAPH EXPOSITORY ESSAY.

Answers may vary.

Lesson 15

1 CHOOSE THE BEST DESCRIPTIVE WORDS AND PHRASES.

Answers may vary.

2 ADD TRANSITIONS.

Answers may vary. Some possible answers are:

1. It is hard to believe, but no one remembers the two men who rowed across the Atlantic. *Or* It is hard to believe, yet no one remembers the two men who rowed across the Atlantic.
2. Harbo and Samuelson wanted adventure. Instead they almost died.
3. Like early explorers, Harbo and Samuelson were looking for adventure. *Or* Early explorers wanted adventure, and Harbo and Samuelson were looking for adventure, too.
4. Although no one remembers Harbo and Samuelson today, in their day they were famous for a time. *Or* No one remembers Harbo and Samuelson today. However, in their day, they were famous for a time.

3 WHAT WILL YOU WRITE ABOUT?

Answers may vary.

4 WRITE A PERSUASIVE PARAGRAPH.

Answers may vary.

Lesson 16

1 TRY YOUR HAND AT USING DETAILS.
Answers may vary.

2 IS IT ONE OR MORE THAN ONE?
Answers may vary. Some possible answers are:
1. Rosella Rice writes that Johnny Appleseed has long hair and a beard.
2. We bake apple pies for holidays, and they disappear quickly.
3. Insects damage apple trees no matter how hard farmers try to stop them.

3 WHAT WILL YOU WRITE ABOUT?
Answers may vary.

4 WRITE A PERSUASIVE PARAGRAPH.
Answers may vary.

Lesson 17

1 IS IT ONE OR MORE THAN ONE?
Answers may vary.

2 USE PRONOUNS IN SENTENCES.
1. He and I share lunch sometimes, but we always use separate dishes and forks.
2. She and Bill try hard to eat healthy food, but they sometimes eat fast-food lunches.
3. Bill gave her and me the list of things we should do to stay healthy.

3 WHAT WILL YOU WRITE ABOUT?
Answers may vary.

4 WRITE A PERSUASIVE PARAGRAPH.
Answers may vary.

Lesson 18

1 TRY YOUR HAND AT USING DETAILS.
Answers may vary.

2 USE PRONOUNS IN SENTENCES.
1. Walter, who is worried about being late, hurries into the bathroom.
2. Ruth puts the breakfast on the table that has Walter's paper on it.
3. Travis probably wonders whom he can ask next for the fifty cents.

3 WHAT WILL YOU WRITE ABOUT?
Answers may vary.

4 WRITE A THREE-PARAGRAPH EXPOSITORY ESSAY.
Answers may vary.

Lesson 19

1 TRY YOUR HAND AT USING DETAILS.
Answers may vary.

2 USE PRONOUNS IN SENTENCES.
1. What is that fruit?
2. To whom did he give the breakfast?
3. Whose is that breakfast?

3 WHAT WILL YOU WRITE ABOUT?
Answers may vary.

4 WRITE A THREE-PARAGRAPH EXPOSITORY ESSAY.
Answers may vary.

Lesson 20

1 TRY YOUR HAND AT USING DETAILS.
Answers may vary.

2 USE PRONOUNS IN SENTENCES.
Answers may vary. You may need to review the different uses in sentences of *who* and *whom*.

3 WHAT WILL YOU WRITE ABOUT?
Answers may vary.

4 WRITE A THREE-PARAGRAPH EXPOSITORY ESSAY.
Answers may vary.

Review

1 LIST DESCRIPTIVE WORDS AND PHRASES TO WRITE ABOUT.
Answers may vary.

2 USE DESCRIPTIVE WORDS AND PHRASES IN SENTENCES.
Answers may vary.

3 WHAT WILL YOU WRITE ABOUT?
Answers may vary.

4 PUT SENTENCES IN CORRECT TIME ORDER.
Answers may vary.

5 WRITE A THREE-PARAGRAPH SUMMARY.
Answers may vary.

6 WRITE A THREE-PARAGRAPH EXPOSITORY ESSAY.
Answers may vary.

7 WRITE A DESCRIPTIVE PARAGRAPH.
Answers may vary.

8 WRITE A PERSUASIVE PARAGRAPH.
Answers may vary.

Challenger Writing 7

Lesson 1

1 CHOOSE THE BEST DESCRIPTIVE WORDS AND PHRASES.

Answers may vary.

2 ADD DETAILS.

Answers may vary. Some possible answers are:

1. Kyle was worried and upset over his little sister Maggie's grim news.
2. Kyle watched the calm sea and the seagulls circling over the slowly moving ship.
3. Three years ago there had been a deadly car accident that left is mom dead and his dad angry and depressed.

3 WHAT WILL YOU WRITE ABOUT?

1. Kyle, Salama, Maggie
2. Kyle has been away for years. His sister Maggie tells him that she is very sick, and he doesn't know how he will get money to help her. His friend Salama steals money from the shipping company to give Kyle to help her. Kyle is worried about taking it, but in the end, Kyle takes it.
3. on a ship
4. as the ship is docking in New York
5. Kyle's sister is sick and needs help.
6. Kyle takes the money after he sees his sister on the dock.

4 WRITE A THREE-PARAGRAPH SUMMARY.

Answers may vary.

Lesson 2

1 CHOOSE THE BEST DESCRIPTIVE WORDS AND PHRASES.

Answers may vary.

2 ADD DETAILS.

Answers may vary.

3 WHAT WILL YOU WRITE ABOUT?

Answers may vary.

4 WRITE A THREE-PARAGRAPH EXPOSITORY ESSAY.

Answers may vary.

Lesson 3

1 CHOOSE THE BEST DESCRIPTIVE WORDS AND PHRASES.

Answers may vary.

2 TRY YOUR HAND AT USING DETAILS.

Answers may vary.

3 WHAT WILL YOU WRITE ABOUT?

1. Henry Manning, Jerome Smith

2. Manning has stolen money from the bank where he works. Before he is arrested, he buries $10,000 under a spruce tree in Jerome Smith's yard. When Manning gets out of prison, he goes to get his money but realizes he can't just dig it up. People will see him, so he changes his appearance and gets a job as a mechanic in the garage where Smith takes his car.
3. in the bank, in a housing division
4. just before Manning is arrested, 3½ years later
5. Manning has stolen money from his bank and wants to hide it so he can have it when he gets out of prison.
6. Manning figures out how he can get the money. He'll wait, work, and save his money, and when the Smiths are ready to move, he'll buy the house.

4 WRITE A THREE-PARAGRAPH SUMMARY.

Answers may vary.

Lesson 4

1 CHOOSE THE BEST DESCRIPTIVE WORDS AND PHRASES.

Answers may vary.

2 ADD TRANSITIONS.

5, 3, 4, 6, 1, 2

The choice of transitions and their placement may vary, but the following are possible answers.

Henry hatches a plan to become friendly with the Smiths.

So Henry strikes up a friendship with Constance Smith.

Jerome Smith writes to Constance that he wants a divorce.

Then Henry starts to visit Constance without the excuse of taking care of her car.

Finally Henry proposes to Constance.

Henry becomes the successful owner of the garage and an auto dealership.

3 WHAT WILL YOU WRITE ABOUT?

Answers may vary.

4 WRITE A THREE-PARAGRAPH EXPOSITORY ESSAY.

Answers may vary.

Lesson 5

1 CHOOSE THE BEST DESCRIPTIVE WORDS AND PHRASES.

Answers may vary.

2 ADD TRANSITIONS.

7, 5, 1, 3, 8, 2, 6, 4

The choice of transitions and their placement may vary, but the following are possible answers.

Alfred has to empty his pockets.

Next, Mr. Carr tells Alfred he is going to turn him over to the police.

Mrs. Higgins asks Mr. Carr what has happened.

Then Mrs. Higgins explains that sometimes it takes a while for people to grow up.

Mr. Carr respects Mrs. Higgins' quiet dignity and goodness.

Mrs. Higgins walks fast and won't let Alfred talk.

Later Mrs. Higgins pours herself a cup of tea and sighs.

Alfred feels like he has never really seen his mother before.

3 WHAT WILL YOU WRITE ABOUT?

1. Alfred Higgins, Sam Carr, Mrs. Higgins
2. Mr. Carr catches Alfred stealing from his drugstore where he works. Mr. Carr says he will turn Alfred over to the police but calls Alfred's mother, who hurries to the drugstore. Her calm and quiet dignity and her goodness convince Mr. Carr to let Alfred go. Alfred can't figure out his mother. When they get home, he sees how old she looks and feels as if he has never really seen his mother before.
3. at night
4. drugstore, street, Higgins' home
5. Alfred has stolen from his employer, Sam Carr.
6. As he looks at his mother, Alfred feels as if his youth is over.

4 WRITE A THREE-PARAGRAPH SUMMARY.

Answers may vary.

Lesson 6

1 CHOOSE THE BEST DESCRIPTIVE WORDS AND PHRASES.

Answers may vary.

2 ADD TRANSITIONS.

The choice of transitions and their placement may vary, but the following are possible answers.

1. People were willing to watch, but not to help. For example, no one called the police.
2. The gang members attacked Harry. They also knocked over the newsstand.
3. The story says a lot about people. First, people in a crowd do what the crowd does. Second, people put their own safety ahead of helping anyone else.

3 WHAT WILL YOU WRITE ABOUT?

Answers may vary.

4 WRITE A THREE-PARAGRAPH EXPOSITORY ESSAY.

Answers may vary.

Lesson 7

1 TRY YOUR HAND AT USING DETAILS.

Answers may vary.

2 ADD TRANSITIONS.

The choice of transitions and their placement may vary, but the following are possible answers.

1. Mrs. Ericson got out of the car, so the inspector felt he could insult Marian. *Or* Because Mrs. Ericson got out of the car, the inspector felt that he could insult Marian. *Or* Mrs. Ericson got out of the car. Consequently, the inspector felt that he could insult Marian.
2. The inspector was mean to Marian, first, because she was African American, and second, because she was a woman.
3. Marian failed the test. As a result, she would not be able to pick up the children after school. *Or* Because Marian failed the test, she would not be able to pick up the children after school.

3 WHAT WILL YOU WRITE ABOUT?

Answers may vary.

4 WRITE A THREE-PARAGRAPH EXPOSITORY ESSAY.

Answers may vary.

Lesson 8

1 TRY YOUR HAND AT USING DETAILS.

Answers may vary.

2 ADD TRANSITIONS.

The choice of transitions and their placement may vary, but the following are possible answers.

1. Although Laurie does bad things, he is not a bad child.
2. Both Laurie's father and mother seem like nice people.
3. Charles the helper hands out crayons. In contrast, Charles who does bad things throws them. *Or* Unlike Charles the helper who hands out crayons, Charles who does bad things throws them.

3 WHAT WILL YOU WRITE ABOUT?

Answers may vary.

4 WRITE A THREE-PARAGRAPH EXPOSITORY ESSAY.

Answers may vary.

Lesson 9

1 TRY YOUR HAND AT USING DETAILS.

Answers may vary.

2 COMBINE THE SENTENCES.

Answers may vary. Some possible answers are:

1. I wonder what her aunt and uncle would say if they knew what their niece was like.
2. Mr. Framton was an odd person anyway if all he talked about was his illnesses. That's what Mrs. Sappleton said. *Or* Mr. Framton was an odd person anyway. Mrs. Sappleton said all he talked about was his illnesses.
3. The spaniel was tired, and the men were covered in mud, but Mrs. Sappleton was happy to see them.

3 WHAT WILL YOU WRITE ABOUT?

Answers may vary.

4 WRITE A THREE-PARAGRAPH PERSUASIVE ESSAY.

Answers may vary.

Lesson 10

1 TRY YOUR HAND AT USING DETAILS.

Answers may vary.

2 COMBINE THE SENTENCES.

Answers may vary. Some possible answers are:

1. Lewis Carroll had a vivid imagination because *Alice in Wonderland* is a very unusual story.
2. Science fiction movies give me the creeps, and I have bad dreams after I see one.
3. I don't like fantasy, but I saw the Disney movie once and it was good.

3 WHAT WILL YOU WRITE ABOUT?

Answers may vary.

4 WRITE A THREE-PARAGRAPH EXPOSITORY ESSAY.

Answers may vary.

Lesson 11

1 TRY YOUR HAND AT USING DETAILS.

Answers may vary.

2 COMBINE THE SENTENCES.

Answers may vary. Some possible answers are:

1. Anika was bored by her job, and she wished for more excitement. *Or* Bored by her job, Anika wished for more excitement.
2. I found it [similar construction] difficult to tell what is real in the story and what is not.
3. Anika was dreaming she was the doctor, or she really was the doctor.

3 WHAT WILL YOU WRITE ABOUT?

Answers may vary.

4 WRITE A THREE-PARAGRAPH EXPOSITORY ESSAY.

Answers may vary.

Lesson 12

1 TRY YOUR HAND AT USING DETAILS.

Answers may vary.

2 COMBINE THE SENTENCES.

Answers may vary. Some possible answers are:

1. His wife died from a fever, but Murlock didn't seem sorry.
2. Murlock awoke because of the noise of the panther dragging the body to the window.
3. If she was dead, how did a piece of the panther's ear get in her teeth?

3 WHAT WILL YOU WRITE ABOUT?

Answers may vary.

4 WRITE A THREE-PARAGRAPH EXPOSITORY ESSAY.

Answers may vary.

Lesson 13

1 TRY YOUR HAND AT USING DETAILS.

Answers may vary.

2 COMBINE THE SENTENCES.

Answers may vary. Some possible answers are:

1. Norman frightens Ethel, and she begins to yell at him. *Or* Norman frightens Ethel, who begins to yell at him.
2. Ethel wants to take her mother's china home with them, and Norman decides to carry one of the boxes. *Or* Ethel wants to take her mother's china home with them, so Norman decides to carry one of the boxes. *Or* Because Ethel wants to take her mother's china home with them, Norman decides to carry one of the boxes.
3. Ethel and Norman seem to joke a lot, which makes the scene funny at times.

3 WHAT WILL YOU WRITE ABOUT?

Answers may vary.

4 WRITE A THREE-PARAGRAPH PERSUASIVE LETTER.

Answers may vary.

Lesson 14

1 TRY YOUR HAND AT USING DETAILS.

Answers may vary.

2 COMBINE THE SENTENCES.

Answers may vary. Some possible answers are:

1. Fyodor was sentenced to death because he had opposed the Tzar.
2. The guards didn't seem to want to execute the prisoners and seemed sorry to do their duty.
3. Fyodor was freed after four years, but he never got over the experience and was marked for life by it. *Or* Although Fyodor was freed after four years, he never got over the experience and was marked for life by it.

3 WHAT WILL YOU WRITE ABOUT?

Answers may vary.

4 WRITE A THREE-PARAGRAPH EXPOSITORY ESSAY.

Answers may vary.

Lesson 15

1 TRY YOUR HAND AT USING DETAILS.

Answers may vary.

2 COMBINE THE SENTENCES.

Answers may vary. Some possible answers are:

1. Schatz was feeling sick, so his father called the doctor, who came right away.

2. Schatz didn't understand that the thermometer used in France is different from the one used here.

3. Schatz wouldn't let anyone in because he thought he could give them his illness.

3 WHAT WILL YOU WRITE ABOUT?

1. Schatz, his father, the doctor

2. Schatz has the flu and thinks he will die. Then his father tells him it was a misunderstanding.

3. during one day

4. Schatz's house, mostly in his room

5. Schatz doesn't realize that the thermometer used in France is different from the one used where he lives. He thinks he will die because his temperature is so high.

6. His father tells Schatz the difference and Schatz relaxes some, but he cries easily the next day.

4 WRITE A THREE-PARAGRAPH SUMMARY.

Answers may vary.

Lesson 16

1 TRY YOUR HAND AT USING DETAILS.

Answers may vary.

2 USE PRONOUNS IN SENTENCES.

Additional sentences vary. Listed below are some possible ideas.

1. What happens to Johnsy is not what she expects. *Instead of dying, she decides to live.*

2. Behrman, who lives downstairs, decides to help Johnsy, whom he likes. *He goes out in the rain and cold to paint one ivy leaf on the wall.*

3. The ending was a surprise to *me*, but I missed the clues that were there. *If I had seen them, I could have guessed.*

3 WHAT WILL YOU WRITE ABOUT?

Answers may vary.

4 WRITE A THREE-PARAGRAPH EXPOSITORY ESSAY.

Answers may vary.

Lesson 17

1 TRY YOUR HAND AT USING DETAILS.

Answers may vary.

2 USE PRONOUNS IN SENTENCES.

Additional sentences vary. Listed below are some possible ideas.

1. The narrator, *who* lives with his aunt and uncle, has a crush on a girl *whom* we only know as Mangan's sister. *The story is about how the narrator wants to impress her.*

2. Not very much happens in the story, *which* is set in Dublin, Ireland, in the early 1900s. *I think Joyce describes teenage love very well.*

3. If the story continued, I wonder *what* would happen next. *Maybe Mangan's sister would make fun of the narrator for not keeping his promise.*

3 WHAT WILL YOU WRITE ABOUT?

Answers may vary.

4 WRITE A THREE-PARAGRAPH EXPOSITORY ESSAY.

Answers may vary.

Lesson 18

1 TRY YOUR HAND AT USING DETAILS.

Answers may vary.

2 UNTANGLE THE CONFUSION.

Answers may vary. Some possible answers are:

1. Getting credit for ideas, according to Fromm, is important to a having-individual. *Or* According to Fromm, getting credit for ideas is important to a having-individual.

2. This idea of "having" as something to do with private property confused me when I started to read the article.

3. Material rewards are not necessarily the only way to encourage people in their work roles.

4. [Students may revise confusing sentences in which the problem is something other than misplaced modifiers. Accept those answers, and note the problem that was corrected, such as an omitted word.]

3 WHAT YOU WILL WRITE ABOUT?

Answers may vary.

4 WRITE A THREE-PARAGRAPH EXPOSITORY ESSAY.

Answers may vary.

Lesson 19

1 TRY YOUR HAND AT USING DETAILS.

Answers may vary.

2 UNTANGLE THE CONFUSION.

Answers may vary. Some possible answers are:

1. Doctors didn't give **Leslie [him]** long to live because of his size and his cerebral palsy.

2. The narrator was helpful **to** me in figuring out what was going on.

3. I was worried about what the belt **was** for when the narrator started talking about it.

3 WHAT WILL YOU WRITE ABOUT?

Answers may vary.

4 WRITE A FIVE-PARAGRAPH DESCRIPTIVE ESSAY.

Answers may vary.

Lesson 20

1 TRY YOUR HAND AT USING DETAILS.

Answers may vary.

2 UNTANGLE THE CONFUSION.

Answers may vary. Some possible answers are:

1. Jason and Liam were reading the story, and it made Liam [Jason] think of Anna's brother.
2. Gladys told May that she thought May had made a mistake with Leslie. *Or* In talking to May, Gladys said that May had made a mistake with Leslie.
3. The doctor saw Leslie regularly but offered little hope. He gave Joe some advice early on about a home for Leslie.

3 WHAT WILL YOU WRITE ABOUT?

Answers may vary.

4 WRITE A FIVE-PARAGRAPH EXPOSITORY ESSAY.

Answers may vary.

Review

1 BRAINSTORM DESCRIPTIVE WORDS AND PHRASES TO WRITE ABOUT.

Answers may vary.

2 USE DESCRIPTIVE WORDS AND PHRASES IN SENTENCES.

Answers may vary.

3 WHAT WILL YOU WRITE ABOUT?

1. T-chart
2. Five W's and H
3. brainstorming
4. listing
5. cause-and-effect chain
6. mapping
7. table

4 WHAT WILL YOU WRITE ABOUT?

Students may suggest additional tools for items 3, 5, 6, and 7. Accept answers supported by good reasoning.

1. T-chart
2. cause-and-effect chain
3. Five W's and H
4. listing
5. brainstorming
6. mapping
7. chart

5 CONNECT IDEAS.

1. transitions that show time order
2. transitions that add information
3. transitions that show cause and effect
4. transitions that show comparison and contrast

6 WRITE A THREE-PARAGRAPH SUMMARY.

Answers may vary.

7 WRITE A FOUR-PARAGRAPH EXPOSITORY ESSAY.

Answers may vary.

8 WRITE A THREE-PARAGRAPH PERSUASIVE ESSAY.

Answers may vary.

Challenger Writing 8

Lesson 1

1 UNTANGLE THE CONFUSION.

1. Dr. Lynn's cabinet trick inspired Houdini. Years later, Houdini was doing the same trick.

2. I have never **been** interested in magic, but Houdini's story is interesting and his death was very strange.

3. Captain Angle was puzzled by how Houdini had gotten himself out of the four pairs of irons.

4. It would be interesting to see Houdini and a modern escape artist like David Copperfield work together. I bet Houdini (Copperfield) would be better.

5. Answers may vary. (Point out that now that students know this about their writing, they should be aware of it as they edit.)

2 WHAT WILL YOU WRITE ABOUT?

Answers may vary.

3 HOW WILL YOU ORGANIZE YOUR SUMMARY?

The order is determined by the biographical sketch.

4 WRITE A FIVE-PARAGRAPH SUMMARY.

Answers may vary.

Lesson 2

1 UNTANGLE THE CONFUSION.

1. A person puts on cosmetics and lotions and uses hair color to look younger, better, and more attractive than the person really is.

2. The writer says that putting on cosmetics is like putting on a new skin that the user thinks is more attractive than her natural one.

3. Cosmetics—all those lotions, oils, make-up, and hair color—are an attempt to fool others and ourselves. *Or* All those lotions, oils, make-up, and hair color are an attempt to fool others and ourselves.

4. Answers may vary. (Point out that now that students know this about their writing, they should be aware of it as they revise.)

2 WHAT WILL YOU WRITE ABOUT?

Answers may vary.

3 HOW WILL YOU ORGANIZE YOUR ESSAY?

Answers may vary.

4 WRITE A FIVE-PARAGRAPH EXPOSITORY ESSAY.

Answers may vary.

Lesson 3

1 IS IT ONE OR MORE THAN ONE?

1. They have probably enjoyed reading the tabloid headlines.

2. Reality shows are fun to watch, and I enjoy them, but some of them seem too silly to be real.

3. Are people really that strange when you get them together in a contest for a long period of time?

4. Tabloids send reporters to check out stories, but sometimes it seems as if they make up the stories.

5. Answers may vary. (Point out that now that students know this about their writing, they should be aware of it as they revise.)

2 WHAT WILL YOU WRITE ABOUT?

Answers may vary.

3 HOW WILL YOU ORGANIZE YOUR ESSAY?

Answers may vary.

4 WRITE A FIVE-PARAGRAPH EXPOSITORY ESSAY.

Answers may vary.

Lesson 4

1 IS IT ONE OR MORE THAN ONE?

1. Veblen's ideas of ownership are not easy to understand, but once you do, the ideas make sense.

2. People who have lots of money sometimes dress in sloppy clothes. They think it's cool.

3. Have you seen some of the pictures in the tabloids of celebrities in torn, old clothes? What were they thinking to be out like that?

4. Answers may vary. (Point out that now that students know this about their writing, they should be aware of it as they revise.)

2 WHAT WILL YOU WRITE ABOUT?

Answers may vary.

3 HOW WILL YOU ORGANIZE YOUR ESSAY?

Answers may vary.

4 WRITE A FIVE-PARAGRAPH EXPOSITORY ESSAY.

Answers may vary.

Lesson 5

1 ADD TRANSITIONS.

6, 4, 5, 7, 1, 3, 2

The words in bold below are possible uses of transitions.

The young woman drops her book and Mr. Parkenstacker picks it up and returns it to her.

Then the young woman says that she prefers talking over reading in the fading light.

The young man gives up flirting when the young woman takes offense at it.

Soon the young woman says that she wants to talk to a natural man, not one that is interested in her for her money.

After a while, the young woman says that she is being chased by two rich men who want to marry her.

Later, the young woman says that no position is too humble if the man is the right man.

Finally, Mr. Parkenstacker says that he is a cashier in the restaurant across the park.

2 WHAT WILL YOU WRITE ABOUT?

1. girl in gray, Mr. Parkenstacker
2. They talk on the park bench. She leaves, telling him not to follow. He follows and sees her go into the restaurant and take up her job as the cashier. He gets into his waiting car.
3. early evening
4. city park
5. The young man has seen the young woman in the park before and wants to meet her.
6. The roles are reversed. The young woman who pretends to be rich is the poor cashier in the restaurant, and the young man who pretends to be poor is rich, with a waiting car and driver.

3 HOW WILL YOU ORGANIZE YOUR SUMMARY?

The order is determined by the events in the story.

4 WRITE A THREE-PARAGRAPH SUMMARY.

Answers may vary.

Lesson 6

1 ADD DETAILS.

Answers may vary. Some possible answers are:

1. Marco Polo traveled slowly across the hills and valleys of the huge, barren Lop Nor Desert.
2. Kublai Khan had a moveable palace with gold and silver walls that were held together by silk cords.
3. Kublai Khan had a very impressive messenger service by which messages were carried three ways: by runners, by men on horseback, and by men on faster horses galloping 300 miles in a day.

2 WHAT WILL YOU WRITE ABOUT?

Answers may vary.

3 HOW WILL YOU ORGANIZE YOUR ESSAY?

Answers may vary.

4 WRITE A FIVE-PARAGRAPH ESSAY.

Answers may vary.

Lesson 7

1 ADD TRANSITIONS.

The words in bold below are possible uses of transitions.

1. Lewis's journal is very important in understanding the expedition. **First,** the journal explains how Lewis met the Shoshone. **Second,** Lewis reveals his attitude toward Native Americans in it. **Third,** the journal explains the risks that Lewis took.

2. Lewis took many risks. **For example,** he gave Cameahwait his gun and told him to shoot him if the chief didn't believe him.
3. Lewis told Cameahwait that the government would protect the Shoshone from their enemies **as well as** send the Shoshone trade goods. *Or* Lewis told Cameahwait that the government would protect the Shoshone from their enemies. **In addition,** it would send the Shoshone trade goods. *Or* Lewis told Cameahwait that besides protecting the Shoshone from their enemies, the government would also send the Shoshone trade goods.
4. Answers may vary.

2 WHAT WILL YOU WRITE ABOUT?

Answers may vary.

3 HOW WILL YOU ORGANIZE YOUR ESSAY?

Answers may vary.

4 WRITE A FIVE-PARAGRAPH EXPOSITORY ESSAY.

Answers may vary.

Lesson 8

1 ADD TRANSITIONS.

The words in bold below are possible uses of transitions.

1. **Like** the ice floes, the ship was breaking up.
2. The crew played football and hockey for exercise, and killed seals for food as well as trained the dog teams. *Or* The crew killed seals for food as well as trained the dog teams. They played football and hockey for exercise, too.
3. When the ice floe broke in half, the men were fearful. **In contrast,** the two seals were at home on their floe. *Or* When the ice floe broke in half, the men were fearful, **unlike** the two seals that were at home on their floe. *Or* When the ice floe broke in half, the men were fearful. On the other hand, the two seals were at home on their floe.
4. Answers may vary.

2 WHAT WILL YOU WRITE ABOUT?

Answers may vary.

3 HOW WILL YOU ORGANIZE YOUR ESSAY?

Answers may vary.

4 WRITE A FOUR-PARAGRAPH EXPOSITORY ESSAY.

Answers may vary.

Lesson 9

1 ADD TRANSITIONS.

1. The cable of the bathysphere went slack and then jerked tight **because** the ship was rocking. *Or* The ship was rocking. **Consequently,** the cable of the bathsphere went slack and then jerked tight.
2. The bathysphere had no electric power of its own. **As a result,** Beebe and Barton relied on oxygen tanks and a power cable hooked to the ship on the surface. *Or* **Because** the bathysphere had no electric power of its own, Beebe and

Barton relied on oxygen tanks and a power cable hooked to the ship on the surface.

3. The dives of these men were very important **because** we now know a great deal about the ocean floor. *Or* **As a result** of the dives of these men, we now know a great deal about the ocean floor. *Or* **Because of** the dives of these men, we now know a great deal about the ocean floor.

4. Answers may vary.

2 WHAT WILL YOU WRITE ABOUT?
Answers may vary.

3 HOW WILL YOU ORGANIZE YOUR ESSAY?
Answers may vary.

4 WRITE A FIVE-PARAGRAPH EXPOSITORY ESSAY.
Answers may vary.

Lesson 10

1 ADD DETAILS.
Answers may vary. Some possible answers are:
1. Greek teachers and students had questions about the skies. They wanted to know things like whether the sun moved around the planets and if the Earth was the center of the universe.
2. The mission of the Huygens is important because it was the first spacecraft to land on the moon of another planet.
3. Skylab broke up. It fell to Earth in 1979 with many pieces of it landing in the Indian Ocean and Australia. *Or* When Skylab broke up and fell to Earth in 1979, pieces fell into the Indian Ocean and on Australia.
4. Scientists decided in 2006 that Pluto is not a planet but a dwarf planet. Unlike the other planets, it is small and made of ice.

2 WHAT WILL YOU WRITE ABOUT?
Answers may vary.

3 HOW WILL YOU ORGANIZE YOUR ESSAY?
Answers may vary.

4 WRITE A FIVE-PARAGRAPH PERSUASIVE ESSAY.
Answers may vary.

Lesson 11

1 ADD DETAILS.
Answers may vary. Some possible answers are:
1. Rachel Carson wrote "Fable for Tomorrow" to warn people about the dangers of pesticides.
2. DDT lasts a long time, so it remains in the soil and can harm people for many years.
3. People praised Carson for her efforts to save the Earth from harmful chemicals.
4. Because of Rachel Carson's work, 40 states passed laws to limit pesticides.

2 WHAT WILL YOU WRITE ABOUT?
Answers may vary.

3 HOW WILL YOU ORGANIZE YOUR ESSAY?
Answers may vary.

4 WRITE A FIVE-PARAGRAPH PERSUASIVE ESSAY.
Answers may vary.

Lesson 12

1 WHAT DO YOU MEAN?
Answers may vary. Some possible answers are:
1. The Amazon rainforest is worth saving because it has so many native plants that can be used for medicines.
2. Different groups have different proposals for saving the rainforest. One is "carbon credits." *Or* Different groups have different proposals for saving the rainforest, one of which is "carbon credits."
3. Ecotourism and bio-prospecting are two ways to save the rainforest, but not everyone agrees with these proposals. *Or* Ecotourism and bio-prospecting are two ways to save the rainforest; however, not everyone agrees with these proposals.
4. Answers may vary.

2 WHAT WILL YOU WRITE ABOUT?
Ecological importance of the rainforest, global warming and the impact of the carbon cycle, cultures in the rainforest

3 HOW WILL YOU ORGANIZE YOUR ESSAY?
The order is determined by the article.

4 WRITE A FIVE-PARAGRAPH SUMMARY.
Answers may vary.

Lesson 13

1 WHAT DO YOU MEAN?
Answers may vary. Some possible answers are:
1. Brower and Park agree on the beauty of the valley, but they don't agree on whether the copper should be mined. *Or* Brower and Park agree on the beauty of the valley. They don't agree on whether the copper should be mined.
2. Park is concerned about the standard of living of future generations, whereas Brower is worrying about people today. *Or* Park is concerned about the standard of living of future generations. Brower worries about people today.
3. Park brings up Minas Gerais to prove his point, and Brower turns it around to prove his point. *Or* Park brings up Minas Gerais to prove his point. Brower turns it around to prove his point.
4. Answers may vary.

2 WHAT WILL YOU WRITE ABOUT?
Answers may vary.

3 HOW WILL YOU ORGANIZE YOUR ESSAY?

Answers may vary.

4 WRITE A FIVE-PARAGRAPH EXPOSITORY ESSAY.

Answers may vary.

Lesson 14

1 WHAT DO YOU MEAN?

Answers may vary. Some possible answers are:

1. T.J. had had his own land in Alabama, and he had grown cotton and corn. *Or* T.J. had had his own land in Alabama where he had grown cotton and corn.
2. The other boys weren't so sure about T.J.'s idea, but T.J. was so sure that they joined him.
3. T.J. was different from the other boys. His hair was white and he talked in a soft, gentle way. *Or* T.J. was different from the other boys with his white hair and his soft, gentle way of talking.
4. Answers may vary.

2 WHAT WILL YOU WRITE ABOUT?

Answers may vary.

3 HOW WILL YOU ORGANIZE YOUR ESSAY?

The natural order of the event requires chronological order for the essay.

4 WRITE A FIVE-PARAGRAPH EXPOSITORY ESSAY.

Answers may vary.

Lesson 15

1 WHAT DO YOU MEAN?

Answers may vary. Some possible answers are:

1. I was surprised at the ending because I thought T.J. would get his garden. *Or* I thought T.J. would get his garden, so I was surprised at the ending.
2. I guess he did get his garden, but it just wasn't cotton and corn. *Or* I guess he did get his garden. It just wasn't cotton and corn.
3. The building owner saw the dirt, and he was right that the roof could fall in. *Or* The building owner, who saw the dirt, was right that the roof could fall in.
4. T.J. was having a hard time understanding. The man just turned away.
5. The other boys wanted to believe, but Blackie understood that they had no right to the roof. *Or* The other boys wanted to believe. However, Blackie understood that they had no right to the roof. *Or* Although the other boys wanted to believe, Blackie understood that they had no right to the roof.

2 WHAT WILL YOU WRITE ABOUT?

Answers may vary.

3 HOW WILL YOU ORGANIZE YOUR ESSAY?

Answers may vary.

4 WRITE A FIVE-PARAGRAPH EXPOSITORY ESSAY.

Answers may vary.

Lesson 16

1 WHAT DO YOU MEAN?

Answers may vary. Some possible answers are:

1. Living in the early 19th century was hard work, and I wouldn't have liked it. *Or* Living in the early 19th century was hard work. I wouldn't have liked it. *Or* I wouldn't have liked living in the early 19th century because it was hard work.
2. Wing chairs had "wings" so that people could keep warm, but servants didn't have wing chairs or fireplaces in their rooms. *Or* Wing chairs had "wings" so that people could keep warm. Servants didn't have wing chairs or fireplaces in their rooms.
3. Keeping a fire going all night was important because it was too hard to start a new fire every morning. *Or* It was important to keep a fire going all night because it was too hard to start a new fire every morning. *Or* Because it was such hard work to start a new fire every morning, it was important to keep a fire going all night
4. Alonzo Phillips went door to door to sell his matches, so it took a long time for matches to catch on with the public. *Or* Because Alonzo Phillips went door to door to sell his matches, it took a long time for matches to catch on with the public.
5. The Industrial Revolution changed 19th-century living dramatically because of labor-saving devices that made homes more comfortable and gave people more free time. *Or* Nineteenth-century living changed dramatically during the Industrial Revolution because of labor-saving devices that made homes more comfortable and gave people more free time. *Or* Labor-saving devices invented during the Industrial Revolution made homes more comfortable and gave people more free time. The result was a dramatic change in 19th-century living.

2 WHAT WILL YOU WRITE ABOUT?

Answers may vary.

3 HOW WILL YOU ORGANIZE YOUR ESSAY?

Answers may vary.

4 WRITE A FIVE-PARAGRAPH EXPOSITORY ESSAY.

Answers may vary.

Lesson 17

1 WHAT DO YOU MEAN?

Answers may vary. Some possible answers are:

1. I have a friend who will argue over anything, and the play reminds me of her. *Or* The play reminds me of a friend who will argue over anything.
2. Ivan is only trying to show that the two families have been friendly for many years, but Natalia becomes angry.

3. There is so much shouting that Stepan rushes back into the room and joins the argument. *Or* Because of the shouting, Stepan rushes back into the room and joins the argument. *Or* Hearing so much shouting, Stepan rushes back into the room and quickly joins the argument.

4. All three of them seem silly to me, and they probably could argue over whether the sun is shining. *Or* All three of them seem silly to me. They probably could argue over whether the sun is shining.

5. Natalia has no principles because she is desperate to get married. *Or* Because she is desperate to get married, Natalia has no principles. *Or* Desperate to get married, Natalia has no principles.

2 WHAT WILL YOU WRITE ABOUT?
Answers may vary.

3 HOW WILL YOU ORGANIZE YOUR ESSAY?
1. order of importance
2. Order of importance is the most typical pattern for developing an essay explaining an opinion. (Students should actually mark the reasons in the order in which they will use them.)

4 WRITE A FIVE-PARAGRAPH EXPOSITORY ESSAY.
Answers may vary.

Lesson 18

1 TRY YOUR HAND AT DETAILS.
Answers may vary.

2 WHAT WILL YOU WRITE ABOUT?
Answers may vary.

3 HOW WILL YOU ORGANIZE YOUR ESSAY?
Students should indicate that they are going to organize their essays according to the order of importance of their reasons. (Students should actually mark the reasons in the order in which they will use them.)

4 WRITE A FIVE-PARAGRAPH EXPOSITORY ESSAY.
Answers may vary.

Lesson 19

1 CHOOSE THE BEST DESCRIPTIVE DETAILS.
Answers may vary.

2 WHAT WILL YOU WRITE ABOUT?
Answers may vary.

3 HOW WILL YOU ORGANIZE YOUR ESSAY?
Answers may vary.

4 WRITE A FIVE-PARAGRAPH EXPOSITORY ESSAY.
Answers may vary.

Lesson 20

1 TRY YOUR HAND AT USING DETAILS.
Answers may vary.

2 WHAT WILL YOU WRITE ABOUT?
Answers may vary.

3 HOW WILL YOU ORGANIZE YOUR ESSAY?
order of importance

4 WRITE A FIVE-PARAGRAPH EXPOSITORY ESSAY.
Answers may vary.

Review

1 WHAT WILL YOU WRITE ABOUT?
1. brainstorming
2. Venn diagram
3. chart
4. T-chart
5. listing
6. 5 W's and H

2 HOW WILL YOU CONNECT IDEAS?
1. transitions that show time order, 2. add information, 3. compare and contrast, 4. show cause and effect

3 WRITE A WRITING GUIDE.
Students should include the following items in their writing guides:

Paragraph 1, Introduction: State topic, opinion, three reasons/examples to support the opinion

Paragraph 2, Body: Develop first reason/example, use details, use transitions

Paragraph 3, Body: Develop second reason/example, use details, use transitions

Paragraph 4, Body: Develop third reason/example, use details, use transitions

Paragraph 5, Conclusion: Restate topic, opinion, reasons/example, tie up ideas in a final statement

4 GATHER, PLAN, AND WRITE A FIVE-PARAGRAPH ESSAY.
1. Review pieces of writing, and list ways the writing has improved.
2. Students should create a list.
3. Students should understand that they need to pick the ways that show the most improvement and are the easiest to explain.
4. Students should create a chart of three columns and then write across the top the three ways that they chose.
5. Students should recognize that adding details before they actually begin to write means that they are more likely to have a number of details to use rather than trying to think of details and write at the same time.
6. order of importance
7. Answers may vary.